DAILY
DEVOTIONS

Published by Concordia Publishing House
3558 S. Jefferson Avenue, St. Louis, MO 63118-3968
1-800-325-3040 • www.cph.org

Unless otherwise indicated, all Scripture quotations are from the ESV Bible® (The Holy Bible, English Standard Version®), copyright © 2001 by Crossway Bibles, a publishing ministry of Good News Publishers. Used by permission. All rights reserved.

Scripture quotations marked NKJV™ are taken from the New King James Version®. Copyright © 1982 by Thomas Nelson, Inc. Used by permission. All rights reserved.

Scripture quotations marked NIV are taken from the Holy Bible, New International Version®. NIV®. Copyright © 1973, 1978, 1984 by Biblica, Inc.™ Used by permission of Zondervan. All rights reserved.

Hymn texts with the abbreviation LSB are from Lutheran Service Book, copyright © 2006 Concordia Publishing House. All rights reserved.

Hymn texts with the abbreviation TLH are from The Lutheran Hymnal, copyright © 1941 Concordia Publishing House. All rights reserved.

The catechism quotations from Martin Luther are taken from Luther's Small Catechism with Explanation, copyright © 1986, 1991 Concordia Publishing House. All rights reserved.

Cover image © istockphoto.com. Interior images © istockphoto.com.

Manufactured in the United States of America

Library of Congress Cataloging-in-Publication Data

Daily devotions : drawn from 75 years of Portals of prayer.
   p. cm.

  ISBN 978-0-7586-3141-1

  1. Devotional calendars—Lutheran Church—Missouri Synod. 2. Lutheran Church—Missouri Synod—Prayers and devotions. I. Portals of prayer.

  BV4810.D235 2011
  242'.2—dc23
                                     2011031499

1 2 3 4 5 6 7 8 9 10   20 19 18 17 16 15 14 13 12 11

DAILY
DEVOTIONS
from
75 YEARS OF
PORTALS *of* PRAYER

CONCORDIA PUBLISHING HOUSE • SAINT LOUIS

PREFACE

—⚏—

For seventy-five years, *Portals of Prayer* has provided God's
Word as a source of assurance, comfort, and strength for the
Christian. Over the years, these portable devotion booklets
have been found on the table after breakfast and dinner, in purses, brief-
cases, and on desks at work, in doctors' and dentists' waiting rooms, in
nursing homes, hospitals, prisons, and college campuses, and in military
rucksacks and loadout bags carried by troops around the world. From its
beginning, the purpose of *Portals of Prayer* has been to deepen faith by
grounding it in the Holy Scriptures, which testify to Jesus Christ as our
only Savior, and to encourage Christian living amid the challenges of our
world. Its influence is widespread, with readers of each current quarterly
issue numbering over a million.

The first issue of this devotional booklet was published in Lent 1937
with the title *Standing in His Grace*. For the first several years, the booklets carried a variety of names such as *He Loved Me*, *Walking with God*,
Streams of Living Water, and *Quiet Moments with God*. Beginning in the
spring of 1948, the periodical took the name *Portals of Prayer* for each
issue. Other changes have happened over the years as well. First delivered seven times a year, *Portals of Prayer* became a bimonthly devotional
in 1959, and quarterly publication began in 1981. A German language
counterpart, *Tägliche Andachten*, was published from 1937 to 1999. A
Spanish language version, *Portales de Oración*, began in 2008, and a
braille edition has been available since 1956. And while the devotional
has always been available in the familiar "pocket-size" edition, new
sizes and formats have joined it over the years. A large-size "sight-saver"
print edition was introduced in the '70s; a digest-size print edition began
in 2010. Over the years, the reach of *Portals of Prayer* was extended as
the daily devotions were made available on long-playing (LP) record
albums and audiocassettes, as well as being broadcast on numerous
radio stations. Today, *Portals of Prayer* continues to adapt to the changing times and can be accessed on the World Wide Web and downloaded
onto computers and smart phones.

The devotions selected for this book come from every issue of *Portals of Prayer*. Many appear on the same day of the year they originally appeared; some will even make note of a historical event that happened on the original date the devotion was published. With over 27,000 readings to choose from, some excellent devotions and authors had to be overlooked. The devotions selected for this anniversary book represent the great number of topics discussed, the different approaches to the subjects, and the various writing styles and personal gifts of the authors. Despite the span of years, the variety of authors, or even the topics that are written upon, one thing above all connects the devotions together: the Gospel of God's love and mercy in Christ Jesus.

It is the prayerful hope of the publisher that this anthology of brief meditations will find its way into thousands of hands, bringing hope, courage, and guidance for every circumstance of daily living.

ORDER OF FAMILY WORSHIP

Leader: In the name of the Father and of the Son and of the Holy Spirit.

All: Amen.

Leader (*With all repeating each phrase*): Lord, have mercy. Christ, have mercy. Lord, have mercy.

A PSALM may be read by the leader or by the family in response.

All: Glory be to the Father and to the Son and to the Holy Spirit; as it was in the beginning, is now, and will be forever. Amen.

THE SCRIPTURE READING

THE MEDITATION

THE PRAYER

THE LORD'S PRAYER

Leader: Let us bless the Lord.

All: Thanks be to God.

Leader: The almighty and merciful God, the Father, the Son, and the Holy Spirit, bless us and keep us.

All: Amen.

January

Glory be to the Father and to the Son and to the Holy Spirit; as it was in the beginning, is now, and will be forever. Amen.

January 1
New Year's Day

—⚬—

Read Malachi 3:6–12
Psalm 145
I the LORD do not change. *Malachi 3:6*

A Changeless God
for a Changing World

O ne word that can aptly describe our modern world is
change. Nothing seems to last. Nothing seems to stand
still. Our scientists constantly search, discover, and produce new gadgets to make our lives more comfortable and more
pleasant. Everything is constantly changing, making us feel at
times as if we were in some never-ending race.

And not all the changes that take place are pleasant. At times,
we can become frightened by what is happening around us, particularly when the changes are beyond our control.

In the midst of this fast pace, we hear the words of God, spoken
through Malachi: "I the LORD do not change." What a refreshing
thought! What a joy to know that in the midst of this race we
call living, our God is constant and dependable, not affected by
our insatiable desire and need for change. Instead, He continues
to love us, remaining faithful to all the promises He has made in
His Word, particularly His promise of salvation through faith in
His Son, our Lord and Savior Jesus Christ, whom the Scriptures
describe as the same yesterday, today, and forever.

O gracious and merciful Father, grant that in the midst
of a changing world we may always hold steadfast to You,
our changeless Lord; through our Savior Jesus Christ. Amen.

—⚬—

January 1, 1988
On this date in 1988, American Lutheran Church and Lutheran Church
in America join together with Association of Evangelical Lutheran Churches
to form the Evangelical Lutheran Church in America (ELCA)

January 2

—◊—

Read Psalm 31
In your hearts honor Christ the Lord as holy. *I Peter 3:15*

WALKING WITH OUR FRIEND

I said to a man who stood at the gate of the year: 'Give me a light that I may tread safely into the unknown,' and he replied, 'Go out into the darkness, and put your hand into the hand of God. That shall be to you better than a light and safer than a known way.'" Every day we are to cling to God's hand and make the common things of life an act of worship.

Mother, as you sweep and dust and make the beds, God is by your side. Talk with Him there! He is the God of the commonplace. Sanctify the Lord Jesus in your heart, and your home becomes a cathedral with the light of heaven flowing in.

Father, you may grow weary with the daily grind. Talk with God across your fields, your work table, or your desk. Your heart was made to fellowship with God. You do not need a change of work, greener fields; what you need is more of God for the everyday common things.

Yes, God is the God of the common folks who trust in Him; He is the God of common things. When He comes to us, each lowly task becomes a holy sacrifice for His glory. Common folks, under the radiance of His presence, are the kings of the universe. There is something rich and satisfying about their lives. They possess a secret place of hidden joy that the world can never know. They are "laborers together with God." Their life is hid with Christ in God. They walk through life arm in arm with Him who will ever sustain and uphold them.

Lord, I would walk with Thee all through the day, that my life may be ceaseless worship. Amen.

—◊—

January 6, 1947

January 3

—⁂—

Read Isaiah 43:1–13
The disciples were first called Christians. *Acts 11:26*

His Name Is Our Name

The persecution that followed the stoning of Stephen scattered most of the believers from Jerusalem, the center of the Mother Church. Wherever they went, they shared the Gospel, mostly with Jews.

Outwardly, the new disciples looked no different from their friends and relatives. But spiritually, they were plainly different: they believed on Christ and lived like Him. If this be so, said the people of Antioch, let them be called "Christians."

The name is a happy choice. The disciples of Christ are no mere followers. Paul would say they are wedded to Christ by faith. As a bridegroom gives his bride his name, so Christ, the heavenly Bridegroom, gives His Bride, the Church, His name.

Furthermore, the disciples are intimately bound to Christ through Holy Baptism. Paul says that in Baptism, we "put on" Christ. We are "christened," we say. Paul might say, "Christ dwells in you by faith" or "Let Christ be formed in you."

"Christian" symbolizes more, therefore, than local church membership. It signals that the Father in heaven has numbered us among His sons and daughters, that He has filled us with the righteousness of His Son, that He has declared us to be "little Christs."

Let us strive to keep unspotted that name of which we are unworthy.

Blessed Lord Christ, whose name is above every name, help us to keep Thy name holy. Amen.

—⁂—

January 3, 1959
On this date in 1959, Alaska is admitted as forty-ninth U.S. state

January 4

—⚡—

Read Titus 3:4–7

"Truly, truly, I say to you, unless one is born of water and the Spirit, he cannot enter the kingdom of God. That which is born of the flesh is flesh, and that which is born of the Spirit is spirit. Do not marvel that I said to you, 'You must be born again.'" *John 3:5–7*

YOU MUST BE BORN AGAIN

Nicodemus could not understand this. Nor can we. The new birth is a mystery. Equally so, it is a necessity. With a finality that permits no argumentation, Jesus declares solemnly: "You must be born again." And "you" means all men without distinction of time or race, station or place.

As we read the whole of this report of Christ's midnight talk with learned Nicodemus, it becomes clear to us that there must be a new birth for each of us, even though we never can fathom the mysterious process of regeneration. For we are all the children of Adam and Eve. From these sin-defiled parents, we all have inherited the taint of sin. Original sin may be an unpopular, and to many an unknown, doctrine of Scripture. But it is a stubborn fact that daily stares each one of us in the face. We see it in our children even as our parents saw it in us. "That which is born of the flesh is flesh." All nature testifies to the fact that like begets like. "That which is born of the Spirit is spirit." Every regenerated and believing child of God knows how true that is.

As we thank God for our redemption by the shed blood of Christ, so let us bless His Spirit for the gracious washing of regeneration in Holy Baptism. May our lives testify to the fact that we have been born again.

For the blessings of Holy Baptism we thank Thee, dear Lord. Grant that we who have been baptized into Christ may daily put on Christ. Help us day by day to bear in mind that, as Christ rose from the dead by the glory of the Father, even so we also should walk in newness of life. Amen.

—⚡—

Read Psalm 23
And they shall call His name Immanuel (which means,
God with us). *Matthew 1:23*

IMMANUEL

It happened at Bethlehem. One moment, the earth and mankind were separated from God. The next moment, a Child was born, and God was with us here on earth, one of us, sharing our little life, holding our sins in His forgiving hands, lifting us into His heaven.

Our Savior has many great names, but none greater than this: Immanuel! In one word we discover who He is and what He did. He is the eternal God, and He came to live with us.

Men like to say that they look for God and seek Him everywhere—in the majesty of the stars, in the far reaches of the universe, in the beauty and wonder of nature. But they can find Him there only after He has found them at the manger and the cross. Once He lay in the manger and walked to the cross, and now He lives forever in His Word. Seeking Him there, we shall always find Him, because He is already here and has found us.

This is the magnificent, central truth of our faith. God with us! The world goes hurrying by, and the years of the world rush toward eternity. But we have no part in all of its hurry and confusion. Our souls are at rest, because they rest in Him who came to the place where we were and who will stay with us world without end.

O heavenly Father, we thank Thee with all our heart that Thou hast sent Thy Son to be our Redeemer, Companion, and Friend—our Immanuel— all the days of our life. Amen.

—ɰ—

January 5, 1948

JANUARY 6

—w—

Read I Kings 8:22–30
His disciples remembered that it was written,
"Zeal for Your house will consume Me." John 2:17

ZEALOUS IN WORSHIP

Jesus had just done a sensational thing in the temple. He had driven out the sheep and oxen. He had upset the tables of the money-changers and thrown their money onto the floor. Jesus was deeply moved. The beautiful temple of God, intended alone for the worship of God, had been turned into a house of merchandise.

The Christian Church, like the ancient temple, is the house of God, and we Christians go there to worship and to pray. Both the teaching and the symbolism of the Church are there to build us up in our precious faith. The altar is there to assure us of God's presence. On it, in sacred vessels, lie the bread and the wine, the earthly elements of the Lord's Supper, which convey to us the merits of Christ's suffering and death. The open Bible is "a lamp to [our] feet and a light to [our] path" (Psalm 119:105). And the pulpit brings us the Good News of the Gospel that "God so loved the world, that He gave His only Son, that whoever believes in Him should not perish but have eternal life" (John 3:16).

Our duty as Christians is to be zealous in our worship and to insist that the church remain the house of God's Word and Sacraments. When we attend the divine services in such a church, we receive spiritual blessings that satisfy the longings of the human soul. Christ is held up as the loving Savior of the world, and by receiving Him as our personal Savior, we receive peace and hope and the assurance of salvation.

—w—

January 6, 1942

January 7

—⁊⁊—

Read Ephesians 4:13–15
We are to grow up in every way into Him who is
the head, into Christ. *Ephesians 4:15*

A MATURE CHRISTIAN

A young girl said to her mother after a visitor had left their home: "If I could be like that old lady—so beautiful, sweet, and lovable—I wouldn't mind growing old." The wise mother answered: "If you want to be that kind of an old lady, you'd better begin right now. She doesn't impress me as being a piece of work that was done in a hurry. It has taken a long time to make her what she is."

In these days when people flash to prominence overnight and oftentimes fade into oblivion in a day, it is good for us to remember that this is not God's way of developing fully Christ-centered lives. Christian maturity will never be achieved by a sudden rush into the limelight. It comes only after a long climb up the rocky hill of life.

A mature Christian is not lopsided. He is well developed, having "breadth" as well as "length," "depth" as well as "height." He is filled with the fullness of Christ and grounded in love.

God takes time to develop such a Christian. Our heavenly Father is not a God of shortcuts. He has a school, and His hours are long. His lessons are not easily learned. It takes many hours of meditation and prayer, many sessions at "Jesus' feet," a lifetime of tribulations and blessings, before we emerge as "mature Christians." Such character is not the result of an overnight rally.

—⁊⁊—

January 9, 1949

Read Ruth 2
For each will have to bear his own load. *Galatians 6:5*
Bear one another's burdens, and so fulfill the
law of Christ. *Galatians 6:2*

A BALANCED LIFE

These two passages seem to contradict each other. In reality, both are essential parts of a pattern of life that God in His wisdom has ordained for a world such as this.

Every person must bear the responsibility for what he or she is and does. He may plead that heredity and environment have conspired against him and left him no choice. But a righteous God says to him: "Thou art the man."

Every person, according to ability, has an obligation toward the life and work of the world. In the home, the church, the place of employment, the community, and the world at large, one must be a co-worker with God and with others for the welfare of all concerned.

Every person must bear the burden of his cross. To court the sympathy of others through habitual self-pity and whining is one of several ways of trying to unload upon others what we ourselves should accept as part of God's plan of love for us.

But there are burdens that require more than one set of shoulders. When a fellow Christian has been overtaken with a fault; when deep sorrow enters the home and heart of another; when sickness, unemployment, or misfortune have left the purse empty and the cupboards bare, the Law of Christ, the great Burden-Bearer, demands that we stand alongside the afflicted person and make part of that load our own.

Thus the two passages belong together. One is a challenge to rugged manhood and womanhood; the other is a call to sympathetic helpfulness.

January 5, 1951

JANUARY 9

—ɯ—

Read John 1:14–28
...full of grace and truth. John 1:14

FROM THE HEART OF GOD

There was nothing sensational about Jesus' entry into the world. When He came, the world was bathed in glory—and the world did not even notice it.

That is how He chose to come—not full of pomp and splendor, but "full of *grace* and *truth.*" These are lovely words—there is music in them and beauty. That is because they come straight from the heart of God and because they belong to His inmost nature.

The Word who has appeared is full of grace. He loves those who do not deserve it; He forgives those who should be punished; He reaches out to embrace those who have rejected Him. That is what grace means. That grace is found alone in Christ.

But He is also full of truth. He is not merely truthful; He is truth itself. He is the answer to this age-old question: "What is truth?" He never will deceive us; His promises cannot fail. We can rely on Him—all through life and in the hour of death.

There is a world of comfort here. When our sins arise to plague us—the angry word, the jealous pang, the foolish pride—it is good to know that our Lord is full of grace.

And when life seems to turn against us, when hopes lie shattered and friendships fail, it is good to know that there is a Word of eternal truth that we can trust for time and eternity.

Let Thy grace, O Lord, cover our many sins, and Thy truth be our guide through life. Amen.

—ɯ—

January 9, 1946

Read Daniel 6
But Peter and the apostles answered, "We must obey
God rather than men." *Acts 5:29*

THY WILL BE DONE

The lines in this instance were sharply drawn. Jesus had commanded the apostles to preach the Gospel to every creature. The high priest forbade them to do so. The apostles were thus confronted with an inevitable choice between the two. They obeyed Jesus.

In a free country, authorities do not have the power to make such demands on us. But life situations develop in which we also must decide between God's will and that of man.

Young people in high school and college may have to choose between what textbooks and instructors teach as scientific fact and what the Word of God reveals on the same subjects. Employees may be asked to practice dishonesty, such as misrepresenting goods or making unnecessary repairs, to increase the profits of the employer. Professional people at times have to choose between what is right and what is wrong. In our social life, we face the choice between popular sinful pleasures and the will of God.

Obeying God rather than men in these instances calls for a heroic faith. We may suffer ridicule, financial loss, or isolation. And yet, even when our best intentions fail, we have a Savior who died for our sins, even these. And by His gracious mercy, we will not suffer the punishment for our sins because that punishment has already been borne for us by Jesus.

When Thou seest me waver,
With a look recall
Nor for fear or favor
Suffer me to fall. Amen. (TLH 516:1b)

January 10, 1958

January 11

Read John 19:1–7

Behold the Man!

Whether or not Pilate witnessed any part of the merciless scourging and the blasphemous mockery, Scripture does not record. However, he now saw Christ enduring excruciating pain and wearing the mock regalia. Undoubtedly, Pilate felt satisfied that Christ's appearance was sufficiently pathetic to serve the purpose he had in mind. He still wanted to release Christ. He led Him out before the multitude and, perhaps pointing at Him, said to the people: "Behold the man!" (John 19:5). There we have the picture of the thorn-crowned Christ with blood trickling down His cheeks and the purple robe on Him, the well-known painting *Ecce Homo*—"Behold the Man."

Pilate sought to arouse the sympathy of the Jews. A mere glance should have sufficed. Jesus must have been a pathetic sight.

The Roman governor called Christ "the man." That is all Jesus meant to him.

Pilate also intended his words to be a stinging rebuke to the Jews. He meant to say: "Look at your King. Such a disfigured man is your King."

The Jews had no sympathy. The view of Christ enraged them all the more, and they cried the more fiercely: "Crucify Him!"

We thank God that we are permitted to behold Christ as He appeared before Pilate and the multitude. By God's grace, we know He was crowned with thorns that we might be crowned with glory. He wore the scarlet robe that we might be clad in the royal wedding garment, the robe of Christ's righteousness.

April 12, 1943

Read 1 Samuel 24:1–17
Love your enemies and pray for those who persecute you. *Matthew 5:44*

IN HIS STEPS

Who is my enemy? The person who has lied about me, the person who has sown the seeds of strife among my friends and relatives, the person who has beaten me out of hard-earned money.

Jesus says that I should love him, bless him, do good to him. He does not give me time to allow my feelings to cool off. He says: "Do it today before the sun sets." He is demanding the impossible. The wounds are too deeply rooted in my heart.

That is the voice of flesh and blood. But Jesus does not ask flesh and blood to do that which is beyond its powers. He appeals to the Christians as God's children. He says: "Pray for them." Pray to your Father in heaven, who "makes His sun rise on the evil and on the good, and sends rain on the just and on the unjust" (Matthew 5:45). Pray in the name of Jesus, whose sensitive soul felt the full impact of insult, whose body quivered under the hammer blows at Calvary, but who, nevertheless, prayed: "Father, forgive them, for they know not what they do" (Luke 23:34).

As we thus kneel in the presence of God, who so loved, so forgave, who daily forgives us our many sins, something happens. Power from on high takes hold of our stubborn hearts. Anger gives way to love; bitter thoughts and words give way to blessing. We do good.

Thus victory is achieved not only over self, but often also over the enemy. While enmity repaid with enmity widens the gap, love tends to lessen it and reunite the broken friendship.

*May Thy love to me, Lord Jesus, warm my heart with love
even to my enemies. Amen.*

—〰—

January 12, 1950

January 13

—W—

Read John 17: 20–26
I will come again and will take you to Myself, that where I am you
may be also. *John 14:3*

Where I Am You May Be Also

No one can trace the trend of the Savior's thoughts during the closing scenes of His earthly life without being deeply impressed by the *one* compelling force that lay behind His every word and deed: His affectionate attachment to His faithful few and His deep desire that His intimate and free companionship with them be continued in His Father's house above.

Thus, for instance, in His High Priestly Prayer in the Upper Room that night, after imploring the Father's many blessings upon all Christians of all times, He climaxes this prayer of prayers with the jewel of all petitions: "Father, I desire that they also, whom You have given Me, *may be with Me where I am*, to see My glory that You have given Me" (John 17:24, emphasis added). He shares with His Father a desire that, when He repeats it to His disciples, becomes a promise: "I will come again and will take you to Myself, that where I am you may be also."

Jesus has secured His Father's approval and permission to bring His friends into His Father's house. By His death of reconciliation, He has unlocked the door of His Father's home. *Heaven is now an open house!* "Where I am you"—you who have come to the Father by Me—"may be also." What greater delight, what higher ecstasy can the sin-bound soul envision than to spend the endless ages of the world to come in the Father's house with Jesus!

Draw us to Thee, For then shall we
Walk in Thy steps forever
And hasten on Where Thou art gone
To be with Thee, dear Savior. (LSB 701:1)

—W—

January 13, 1944

JANUARY 14

—∞—

Read Ecclesiastes 12:1–7
Psalm 103
For He knows our frame; He remembers that we are dust. *Psalm 103:14*

HE KNOWS WHO YOU ARE

We often say, "I'm only human!" It is true—we are not perfect. We are not God. God knows that too. "He remembers that we are dust." But this is no excuse for doing things unbecoming to God. The fact that we are mortal will not cause God to look the other way.

Many excuse themselves from taking the road of repentance, saying they are only human. But that is all it is—an excuse—and one that our Lord cannot accept.

In the beginning, God created man holy, and He expects us to be holy now. He isn't being difficult. It is simply that anything unclean cannot hold up in His holy presence. It is like fire and straw. God is pure, like a consuming fire, and straw cannot hold up in the presence of fire.

How, then, can we frail humans stand before God? It is impossible with us, but not with God. He doesn't treat us as we deserve. In Jesus, who is true man but also true God, our sins have been removed. Now the perfect record of Jesus is ours. He knows who we are. In Jesus, we are His beloved. The Holy Spirit, through Word and Sacrament, kindles in us the purifying fire of God's pure love and enables us to live as the children of God.

Dear Father, thank You for knowing me so well and loving me
so much in Jesus Christ, my Savior. Amen.

—∞—

January 14, 1994

January 15

—ᴍᴍ—

Read Psalm 38
The sacrifices of God are a broken spirit; a broken and contrite heart,
O God, You will not despise. *Psalm 51:17*

The Dust of Repentance

The first step to God is always through the dust of repentance. God hates pride. The story of the Pharisee and the publican shows this. The Pharisee who paraded his virtues and gave himself straight A's on his report card found that in God's reckoning he had straight F's. The publican who humbled himself was exalted.

The sacrifice that pleases God is the sacrifice of a broken heart and a contrite spirit. God's healing is for crushed hearts. If we draw near to God with an honest heart, we will come confessing our sins. We may come to God in words such as these: "I confess that I have not deserved Thy mercies, for I have often failed to keep Thy Commandments. I know that I have no right to stand before Thee on any record of my own. I have been so slow in my spiritual growth. I have failed often to let my testimony to Thee be clear and true in word and deed. I have been sluggish in my prayer life. I have failed to be loyal and true and sincere and honest. Often I have discredited Thy holy name, which I profess to love. Forgive me, for Jesus' sake."

The Lord will heal the broken heart that seeks the remedy of the Savior's grace. "A bruised reed He will not break, and a faintly burning wick He will not quench" (Isaiah 42:3). God is always ready to stoop down to the lamb caught in the thorns. He will kiss and dry our tears of repentance. The humble ones who come to Him in the tattered rags of their own righteousness will be clothed by Him in the royal robes of their Savior's grace.

Holy Spirit, inscribe deep in my heart: "God opposes the proud,
but gives grace to the humble" (James 4:6). Amen.

—ᴍᴍ—

January 15, 1953

Read Luke 4:14–22
And the Word became flesh and dwelt among us, and we have seen
His glory, glory as of the only Son from the Father, full of grace and truth.
John 1:14

FULL OF GRACE AND TRUTH

John and his fellow disciples saw divine glory in Jesus where others observed nothing but humiliation. So it is with all believers. Our faith sees in Him the majesty, beauty, purity, and splendor of God. To us, He is the only-begotten of the Father. He has done for us what only God could do. He has vanquished Satan, conquered sin, hushed the threatening voice of the Law, and overcome death. He has broken our stubborn will, burst our fetters, and filled our hearts with inexpressible and precious joy. May others think of Him what they will; to us, He is the only-begotten of the Father.

And He is full of grace. He was this in His dealings with the suppliants and the penitent in the days of His flesh, and He has been thus with us. If He had not been full of grace, we could never be what we now are. He drew us to Himself when we would turn from His grace, and by the power of His love we were brought to the mercy seat as brokenhearted penitents.

And He is also full of truth. His words and promises have been yea and amen; we have never vainly confided in Him. He has been to us a "friend who sticks closer than a brother" (Proverbs 18:24), the faithful Bridegroom of our souls, the most blessed Comforter in distress. Our Lord Jesus is all grace and no judgment, all truth and no deception. He is full of grace and truth, for He is the only-begotten of the Father.

—⟋⟍—

January 16, 1938

Read Romans 8:18–27
Psalm 62
God shows His love for us in that while we were still sinners,
Christ died for us. *Romans 5:8*

GRACE BEYOND COMPARE

As we comb through the Old and the New Testaments, we find passage after passage telling us how much God loves us. Although different writers say it in different ways, the message is always the same: in spite of our sinfulness, in spite of our rebellious nature and nasty disposition, God loves us so much that He paid the ultimate price for our redemption.

In today's verse, we find one of the clearest statements regarding the grace of God in Jesus Christ. St. Paul said it all in just seventeen words. God, out of love for you and me, gave His most precious possession—His only-begotten Son—that you and I might be forgiven and reconciled to Him. And He didn't wait for us to try to deserve it. On the contrary, while we were still disobedient, nasty, and selfish individuals, Christ took upon Himself our sin so that we would not have to suffer the death God's justice demands. Jesus Christ gave up His life so that we could have ours to enjoy and to live with Him now and for all eternity.

Heavenly Father, I thank You for being gracious and merciful to me in Jesus, my Savior. Amen.

—⁓—

April 17, 1993

January 18

—⟋⟍—

Read 1 Corinthians 3:11–16
Psalm 127
It is no longer I who live, but Christ who lives in me. *Galatians 2:20*

Standing on Christ

The religion of St. Paul did not stand on its head or on its hands but on Christ. "I decided to know nothing among you except Jesus Christ and Him crucified" (1 Corinthians 2:2). We, too, must put Jesus Christ squarely into the center of our lives. Only then is our faith and religion right side up. We are to fix our eyes on God as He takes His mind off the stars and fastens them on Abraham, promising him the greater Son, the Messiah. Then God gave His people the Ten Commandments, yet declared that "by works of the law no human being will be justified" (Romans 3:20). God sent His Son into our world and to the cross to make good for our many transgressions. All this He did because He loved the world and does not want us, or anyone, to perish.

That is the way to heaven. No man comes to the Father but by His Son. This faith fills us with the joy of forgiveness. It sends us out to make known abroad this joyful message. We do not do this by nature. We act and live this way because Christ is in us. In Christ, we are new creatures. He has washed and cleansed us, restored us to grace, and made us heirs of life eternal. Jesus is our all in all. Therefore, Paul declares: "It is no longer I who live, but Christ who lives in me."

Open our hearts to You, precious Savior, that You may live and rule within and the we be useful to You now and always. Amen.

January 18, 1967

JANUARY 19

Read Psalm 51
Blessed is the one whose transgression is forgiven, whose sin is covered.
Psalm 32:1

THE JOY OF FORGIVENESS

Into our lives come experiences that cut deep into our memory. They will never be forgotten. We have been frightened as a child, and the scare gave us a complex that makes us afraid to be in a small room, to associate with a big-built person, to stay in bed during a thunderstorm. We have been humiliated, and the bitter incident has shadowed our entire outlook on life.

King David, likewise, had many experiences that burned themselves deeply into his mind and heart. He had fought Goliath, and the thrill was never forgotten. He had taken the spear one night from Saul's side and was thankful that he had not slain the king.

But the most blessed experience—so David confesses—came to him when he learned that his sins were forgiven. His sins haunted him in the still night watches. He tossed on a sleepless bed, conscious of his shameful transgressions. The ghost of Uriah did not let him rest. Then he confessed his sins to God and found forgiveness. Once more, he was at peace with God. He exclaims: "Blessed is the one whose transgression is forgiven, whose sin is covered."

How is this blessed experience obtained? Sin must be canceled, and it can be canceled only through the precious blood of Jesus. His righteousness covers us and removes our sin from God's sight. Our sin is not counted against us as we come to the cross, trusting in the merits of Jesus, who died for us. This is the most blessed experience that anyone can have. Through His Son, we are reconciled to God. We are certain that heaven is our home.

Gracious Lord, through Jesus' precious blood, blot out all our sins and remember them no more. Amen.

January 19, 1941

January 20

Read John 3:16–21
Psalm 54
The reason the Son of God appeared was to destroy the works
of the devil. *1 John 3:8*

No Condemnation

During Jesus' ministry, penitent publicans came to Him, and He took them in. When an adulteress was flung at His feet, Jesus acknowledged her. On the cross, He promised paradise to a man who had been an evildoer. The Scriptures teach that Jesus never refused anyone—regardless of the wretchedness of the past—if only that individual penitently confessed his or her sins and looked in faith to Him as the Savior. In John 6:37, He said, "Whoever comes to Me I will never cast out."

And Jesus will not refuse us. Even as churchgoers, we may think of ourselves as of no worth, but that is the devil's lie. We may think we are deserving only of hell and that God's grace is too small to cover all our misdeeds, but that is only the lying voice of him whom Revelation 12:10 calls "the accuser of our brothers." The truth of the Scriptures, which cannot lie, is this: "God did not send His Son into the world to condemn the world, but in order that the world might be saved through Him" (John 3:17). It is for the very purpose of our salvation that Jesus came to endure the eternal and temporal punishment for our transgressions, that we might be spared the consequences of our iniquity in torment and perdition.

Gracious Lord, impress on us the magnitude of Your mercy and the vast outreach of Your redemption. Amen.

January 20, 1983

January 21

—꿈—

Read John 3:1–8
Psalm 145
Your kingdom come. *Matthew 6:10*

The Kingdom Here and Now

As a boy, I spent the weeks before Christmas searching for hidden gifts. I scoured closets and peeked under beds, trying to find the presents my parents had bought for me. The gifts were hidden, but I knew they must be around somewhere.

As adults, we often imagine God's kingdom to be a little like those gifts. We believe God has good things in mind for us. But we look high and low, not quite sure where to find them. God's kingdom, like those Christmas packages, may seem hidden or far off.

God is not trying to hide His kingdom from us. He puts His kingdom right out in the open and beckons us to receive it in faith. His kingdom comes to us when God gives us faith and trust in Jesus so that we respond with new obedience to His Word. Through His Church, God delivers His eternal kingdom of life and salvation to each of us, whenever the Gospel of Jesus is proclaimed, whenever Holy Baptism is administered in His name, and whenever Christ's body and blood are fed to His faithful people.

Father, by Your Word and Holy Spirit, deliver Your kingdom to us as we hear about Jesus. Lead us to trust Him wholly with the faith You so kindly have given us. Amen.

—꿈—

January 20, 2008

January 22

—∞—

Read Genesis 15:1–7
Blessed are those who have not seen and yet have believed. *John 20:29*

MORE THAN MEETS THE EYE

We are usually more completely convinced of something if we have seen it with our eyes. We are so constituted that if we can see and handle something, we think we have proof and can be sure. This can get in the way of faith.

God has, to some extent, revealed Himself in the works of nature. From what we see in the universe, we know God is wise and powerful. We know He is a great God. We can handle and see evidence of this all around us. But there is more than meets the eye in the message God has made known to us in Jesus Christ. Thomas, for example, heard from the other disciples that Jesus was no longer dead. But he had to see before he was ready to believe.

Logically, some of God's promises don't make sense to us. Why should God care so much for us as to pay the supreme price to restore life to us—not gold or silver but the blood of His own Son? But that is what the Gospel tells us. St. Paul says this is foolishness to some. So it would be also to us if we accepted as true only what the eye can see. But we live by faith and not by sight. We take God at His promises and are enriched by His many blessings.

Thanks and praise to You, O God, for the gift of faith. I believe, help my unbelief. Amen.

—∞—

January 22, 1973
On this date in 1973,
the Supreme Court decision
in *Roe v. Wade* makes abortion legal in U.S.

January 23

Read John 1:9–14
Psalm 65
For by grace you have been saved through faith. And this is not your own doing; it is the gift of God. *Ephesians 2:8*

The Gift of God

Grace, salvation, faith. All of this is God's gift to us—a gift, given without expectation or possibility of repayment. A gift to mark the occasion of God's love for us. A gift we did nothing to earn. A gift given when we gave no invitation to a party. A gift given for the best reason of all—just because God loves us and desires to give His Son. A gift wrapped in the person of our Lord and Savior Jesus Christ, a gift from God and of God.

The all-powerful, all-righteous God is both the giver and the gift. What did you get for Christmas? You got God. What did you get for January 1 and 2 and 23? You got God. What did God give you for all eternity? You got God. By giving you Jesus, God gave Himself to you. By giving you Jesus, God gave Himself for you.

As morning dawns and as evening fades, God is at work, giving Himself to us in Christ Jesus. God is at work in Christ, revealing the Father, full of grace and truth. God is at work by the Spirit, working through the Word, creating children of God for Himself. This is a gift to shout about, a gift to sing about, a gift to brag about. Our boast is in Jesus Christ, our God and Savior.

O Holy Spirit, open our eyes to the wonder of God's glorious gift revealed in Christ. Move us to rejoice in the good gift God is for us. In Jesus' name. Amen.

January 23, 2006

January 24

—⬯—

Read I Corinthians 10:13
Cast your burden on the LORD, and He will sustain you. *Psalm 55:22*

OUR BURDENS

The psalmist is referring to burdens on the heart, not on the back. We all know that mental burdens are often worse than physical ones, and spiritual burdens are worse than both. These words, however, open up a golden opportunity to do something with our burdens.

We should know that burdens are inescapable. They come to high and low, rich and poor, saints and sinners, old and young. We can no more dodge them than we can fly by waving our arms.

Burdens bring temptations. We are tempted to think God is unconcerned. We are tempted to sit in the brew of self-pity. We are tempted to become bitter toward life and people.

David advises us to "cast your burden on the LORD, and He will sustain you." We notice that the first part of this passage is coupled with a promise, namely, "and He will sustain you." This is the key to understanding the first part of the sentence. Our Lord promises to sustain *us*. The burden may still remain, but the weight, the drag, the bitterness will be gone. So it was in the life of the apostle Paul, who complained of his burden, but the Lord said: "My grace is sufficient for you" (2 Corinthians 12:9).

Lord, keep us from becoming embittered under the burdens of life.
For Jesus' sake, strengthen and support us day by day. Amen.

—⬯—

January 24, 1964

January 25

—*◊◊◊*—

Read Matthew 25:31–40
Psalm 35
Brother Saul, the Lord Jesus . . . has sent me. *Acts 9:17*

Sent by the Lord

I t was a highly unlikely meeting. There was Saul, the fierc-est antagonist of the followers of Jesus, face-to-face with Ananias, a leading disciple of Jesus in Damascus. Saul had come to Damascus "breathing threats and murder against the disciples of the Lord" (Acts 9:1). Only something had intervened before he could carry out his plans. Just outside the city, Saul had encountered Jesus, and that encounter reversed the rest of Saul's history. Now he waited, temporarily blind, for further direction. It came in the person of Ananias. What could this man say to a man with Saul's reputation? "Brother Saul, the Lord Jesus . . . has sent me so that you may regain your sight and be filled with the Holy Spirit."

Who but a man in Christ would address his enemy as "Brother" and offer him healing and the promise of forgiveness? But that is the way the Lord sends His disciples into a hostile world. We are still called by God, not to destroy the enemy but to discover our brothers and sisters for whom Christ died. We are still called, not to bring people to their knees in conquest but to bring them to their knees to acknowledge that Jesus is Lord. We are still called, not to rule the world but to serve it with love.

Help us, Lord Jesus, to find our brothers. Amen.

—*◊◊◊*—

January 25, 1970

—⚭—

Read Acts 20:17–35
Psalm 26

To Him who is able to do far more abundantly than all that we ask or
think, according to the power at work within us, to Him be glory in the
church and in Christ Jesus throughout all generations, forever and ever.
Amen. *Ephesians 3:20–21*

TO HIM BE ALL GLORY!

The shepherds set the example. They praised God "for all
they had heard and seen" about the Christ Child (Luke
2:20). The angels did the same as they sang, "Glory to
God in the highest" (Luke 2:14).

What is the message that shepherds proclaim and that makes
angels sing? Salvation! It is the wonderful message that God in His
love sent His Son to make us His sons and daughters.

God sent a Savior to rescue us. St. Paul says it simply and
powerfully: "While we were still sinners, Christ died for us"
(Romans 5:8). We are now among God's holy ones who "have
washed their robes and made them white in the blood of the
Lamb" (Revelation 7:14), who stand before the throne of glory
praising God for His salvation.

It is the privilege of the Holy Christian Church throughout the
world to praise God constantly. Glory be to the Father, whose everlasting love has made us His children. Glory be to the Son, whose
sacrifice on Calvary paid the debt of all our sins. Glory be to the
Holy Spirit, who has brought us to faith and who strengthens and
preserves us to eternity. To Him be all glory in the Church forever!

Praise God, from whom all blessings flow;
Praise Him, all creatures here below;
Praise Him above, ye heav'nly host:
Praise Father, Son, and Holy Ghost. Amen. (LSB 805)

—⚭—

JANUARY 27

—ᴍᴍ—

Read John 4:27–38
Stretch out your hand over the sea, that the water may come back
upon the Egyptians. *Exodus 14:26*

USING GOD'S RESOURCES

T he sea was before the Israelites, and the Egyptian army
was behind them. The hills cut off escape to the side.
Yet the word they heard from God through Moses was
"Fear not!"

How often it seems to us that the challenges of life are too
much! We rest fairly secure when we have resources of our own
to overcome problems. But there come times when, in Martin Luther's words, "with might of ours can naught be done." And what
we do as the Church often seems to fail. We view the world around
us and feel that the progress of the Gospel is so slow. We try to
share Christ with a friend and get nowhere. The opportunities are
so great, but our best efforts seem so small.

Then the Lord comes to us and says, "Fear not!" He invites
us to use His resources. He gives us life and salvation. He gives
us hope for the future. He gives us the power and the needed
resources for every challenge of life. These resources are available
to us because God sent His Son, Jesus Christ, into the world to lay
down His life on the cross so that we might have life and hope.
God's resources are never exhausted. Use them!

*Lord, give us the faith and wisdom to use Your resources, Word and
Sacraments, that we may grow in grace. Amen.*

—ᴍᴍ—

January 27, 1973
On this date in 1973, signing of Paris Peace Accords

Read 2 Corinthians 1:1–7
Psalm 92
If we are afflicted, it is for your comfort and salvation. *2 Corinthians 1:6*

TRIUMPH OVER TRAGEDY

When the brilliant William Moon of England was at the height of his mental powers, his future looked promising. Then tragedy struck—he became blind! At first, he exclaimed, "What are my abilities worth now that I am shut up here in my room?" However, slowly he began to realize God had a wise purpose in allowing him to be afflicted. Because his eyes were sightless, he began to develop a unique system of the alphabet to assist others in a similar condition. It soon was adapted to fit the languages of many countries. More than four million blind persons were thus enabled to read the Bible. They found that the kind of embossed type he used was easy to learn.

Even though Moon's efforts were later superseded by those of Louis Braille, it was Moon's pioneering work that helped make possible the latter system that ultimately replaced it. William Moon became a missionary in an unusual way and brought "comfort and salvation" in Christ to many. Out of his tragedy came a great triumph.

Every child of God, regardless of trial or handicap, similarly can be used to bless others. Christ helps us triumph over tragedy.

Lord, help us, even in our affliction, to see how others may be benefited and how it may be for our comfort and salvation. Amen.

—w—

January 28, 1986
On this date in 1986, space shuttle *Challenger* disaster occurs

JANUARY 29

—ɷ—

Read Genesis 7:17–8:1
Psalm 111
But God remembered Noah. *Genesis 8:1*

NOT FORGOTTEN

Have you ever really thought about Noah's plight? At the end of Genesis 7, he had been in the ark for five months. Everything was covered with water. There were no visible signs of anything but endless water everywhere! Noah is listed in Hebrews 11 as one of those heroes of faith who are cheering us on, but there had to have been times when he wondered a bit if maybe God had forgotten him!

"But God remembered Noah." Regardless of our circumstances and how we might feel, God does not forget His people. Only once did God forsake one of His own. That was on a cross, where in one terrible moment His own Son took our place and paid the price for our sins. Through faith in what took place on the cross, we have become the never-to-be-forgotten, never-to-be-forsaken children of God.

"But God remembered Noah." What comfort we find in those words! Things will go wrong in our lives from time to time. Sometimes it might seem that there is no way out of a difficult problem and no visible sign of hope in sight. We may feel adrift and forgotten. That's when we need to remember that God doesn't forget! We can fill in the blank with our own name: But God remembered _____!

Father, give us the hope that comes from remembering that You never forget us. In Jesus' name we pray. Amen.

—ɷ—

January 29, 2001

JANUARY 30

—ᴍ—

Read 2 Timothy 2
Psalm 89:1–14
If we are faithless, He remains faithful—for He cannot deny Himself.
2 Timothy 2:13

HE WHO PROMISES IS FAITHFUL

When someone promises something, we either trust that promise or we don't. If the person making the promise has been faithful in the past, we tend to trust the promise. If that person has let us down a time or two, we may mistrust the promise.

In his Second Letter to Timothy, Paul shares some promises of God that motivate him to endure suffering. Paul says, "The saying is trustworthy, for: If we have died with Him, we will also live with Him" (2 Timothy 2:11). Paul reminds himself and fellow Christians of the promise of new birth given in Baptism (Romans 6:3–4). Paul shares another promise of Jesus: "If we endure, we will also reign with Him" (2 Timothy 2:12). Jesus gave this promise for those who remain in the faith until the end (Mark 13:13). After Paul shares God's promises with Timothy, he reminds him that the Promiser "remains faithful—for He cannot deny Himself."

When we need encouragement as did Timothy, we turn to the cross of Jesus. On the cross, our promised redemption is made complete. In Word and Sacrament, this promise touches us in our very body and soul. We need only to look to His cross to know that He who promises is faithful.

Heavenly Father, we thank You for Your promises, for we know that what You promise is true. Amen.

—ᴍ—

January 11, 2011

JANUARY 31

—⟡—

Read Hebrews 11:1–22
Psalm 112
This is the victory that has overcome the world—our faith. *1 John 5:4*

HEROES OF FAITH

Abraham, Isaac, Jacob, and Joseph were great men, but such greatness is not to be found only in the lives of those who are head and shoulders above ordinary people. Simple men and women in the common walks of life may be equally great, as was the woman who pleaded for her daughter (Matthew 15:21–28) or the Roman soldier who asked Jesus to heal his servant (Matthew 8:5–10).

Even today, it is possible by the grace of God to be great in His sight. To suffer injury or loss without complaining, to make sacrifices for the welfare of others, to be cheerful in a long and painful illness, to refuse to make compromises with the truth even under severe pressure, to boldly confess Christ when ridiculed or when life is endangered—all this is part of a heroic life that may be ours with the help of God.

Victories on the battlefield, in athletic contests, and in business enterprises are highly regarded, yet they pale into insignificance beside the faith that the Holy Spirit implants in us, faith that leans on God's wisdom and power and is rooted in the sacrifice Christ made for us on the cross.

Thanks be to God, who gives us the victory through our Lord Jesus Christ. Amen.

—⟡—

January 31, 1966

February

Thank You, Father, for
remembering even me
when You gave the gift
of eternal life through
your Son, Jesus Christ.
Amen.

February 1

—ɯɯ—

Read John 13:1–10
What I am doing you do not understand now, but afterward
you will understand. *John 13:7*

NOW AND HEREAFTER

Here is a word of light and comfort for every troubled and perplexed heart. Peter questioned the Master's doings; he could not understand them. At first, he refused to let Jesus have His way. But after hearing the Master's firm and reassuring words, he gladly yielded and thus received the blessing.

How like Peter we are! We, too, want to understand God's ways, but we cannot. His thoughts are not our thoughts; His ways are not our ways. And so our proud intellect refuses to assent, our stubborn heart refuses to yield. We murmur and complain, rebel and repine. Our Lord must then speak firmly to us: "If you will not let Me have My way with you, then you can have no part with Me."

Yet such is the compassion of our Savior that He at once adds the word of promise and assurance: "Afterward you will understand." And always the promise comes true. Countless believers will testify to the fact that this "afterward" began for them already in this life, that in later years they could see clearly that God had loved them dearly. They then understood that His thoughts were higher than their thoughts, His ways better than their ways. And the unnumbered saints made perfect in heaven will declare in an eternal afterward that God made no mistake, that He truly led them in paths of righteousness for His name's sake. Here we behold the earthward side of the cloud of sorrow, and it looks dark. Afterward, we shall see the heavenward side of the same cloud, and we shall find it very bright. Trust Jesus. The rainbow of His divine wisdom and love is ever shining above the storm clouds.

—ɯɯ—

February 1, 1939

February 2

—ᵐ—

Read John 17:10–17
To those sanctified in Christ Jesus. *I Corinthians 1:2*

SANCTIFIED IN CHRIST

We are living in an age that has the distinction of being the cleanest in the history of the world. Strict rules of sanitation and cleanliness are insisted upon by all who would lead healthy lives. And it is certainly right and proper that this be so.

If daily cleansing of the body is necessary to physical health and happiness, it should be equally true that a daily sanctification is essential to spiritual health and happiness. Deeply solemn, therefore, is the thought our motto verse suggests: "Sanctification in Christ Jesus." He who "chose us in Him . . . that we should be holy and blameless before Him" (Ephesians 1:4) expects and demands this daily sanctification. The daily sanctification of the soul should be as natural to the Christian as the cleansing of the body.

And although we have become new and holy creatures in Christ, we are still tempted to sin by the weakness of the flesh. And every repeated act of sin, whether in thought, word, or deed, leaves its stain on the soul. The devil, the world, and our flesh place many stumbling stones in our Christian way, and many times our garment of righteousness and holiness bears the polluting stains of our sins of weakness. Each day demands, therefore, that we go in prayer to the throne of grace and petition the Holy Spirit to cleanse and sanctify us anew in the fountain of God's forgiving Word.

Let us bow our heads as Jesus prays to His heavenly Father for us:
"Sanctify them in the truth; Your Word is truth" (John 17:17). Amen.

—ᵐ—

February 2, 1943

FEBRUARY 3

—ᗰ—

Read Philippians 3:7–21
Psalm 92
Our citizenship is in heaven. *Philippians 3:20*

CITIZENS OF HEAVEN

S t. Paul was speaking to people who were "colonists," who lived in one place but had their citizenship in another. He asks them to apply their political situation to their religious life. They were living on earth, but they must conduct themselves by heaven's constitution and bill of rights.

There are few things that the Church of today needs more than this note of other-worldliness. This is not to say that the problems of the world are of no concern to the Christian. On the contrary, he is to be concerned about this world's affairs because it is his Father's world. He must speak the language of this world, but speak it with a decidedly foreign accent. There should be something about her, even when she does what other people do, that indicates that she is doing it from a different motive and perspective.

The heavenly citizenship involves many risks, many trials. But that is what "bearing the cross" is all about. In working out such a citizenship, we need no complicated legal system in order to know what to do. We follow Jesus Christ, who said: "If anyone would come after Me, let him deny himself and take up his cross and follow Me" (Matthew 16:24). To those who in faith follow Him, He gives eternal life.

Heavenly Father, grant us grace so to proclaim Thy Word and so to live, that we may bring many to heaven, our home. Amen.

—ᗰ—

February 3, 1971

Read Matthew 14:13–21
Psalm 107

[Andrew said,] "There is a boy here who has five barley loaves and two fish, but what are they for so many?" *John 6:9*

SOMEBODY NEEDS YOU

More than five thousand people had gathered on a hillside in Galilee to hear Jesus and watch Him heal the sick. When evening came, Jesus had pity on them. He fed that weary, hungry multitude using five loaves and two fish that belonged to a young boy. He used His disciples to organize and serve the crowd.

Jesus helped people by using people. He made Himself dependent on human beings. God still does.

The great commands remain the same: Love the Lord with all your being, and love your neighbor as yourself. We're all meant to be bound together by love.

There is enough food in the world for all to be satisfied. Yet every day, thousands die of malnutrition because food is not distributed fairly. The Lord depends on us, who have daily bread, to share it with those who do not.

Multitudes hunger for the bread of life, the Gospel. They will perish if they don't know God loves them and came to earth to live a life of love in His Son. Jesus' death makes eternal life possible for them. God is depending on us to tell them the Good News.

The Lord doesn't expect us to help the whole world. But He reminds us that someone out there, perhaps someone right in your own neighborhood, needs you.

Dear Lord Jesus, we offer what we have for Your use in helping others.
Open our eyes to the opportunities You give us. Amen.

—⟋⟋—

—⟋⟍—

Read Psalm 139:1–6
Psalm 8
I am fearfully and wonderfully made. Psalm 139:14

MY MAKER

Martin Luther, in his Small Catechism, wasn't satisfied to talk in pious generalities. Repeatedly, he showed how much the truths revealed in the Bible meant to him as an individual. His words reflected his personal faith in his Lord.

Luther didn't settle for "I believe God has made the world." He began his explanation of the First Article of the Apostles' Creed: "I believe that God has made *me*." He went on: "He has given me *my* body and soul, eyes, ears, and all *my* members, *my* reason and all *my* senses." He mentioned specifics such as his house, home, wife, children, land, and animals. He thanked God that "He richly and daily provides *me* with all that *I* need . . . for all which it is my duty to thank and praise, to serve and obey Him" (emphasis added).

Having faith in God means more than being able to recite Bible passages. Faith is not simply words about what God has done. A man may say the right words and subscribe to the correct statements of doctrine and yet not be a Christian.

Faith says this: "God made *me*. Christ is *my* Lord, who has redeemed *me*. The Holy Ghost has called *me*." Faith is *my* hand in the hand of God.

The psalmist didn't just say, "God did a great job." With openmouthed awe he exclaimed: "*I* am fearfully and wonderfully made."

My Maker, be near me and accept my thanks. Amen.

—⟋⟍—

February 5, 1972

Read Revelation 22:13–21

ALPHA AND OMEGA

These words from the last chapter in the Holy Bible are the last words of Jesus Christ, our incarnate Savior, to the Church and to the world at large. In these last words, He calls Himself the Alpha and the Omega, the Beginning and the End, the First and the Last. Only God can talk like that. And Jesus is God. From everlasting to everlasting, He is God. By Him the universe came into being in the beginning, and by Him it shall come to its end in the day appointed. And He is the Beginning and the End of the revelation of God. He has revealed the one true and only God, the ever-blessed Holy Trinity. He has made known to mankind the counsel of God's salvation. He is the God of the holy prophets and apostles. He calls all people to repentance and faith. He promises grace and every blessing to all who obey Him. He threatens the plague of the judgments of God to all who falsify His Word by adding thereto or taking away therefrom. He calls to all the world to make ready for the last judgment. He will surely come. Amen. Yes, He will come. Meanwhile, His Holy Spirit, through the Church, cries to the world, "Come." And Christ again and again cries to the world, "Come." All who thirst for pardon and life shall come. His everlasting salvation is free; let the weary and heavy-laden take it without money and without price.

With the believing Church we answer: "Even so, come, Lord Jesus." We desire to see Him who loved us and gave Himself for us and washed us from our sins in His own blood. Until He comes, He assures us of His grace and love: "The grace of our Lord Jesus Christ be with you all" (2 Thessalonians 3:18).

Lord Jesus, come. Amen.

—ww—

February 6, 1940

Read Mark 12:28–34
Psalm 82
"Which of these three, do you think, proved to be a neighbor . . .?"
He said, "The one who showed him mercy." *Luke 10:36–37*

WHO IS MY NEIGHBOR?

A Bible scholar was testing Jesus. This man had been brought up in a culture that set boundaries for neighbors. He wanted to hear what parameters or limits Jesus would set for those He should care about.

The surprise of the story is that the hero was a Samaritan. Israelites and Samaritans shared a great hatred for one another. The Law expert had been taught that "neighbors"—those we should love—were limited to his own kind.

What are the parameters of our neighborliness? A loving parent will lose sleep and expend unlimited money for his or her child. Would that same parent assist an orphan?

Our society continues with its ghettos fenced in by nationality and race and language. Jesus proposed to the lawyer the new attitude that we love everyone, even our enemies. That attitude was modeled by Jesus, who died for the sins of us all. He thereby opened the gates of heaven to *everyone* who believes in Him—not just one particular group. He demonstrated that "greater love has no one than this, that someone lay down his life for his friends" (John 15:13).

Thank You, Jesus, for dying for us all, that we might have life in Your name. Amen.

—◊◊—

February 7, 1993

Read Luke 23:39–43
Truly, I say to you, today you will be with Me in Paradise. *Luke 23:43*

WELCOME IN THE FATHER'S HOUSE

Of the few persons the Scriptures specifically tell us are now in the Father's house, one was a *criminal*! To a man who had misspent his life in sin and shame, but who in his dying moment had come to faith in the Redeemer, the Savior opened wide the doors of His Father's house and said: "Truly, I say to you, today you will be with Me in Paradise." There was room even for this dying thief in the Father's house above.

Heaven is like that! Its mansions are peopled *not* with those who in this life paraded as the paragons of piety and virtue while spurning the Savior's mercy, but with the vast unnumbered throng of converted "dying thieves," "penitent publicans," and those, both great and small, who have come "out of the great tribulation [and] have washed their robes and made them white in the blood of the Lamb" (Revelation 7:14).

What an inviting, reassuring picture of our Father's house—to remember that the dying thief awaits us there. *His* Savior is *our* Savior. The door by which he entered the Father's house is still open to us: the door of repentance for sin and faith in a divine Redeemer. The same blood that availed for him will avail for us. Yes, verily, "the blood of Jesus Christ His Son cleanses us from all sin" (1 John 1:7).

The dying thief rejoiced to see
That fountain in his day;
And there have I, as vile as he,
Washed all my sins away! **(TLH 157:2)**

—⚏—

February 8, 1944

Read Luke 10:38–42
Psalm 26
Martha, Martha, you are anxious and troubled about many things,
but one thing is necessary. Mary has chosen the good portion,
which will not be taken away from her. *Luke 10:41–42*

ONE THING IS NEEDED

No one is able to please the Lord just by putting out great effort and sacrifice. So often we measure a person's dedication by how busy that person is. But God isn't looking for merely busy people. He desires that we glorify His name. The Lord commanded us to be about our daily business. So perhaps we go into the kitchen, wash dishes, scrub the pots and pans, and mop the floor. We check our watches and see that we have put in a full day of work. Have we served God?

We review our daily activity. We have done what we ought, but did we take time to read God's Word, the Bible? And did we thank Him for His grace in providing eternal salvation for us in His Son, Jesus? When we do not take time every day to reflect on the goodness of the Lord, we end up working very hard, but we miss the one thing needed to live fully to His glory.

Holy Father, forgive us for so often focusing on the immediate tasks
at hand and overlooking daily opportunities to grow in Your grace
and knowledge in Jesus Christ. Amen.

—⁓—

February 9, 2001

FEBRUARY 10

—◊—

Read John 6:1–14
Psalm 116
[Andrew said,] "There is a boy here who has five barley loaves
and two fish, but what are they for so many?" John 6:9

THE POWER OF ONE

One boy did not seem very significant that day in a crowd of five thousand men. His supply of bread and fish would not have gone very far even if he had been willing to share or sell them. But the boy became a good example for us because he made his bread and fish available to Jesus. Jesus' power multiplied them so they were sufficient to feed the vast throng.

Most of us may not feel significant. The abilities we have and the things we possess may not seem important in relieving the misery of the world. Yet today, as in the past, God can do much with our little, if we let Him.

One act of kindness can brighten the whole day for several other people. Those who were helped come into contact with others and can multiply the effect of that one kind deed. One word of forgiveness or encouragement sometimes sets the direction of an entire life.

Let us remember the power of one person—the influence for good that each of us has if he is willing to be available when God wants to use him. Through that one person, God can bless a whole family, change a community for the better, and inspire an entire congregation.

*Lord Jesus, help us to seize every opportunity You give us today
to love You through loving others. Amen.*

—◊—

February 10, 1975

Read 1 Peter 5:6–11
Psalm 51:8–12

Create in me a clean heart, O God, And renew a steadfast spirit
within me. *Psalm 51:10 (NKJV)*

STEADFAST

I like the word *steadfast*. It makes me think of strength, reliability, faithfulness, immovability, and trustworthiness. I would like to be considered steadfast—a steadfast friend, a steadfast worker who is strong and reliable, faithful and immovable and trustworthy.

I try to be steadfast in my faith life. I go to church, make a point of talking to God in prayer, try to live according to Jesus' way of love. For all my efforts, I invariably discover that I'm not the steadfast person I want to be. I stumble and fail. I am unfaithful and weak. I cannot keep my own heart pure or my spirit steadfast.

When I fall, when my heart cries out to God to step in and fix my failings, then it is He who is steadfast. He is strong, faithful, and trustworthy. He gives the gift of the Holy Spirit to draw and keep me close to Him, to strengthen my weak faith, and to remind me of the purity of heart Christ won for us on the cross.

Every day the unfailing, steadfast love of God creates in me a new, clean heart, and in His forgiveness, I am strong.

Faithful God, trustworthy Lord, lead me to rely on You as the source
of my strength and steadfastness. Amen.

—∼∿∼—

February 11, 2007

FEBRUARY 12

—⁂—

Read John 18:33–38
Psalm 119:121–128
Seek first the kingdom of God and His righteousness, and all these things
will be added to you. *Matthew 6:33*

LIFE'S PRIORITY

We live in a time that might be described as the "age of leisure." We have many time-saving devices. We desire shorter work weeks but longer vacations and weekends that are filled with ample "free time." Yet in our pursuit of leisure time, great unhappiness often develops.

Perhaps it is time that we look seriously at the encouragement of Jesus to seek first the kingdom of God. True, we have our jobs by which we make a living. But neither our jobs nor our leisure must become the priority of our lives. We were born—as also Jesus was born—for the purpose of seeking first God's kingdom. This must be the top priority for everyone who hears the Gospel call of the Lord and comes under the transforming power of His Word.

All too many people are so busy making a living that they have forgotten why they are living. The moment we were purchased by the blood of Jesus we became His, and our purpose is to serve Him. It is because all too often we have forgotten this priority that our anticipated joys of leisure time fail to materialize.

Thank You, Lord Jesus Christ, for the privilege of serving You in Your kingdom. Grant that seeking Your righteousness may always be the top priority of my life. Amen.

—⁂—

February 12, 1983

Read Galatians 3:1–14
Psalm 35
By grace you have been saved through faith. And this is not your own
doing; it is the gift of God. *Ephesians 2:8*

EXAMPLE OR SAVIOR?

There are many who try to minimize sin, who say God is a kind, lenient, easygoing Father who will forgive everybody. Preachers have said that Christ's message is all summed up in the Sermon on the Mount and in the Golden Rule. Their whole approach is this: Christ is a great example. Follow Him. Do what He did, live as He lived, be as He was, and you will be saved. To that we answer, "Go ahead and try it." Soon, we find out that we cannot do it. We might just as well come to a man who is struggling in quicksand up to his neck and say to him, "You had better hurry and save yourself before it is too late." What do you think he is trying to do? He *would* save himself if he could, but he can't.

How comforting to the sinner then to hear that God is merciful, that He has *already* made peace with us through His Son, who died for us on the cross! While truth lays bare our sin and shame, mercy pleads, "Forgive and save." While truth insists, "The soul that sins, it shall die," peace nonetheless says to our tortured hearts, "Fear not! Be still!" God's holiness cries out, "Justice must be done!" God's love cries out, "Whoever believes in [Christ] should not perish but have eternal life" (John 3:16).

Dear dying Lamb, Thy precious blood
Shall never lose its power. Amen.

February 14, 1965

Read I John 4:7–11
I Corinthians 13:4–6

In this the love of God was made manifest among us, that God sent His only Son into the world, so that we might live through Him. *I John 4:9*

TRUE LOVE

I f you listen to music from a radio station for an hour, you will discover that there are few songs that don't have love and romance as the theme.

Love is more than just a song. Love is visible. People see it in you. You *show* it. God our Creator *revealed* it. He proved His love when He sent His Son to become a man in Jesus Christ. Out of His love, God ordained that Christ would take the punishment for our sin upon Himself and pay the price for us. "The LORD has laid on Him the iniquity of us all" (Isaiah 53:6).

What is love? It is the total giving of yourself to another with no thought of reward for yourself. In His most trying moment, as the battered Savior walked toward Calvary's cross, He saw some women from Jerusalem weeping. He stopped. "Do not weep for Me," He said, forgetting His own pain, "but weep for yourselves and for your children" (Luke 23:28). Even at that moment, Christ was concerned not for Himself, but that people might believe in Him and so be saved from the coming destruction. True love is patient, does not seek its own, is not arrogant, and bears all things (1 Corinthians 13:4–6). That is God's love. Do you love like that?

Father, fill me with Christ's love, and grant me Your Spirit to love selflessly. Amen.

—⟁—

February 14, 1991

FEBRUARY 15

—⟋⟍—

Read 2 Corinthians 12:7–10
. . . having been buried with Him in baptism. *Colossians 2:12*

BURIED WITH CHRIST

When a man is convicted of murder, the judge pronounces the sentence. In some states, the penalty is death. In others, it is life imprisonment.

All human beings stand before the court of divine justice and are found guilty under God's Law. The Word of God announces death as the penalty for all offenses. "The wages of sin is death" (Romans 6:23).

There is one escape available for the sinner. God Himself provides that way. It is the way of Jesus' death and burial. Jesus died in our stead, and He was buried as though He were the punished criminal. We may now point to His cross and say, "That death was for *our* rebellion. His grave is the grave *we* deserve."

Baptism is the wonderful means God uses to bring me the benefits of Christ's death. The water of Baptism covers my head to signify that the grave covered Christ and my sin. In Baptism, I am joined to Christ, and my sinful self is buried in His grave.

Each day as sin tries to gain the upper hand in my life, I do well to remember my Baptism. The sinner in me is not to be kept alive. I have been buried with Christ.

**O God, give me grace every day to remember my Baptism
and to let my selfish life stay buried with Christ. Amen.**

—⟋⟍—

February 15, 1963

February 16

—ᵡᵡ—

Read Titus 3:5–7
Psalm 51
You must be born again. *John 3:7*

SPIRITUAL REGENERATION

While Christians are conscious that they have been made new creatures in Christ, they cannot describe how this marvelous change occurred. This is not surprising, because spiritual regeneration is a work of the Holy Spirit through the almighty power of God's Word. Holy Scriptures compare the Word to sown seed that grows by itself, and man knows not how (Mark 4:26–28; 1 Peter 1:23).

In His conversation with Nicodemus, Christ compared the Holy Spirit's mysterious work to that of the wind, which cannot be seen but whose power can be observed in the results it produces. The results of regeneration are seen when the Spirit delivers men from Satan's kingdom of darkness into God's kingdom of light, in which they have redemption through Christ's blood, even the forgiveness of sins.

Through God's mercy, the Holy Spirit has performed this gracious work in us, brought us to faith in Christ, and made us God's children and heirs of eternal life. Let our conduct ever show forth His praises.

Create in me a new heart, Lord,
That gladly I obey Your Word.
Let what You will be my desire,
And with new life my soul inspire. (LSB 704:3)

—ᵡᵡ—

February 16, 1968

—ᴍ—

Read Hebrews 12:1–11
Psalm 55
Your rod and Your staff, they comfort me. *Psalm 23:4*

THE SHEPHERD CORRECTS US

A shepherd uses his rod to nudge the straying sheep back in line and into the safety of the flock. The shepherd knows that his sheep need discipline and correction.

Sometimes our Lord must correct us. We wander into foolish places where we have no business going. We lose ourselves in self-interest. We stray into places fraught with danger. We linger, sometimes even wallow, in the dark valley of despair.

Yet Jesus Christ, who died for us and rose again, is always there for us. His saving grace nudges us back into the green and pleasant pastures of His love. He forgives our waywardness and puts us back into the care and protection of His mercy.

The Good Shepherd gives us His Word to correct us. The mirror of His Law shows us that we have sinned and strayed from the path of His righteousness. The grace of God in Jesus Christ then shines brightly into our hearts and lives to comfort and forgive us. The mercy of the Good Shepherd invites us to follow Him, and the protection He provides draws us close to Him.

O Lord, show me my sins, and through Your mercy make me
one of Your own. Amen.

—ᴍ—

February 17, 1997

February 18

—ɯ—

Read I Peter 2:11–25
Beloved, I urge you as sojourners and exiles to abstain from the passions
of the flesh, which wage war against your soul. *I Peter 2:11*

STRANGERS AND PILGRIMS

Man's brief stay here on earth reminds us that we are but strangers and pilgrims here. Even what we refer to as a long life of fourscore years is but a short journey from the cradle to the grave. And from the eternal observation point, where "a thousand years . . . are but as yesterday" (Psalm 90:4), life on earth will seem but a small fraction of time.

Being strangers and pilgrims, and not permanent residents here on earth, reminds us that even though we are in the world, we must never be of the world. It would be foolish to dote on this world as though it were never to end or to neglect the next as though it were never to begin. Strangers and pilgrims will be guided by what Jesus said: "Enter by the narrow gate. For the gate is wide and the way is easy that leads to destruction, and those who enter by it are many. For the gate is narrow and the way is hard that leads to life, and those who find it are few" (Matthew 7:13–14).

Lord Jesus, teach me to know that
I'm but a stranger here,
Heav'n is my home;
Earth is a desert drear,
Heav'n is my home.
Danger and sorrow stand
Round me on every hand;
Heav'n is my fatherland,
Heav'n is my home. Amen. (LSB 748:1)

—ɯ—

February 18, 1952

Read Luke 22:24–26
Psalm 141
We do not have a high priest who is unable to sympathize
with our weaknesses, but one who in every respect has been tempted
as we are, yet without sin. *Hebrews 4:15*

TEMPTED LIKE US

The last time you were tempted to gossip, to cheat, to lie, did it occur to you that Jesus Christ was tempted in the same way? His temptation was even stronger, for He resisted. Once we submit to temptation, we never know how much stronger that temptation would become if we kept on resisting.

Being tempted—being attracted to sin—is an experience known to us all and known also to our Brother Jesus Christ. Being tempted is no sin; only yielding to temptation is sin. The writer says that Jesus was tempted, yet He did not sin.

Sometimes people hesitate to confess a weakness or a sin to their pastor. They feel he would not understand—as though he were never tempted or had never sinned. The writer to the Hebrews sensed this attitude and in a reassuring statement tells us that Jesus understands. He is our Brother; He faced the same temptations we do. He can—and does—sympathize. The Word of forgiveness He speaks comes with genuine understanding of all we have been through. We receive that Word with joy and thanksgiving.

Save us in the day of trial, O Lord, and deliver us from evil. Amen.

—⟋⟍—

February 19, 1974
On this date in 1974, the walkout at Concordia Seminary of The Lutheran Church—Missouri Synod leads to Concordia Seminary in Exile (Seminex)

—␣␣—

Read Matthew 11:7–19
We have become a spectacle to the world, to angels, and to men.
1 Corinthians 4:9

THE MINISTRY: A SPECTACLE

Like it or not, servants of the Church live a kind of fish-bowl existence. The lack of privacy is often annoying. But what is humiliating beyond tolerance is that the invisible world of evil spirits and the very visible world of evil mankind treat the Christian ministry like a "spectacle." A minister is often treated with curious contempt as though he were an oddity at a circus.

The presence in the ministry of unworthy men has, of course, invited such reaction. But not every minister is a hypocrite. Still, the price of the holy office must be paid by those who hold it. Men accused Jesus of having a devil (Mark 3:22), and Herod regarded Him as though He were a magician (Luke 23:8).

It is good to remember that ministers and all Christians are called for service by the Holy Spirit from out of this world. As such, we are to let our light shine, that all may see that our lives glorify God and give honor to Jesus, our Savior.

Therefore, we should uphold one another's hands and give encouragement to one another as members of the household of God who live in grace, reconciled through the blood shed on Calvary's cross.

*Lord of the Church, by Thy humiliation help Thy servants and us
to bear the ridicule of the world. Give true dignity to Thy faithful servants
as they proclaim the Gospel of peace to us. Amen.*

—␣␣—

February 20, 1962
On this date in 1962, John Glenn, aboard *Friendship 7*,
is first American to orbit Earth

—∞—

Read Matthew 20:20–28
Psalm 68

For a day in Your courts is better than a thousand elsewhere. I would rather be a doorkeeper in the house of my God than dwell in the tents of wickedness. *Psalm 84:10*

GREATNESS IN THE SERVICE OF THE LORD

The psalmist makes it clear that he would rather take a humble post in the temple than find comfortable lodging with those who make capital by exploiting others. No doubt we find his choice a good one. We, too, would serve the Lord with gladness.

Too often we arrogantly strive to be great and important people, noticed and honored by others. This was how Jesus' disciples felt, desiring to be the great ones in His kingdom. Our Lord indicated to a mother who wanted the highest seats in His kingdom for her sons that honor comes not by lording it over others but by serving. When the other disciples heard that the mother of these two had asked for preferential treatment, they became quite jealous. Our Lord cleared up the matter by stating that those are great in the Kingdom who out of love for Him serve their fellowmen. Christ said: "As you did it to one of the least of these My brothers, you did it to Me" (Matthew 25:40).

Such loving service the Lord of all is willing to accept. What undeserved honor!

May our service ever be filled with Thy love, for Jesus' sake. Amen.

—∞—

February 21, 1969

Read Matthew 7:24–29
Psalm 11
They were astonished at His teaching, for He taught them as one
who had authority, and not as the scribes. *Mark 1:22*

THE VOICE OF AUTHORITY

What are the voices of authority in your life? Many people do not begin a day without consulting the morning newspaper, watching the first news on television, or listening to the radio. All of these media of communication keep us informed. They have become voices of authority.

According to today's text, Jesus opened the eyes, ears, and hearts of people as He began His ministry in a synagogue at Capernaum. The people responded in amazement as He taught God's Word with divine authority and by His divine power healed a possessed man. Jesus is very different from other religious teachers, because He Himself is the Son of God. His every word is God's Word.

Although our Lord ascended into heaven, He is still present with us in His Word. His is still the voice of authority. His Word still has power to free us from the tyranny of Satan. It imparts the salvation He procured for us. He Himself is the content of His Word. Those who preach and teach this Word are Christ's representatives and therefore speak with His authority.

Blessed are all who hear the teaching of Jesus and believe it!

Dear Lord, thank You for teaching us with authority Your message
of salvation. Amen.

—⁓⁓—

February 22, 1992

—ᚙ—

Read Mark 10:46–52
Psalm 52
He began to cry out and say, "Jesus, Son of David, have mercy on me!"
Mark 10:47

KYRIE ELEISON

B oth misery and mercy were evident at the outskirts of Jericho. Out of the depths of misery, a blind beggar calls to the Son of David for mercy. This man's blindness prompts him to rely on the often unreliable mercy of others. When he cries out to Jesus, the crowd tries to silence him. There is no mercy in the crowd.

Our Lord is different from the crowd, for the Lord is the root and source of mercy. He has ears for the supplication of the blind beggar. No one who cries to the Lord of mercy is turned away empty, for embodied in our Lord Jesus is God's everlasting will to deliver us from the misery brought about by our sin.

The answer of God's mercy to the misery of the blind man is the gift of sight. The answer of God's mercy to the misery of our spiritual, sin-produced blindness is the crucifixion of the Son of David. His wounds are the openings of God's mercy for sinners. On the cross, our misery is wedded to the mercy of God, and out of that blessed union we are given the gift of redemption. During these Lenten days, let the blind beggar be your tutor in the life of prayer. Kyrie eleison! Lord, have mercy!

Son of David, open our eyes to the wonder of Your mercy, which delivers us from sin's misery. Amen.

—ᚙ—

February 23, 1989

February 24

—ⵡ—

Read John 3:11–21
Psalm 132
Jesus . . . suffer[ed] death, so that by the grace of God He might taste
death for everyone. *Hebrews 2:9*

No One Left Out

Who has not felt the sting of being left out of something? Here are a few examples: uninvited to a childhood party, not chosen to play on a team, forgotten by others, unrecognized, bypassed for a promotion, snubbed for a date, turned down for a marriage proposal, left out of a will, probably dying unnoticed and forgotten by history.

Of course, we may sometimes do the same to others, regarding them as unworthy of our notice or consideration. And even if we did care, how could we possibly pay attention to the needs of everyone whose plight comes to our attention? A person would have to be God to exercise that kind of concern and love.

The good news is that God is exactly like that: so superhuman that He not only knows the needs of every human being on this planet—without exception—but also that He cares! He cares not just to the point of remembering, something of which we creatures are hardly capable. He goes beyond remembering and caring to actually doing something to show His love for all people.

"In Christ God was reconciling the world to Himself" (2 Corinthians 5:19). This is what God did.

Thank You, Father, for remembering even me when You gave the gift of eternal life through Your Son, Jesus Christ. Amen.

—ⵡ—

February 24, 1987

—w—

Read Philippians 2:1–16
Psalm 32
For it is God who works in you, both to will and to work for His good
pleasure. *Philippians 2:13*

GOD'S WORKMANSHIP

The beginning and ending verses of the Philippians reading are Law. Here, God instructs us to be of one mind with fellow Christians, be humble, look out for the interests of others, have the mind of Christ, be obedient, work out our salvation, and do all things without grumbling or complaining. God certainly demands a lot from us!

The center of the passage is Gospel. In fact, it is the heart of the Gospel: Jesus led a life holy and pleasing to God, and His death secured forgiveness of our sins. This is certainly Good News! Through Jesus, we are free from our bondage to sin, that which prevents us from knowing the will of God expressed in His Law; thus we are actually able to live in a way that is pleasing to God. Through Christ, "It is God who works in you, both to will and to work for His good pleasure" (v. 13). What an incredible God we have! He so desires a relationship with us that He sent Jesus to live, die, and be resurrected in order that we would be freed to do the same. And through Christ, God continues to work in us, enabling us to desire His will and live out His good pleasure.

*Dear God, I praise You for Your loving kindness, and I thank You
for helping me to live a life pleasing to You. May Christ so reign in my life
that I am free to live fully for You. Amen.*

—w—

February 25, 2011

FEBRUARY 26

—∿—

Read Mark 14:22–25
Psalm 136
And whatever you do, in word or deed, do everything in the name of the
Lord Jesus, giving thanks to God the Father through Him. *Colossians 3:17*

HE GAVE THANKS

As Christians, we are to give thanks. In response to Christ's sacrifice for our sins, the gift of faith, and the promise of salvation, all we do should reflect our thanks and praise.

On the night before His death, Jesus took bread and gave thanks and then distributed it to the disciples. He did the same with the wine. The Greek word that means "to give thanks" is *eucharist,* the origin of one of the Church's names for the Lord's Supper, or Sacrament of the Altar.

Just as Jesus gave thanks over the bread and wine, we also give thanks every time we partake of the Eucharist. As we eat and drink, we receive, under the bread and the wine, the body and blood of Christ for the forgiveness of our sins and the strengthening of our faith. In addition, the Eucharist is a foretaste of the heavenly feast to come, when we will gather with all the saints before the throne of God, giving Him thanks forever. Through the Holy Eucharist, God strengthens us to do everything in His name, giving thanks to Him in both word and deed.

Father, as I partake of the feast of thanksgiving in the Eucharist,
strengthen me by Your grace to give thanks to You in all I say and do.
Amen.

—∿—

February 28, 2009

—∿—

Read 1 Peter 2:18–25
He opened not His mouth. *Isaiah 53:7*

THE SUBMISSIVE SUFFERER

The Lamb of God was slain that the sheep gone astray might be regained. He did this of His own free will. "Yes, Father, yes, most willingly I'll bear what You command Me" (*LSB* 438:3). This willing submissiveness of the Savior is an essential element in the doctrine of the atonement. The Lamb of God bore the sin of the world solely because His own great love compelled Him to do this.

Therefore, He silently suffered oppression and affliction. He suffered grievous wrongs, and He was subjected to terrible tortures. Always, He remained patient. "He opened not His mouth."

But He was delivered from the prison and the judgment that He endured for men. Death brought to an end His humiliation. Exaltation followed, and there is none who can declare its duration, who can adequately describe the glory earned by His submissive suffering.

"He was wounded for our transgressions; He was crushed for our iniquities" (Isaiah 53:5). The Prophet once more sings the mighty truth of the Passion, the new song that so thrilled him as it does us and all the saints.

"He died for me." That thought must dominate our lives and ever control our living. So shall the Father's will be made our own, and with similar patience we shall submit to the burdens God may ask us to bear.

Grant me grace, heavenly Father, in willing and patient faith to do and to suffer what Thou commandest. Amen.

—∿—

February 27, 1948

February 28

—⚏—

Read 1 John 2:18–24
Psalm 73

They went out from us, but they were not of us; for if they had been of us, they would have continued with us. *1 John 2:19*

Are You with Us?

They came to the Christian gatherings. They associated with believers. They said all the right things and went through the motions of religion. Then, for whatever reason, they left.

It happened to the community of believers that John was writing to. The people in his congregation likely said, "But they were so active and sincere! What happened?"

Listen, we can go through the motions of religion, have Christian friends, know the liturgy of our Church backwards and forwards, but salvation is still by a personal relationship with Jesus Christ.

How do you know if you are part of God's people? John says that God's people remain together. In Holy Baptism, God put His name on you, made you His child, and gave you salvation. In confirmation class, you were taught the truths of the Christian faith. You may now be an adult member of the Church. But it is important to remain in the fellowship of believers, to attend church regularly, to hear God's Word, and to receive the Lord's Supper frequently. By remaining in the company of God's saints, our faith is strengthened and preserved to life everlasting.

Help me, Lord Jesus, to faithfully remain in the fellowship of Your Church, now and for eternity. Amen.

—⚏—

February 28, 1991
On this date in 1991, First Gulf War ends

FEBRUARY 29

—ᴍ—

Read Luke 12:35–48
Psalm 123
Well done, good and faithful servant. You have been faithful over a little;
I will set you over much. *Matthew 25:23*

GOOD AND FAITHFUL SERVANTS

God has given all people talents with which to operate. He tells us to do business with them till He comes back. There will be a day of reckoning. God Himself will conduct the inquest. Every servant must stand trial.

God does not give talents or endowments equally. To some, He gives many; to others, few. The Lord does not require that we serve Him equally. He simply asks that we faithfully use whatever talent or talents He has given us.

One talent He has given each one of us is to make Him known to people. We do that by our confession and also by our life. Paul therefore said of Christians, "You yourselves are our letter of recommendation, written on our hearts, to be known and read by all" (2 Corinthians 3:2). We are to publish salvation through Christ. God has given this talent to every Christian.

Alive to our faults, we will humbly call ourselves unprofitable servants. But God is gracious and for Christ's sake forgives us our imperfection and calls us "good and faithful" servants. With the love of Christ dwelling in our hearts, we will constantly seek to become better servants.

Dear Savior, help me that I may always lead a life that is faithful to You and helpful in bringing others closer to You. Amen.

—ᴍ—

February 29, 1988

March

Dear God, who calls
and keeps us in Christ
Jesus, be with us and
hold us in the true and
saving faith. Amen.

March 1

—⚏—

If I had not come and spoken to them, they would not have been guilty
of sin, but now they have no excuse for their sin. *John 15:22*

THE CROSS DECIDES DESTINIES

The cross of Calvary holds every man's destiny. Life is
there; death is there. There, sin is forgiven; there, sin is
retained. Truly, Christ is "appointed for the fall and rising of many," and in Him the "thoughts from many hearts may be
revealed" (Luke 2:34–35).

All men have a relationship with Christ. Either they fall before
Him in adoration or rise against Him in opposition. Either Christ
becomes the foundation stone on which they stand or the rock that
will grind them to powder. To some, Christ is a Savior unto life;
to others, a Savior unto death. Jesus is the great revealer. All men
in their view of Him show whether they love darkness rather than
light or light rather than darkness. Thus Jesus, who takes away
sin, also multiplies sin. He forgives the sin of every penitent. To
the impenitent, He says: "The view you take of Me shows what
you are." By rejecting the holiest, the best, the purest One who
ever crossed human horizons, men judge themselves. "This is the
judgment: the light has come into the world, and people loved
the darkness rather than the light because their works were evil"
(John 3:19).

Ponder, ponder now while it is day: "What shall I do with
Jesus?" There is only one answer for us: "My Lord and my God."

*Blessed Redeemer, I take Thee as my Lord and Savior. Strengthen me,
I earnestly beseech Thee, by Thy Spirit, that I may ever remain at Thy side
and in devotion to Thy holy name. Amen.*

—⚏—

March 1, 1946

March 2

—⚹—

Read Psalm 73

Every branch that does bear fruit He prunes, that it may bear more fruit.

John 15:2

The Blessings in Trials

Anyone familiar with the culture of grapes knows how necessary it is to prune them. If left to itself, the vine soon becomes laden with rank growth that saps the strength of the vine and reduces its yield. Therefore, skilled vine-dressers go through the vineyard periodically and mercilessly cut away the useless shoots and leave the vine bleeding at a hundred points. But the vine is the better for the pruning.

"My Father is the vinedresser," says Jesus (John 15:1). He knows better than we ourselves when the rank shoots of pride, selfishness, covetousness, or any other sins are in danger of sapping our spiritual strength. He purges us. "For the Lord disciplines the one He loves, and chastises every son whom He receives" (Hebrews 12:6). Through the trials that He permits to come into our lives, God seeks to draw us closer to Himself, that we may bring forth more fruit.

God is a gracious vinedresser. No stroke of His knife will be a stroke too deep. And in every temptation, He will make a way to escape that we may be able to bear it. Let us in time of trial learn anew the deep meaning of the prayer of Jesus: "Not My will, but Yours, be done" (Luke 22:42). In heaven, we will see clearly how every trial in our life was an instrument in God's hand to keep us united by faith to our Lord and Savior Jesus Christ.

Jesus, lead Thou on Till our rest be won;
And although the way be cheerless,
We will follow calm and fearless.
Guide us by Thy hand To our fatherland. **(LSB 718:1)**

—⚹—

March 2, 1953

MARCH 3

—m—

Read 2 Corinthians 9:6–15
Psalm 35

Because you have asked ... for yourself understanding to discern
what is right ... I now do according to your word. *I Kings 3:11–12*

KNOW WHAT YOU WANT WHEN YOU PRAY

The poet Goethe wrote, "It is important to know as much
as possible about what you want most of all, because
sooner or later you are so likely to obtain it."

"You do not know what you are asking" (Matthew 20:22), Jesus
told James and John when through their mother they had asked
for the privilege of sitting to His right and left in His kingdom.
What people seek—and obtain—is not always good. Judas Iscariot
wanted money, and he got it, but what a burden it turned out to
be! The rich man in Jesus' parable wanted and received a sumptu-
ous lifestyle, but it led to spiritual bankruptcy. On the other hand,
young Solomon knew what he wanted and needed. He prayed for
it, and God gave it to him: a discerning heart. As a bonus, he received also riches, honor, and a long life. If what we pray for is
good for us, God is "able to do far more abundantly than all that
we ask or think" (Ephesians 3:20).

Beyond anything we can desire or imagine—but need so
desperately—is our salvation in Jesus Christ, who at the sacrifice
of His own life gave us life in Him, including eternal life. For this
we should pray most of all.

*Lord, help me search my heart and mind, that I may know and ask
of You what is truly needful for me. Amen.*

—m—

March 3, 1984

March 4

—⟋⟍—

Read Isaiah 53
Psalm 82
... one from whom men hide their faces. *Isaiah 53:3*

ACQUAINTANCE WITH GRIEF

I f there is anything to move us to profound repentance, it is this prophetic picture of the "Man of sorrows" whom Isaiah paints before us. He depicts Him as despised and rejected by men and truly acquainted with the grief, sin, and trouble of the whole world.

The entire life of Jesus, the Man of sorrows, was characterized by grief. If anyone was not a stranger to sorrows and woes, it was our Lord. He saw them on every hand, and He wept over Jerusalem. His personal pain and suffering was even unto drops of blood.

Men turned from Him in scorn. He was "one from whom men hide their faces." We did not esteem Him for what He was. His lowly state made us ashamed; such a Lord we would not own, who was as someone from whom one hides the face and looks the other way.

Yet He is our Savior and Substitute. When He is wounded, He is wounded by and for our sin. When He is beaten, then by His stripes we are healed. Note that there is nothing general or vague. Every word of our salvation is terribly clear and direct, but it is also graciously definite: His correction is our healing. His grief becomes our joy. Such is the love of God!

Dearest Jesus, may the blows and stripes that fell on Thee
Heal up the wounds of sin in me. Amen.

—⟋⟍—

March 4, 1965

March 5

—∞—

Read Galatians 1:3–12
Psalm 139
No man comes to the Father except through Me. *John 14:6*

CHRISTIAN OR ELSE

The Gospel is for all. No one is excluded. The Lord is "not wishing that any should perish, but that all should reach repentance" (2 Peter 3:9). Therefore, Jesus says: "Whoever comes to Me I will never cast out" (John 6:37). From all walks of life they came and were received. Levi, the young tax collector, whose shady deals made him unpopular; Saul of Tarsus, whose self-appraisal made him proud and haughty; the thief on the cross, whose criminal record made him an outcast of decent society. They came and were received and transformed by the power of the cross. To this day, Jesus with outstretched arms pleads with all: "Come to Me, all who labor and are heavy laden, and I will give you rest" (Matthew 11:28).

We must come to Him to find forgiveness and peace. Only through Jesus is heaven's door opened. "No man comes to the Father except through Me." This is final. Narrow? Yes, but true.

Jesus is the way. He made possible our return to God. He climbed Calvary's hill with our sins and paid the penalty in full with His own blood. Now all who believe in Him shall not perish but have everlasting life. So it is Christ.

This truth gives us life. He that believeth in Him hath everlasting life; no man shall be able to pluck us out of Christ's hands. This is Gospel!

Jesus, draw me daily into Thy forgiving arms. Amen.

—∞—

March 5, 1966

March 6

—ᴍ—

Read I Thessalonians 5:5–11
And [he] had lain down and was fast asleep. *Jonah 1:5*

Asleep in a Storm

A ship is storm-tossed on the Mediterranean. Her captain and crew are greatly concerned for their cargo and lives. Yet down in the hold a passenger lies sound asleep. The Bible stays that a drunkard is like a man lying on top of a mast (Proverbs 23:34). But Jonah is not drunk with strong drink. He is drunk with the poison of his sin and rebellion against God's will. His conscience has become numb. He can sleep with a guilty conscience!

Jonah sought relief for a guilty conscience in sleep. Many a littler man has in far less tragic circumstances turned to drink or dope or lust for release from a burdened spirit. But the remedy will not work. No human expedient can permanently still a guilty conscience. A man cannot sleep forever. Sooner or later, he must awaken to reality.

As Christians, we know that we daily sin much, and our sins trouble us, sometimes even cause us sleepless nights. If this no longer happens, beware; the sleep of indifference is all but fatal.

Fully awake to our sinfulness, we turn to the only One who can help—our gracious God. Each new day He comes to us in His Word with the forgiveness His Son has earned for us on the cross. By the sanctifying power of the Holy Spirit, we are then able to struggle against sin and go the way God would have us go.

God, for Jesus' sake, I pray Thee, keep my conscience ever awake,
that I fall not into the sleep of indifference. Amen.

—ᴍ—

March 6, 1960
Stratford Eynon
On this date in 1960, U.S. announces that
3,500 American soldiers will be
sent to Vietnam

MARCH 7

—〰—

Read Matthew 11:28–30
And he arose and came to his father. Luke 15:20

FATHER'S LOVE

S ome lives are strewn with lofty resolutions never kept because they were never really meant: mere expressions of a love turned inward upon self.

But the young man meant it when he said: "I will arise and go to my father, and I will say . . . I have sinned. . . . I am no longer worthy to be called your son" (Luke 15:18–19). Here was no mere good intention, thrown as a sop to an aching conscience. Nor was it said as a noble gesture meant to impress others or to salvage his own wrecked self-esteem—but to be forgotten as soon as said. "He arose and came!"

Here, instead, was repentance and conversion, faith-moved and sure. Here was a going back because the going away was recognized to have been as wrong and ungrateful as it was foolish. Here was a turning to the light because, by experience, the shade of evil had been found to be the harbinger of the night of death. Here was a return from a far country, seen at last to be a shameful land, to the health and purity he had left.

But here, above all, was a heart of pride and self-love broken by the same gentle and remembered love that alone could ever heal it.

Lent, too, is a time of the aching and the breaking heart as we remember the crucified proof of the Father's love. Let us, too, arise and surely, surely come.

Dear Father, though we may go from Thee, in mercy grant us to come back again, for Jesus' sake. Amen.

—〰—

March 7, 1958

—ᴠ—

Read Hebrews 8
Psalm 118

He is able to save to the uttermost those who draw near to God
through Him, since He always lives to make intercession for them.
Hebrews 7:25

OUR PRIEST FOR ALL TIME

To all eternity Jesus is the Priest through whom we have access to the Father. For all time, now and in the future, Jesus is our assurance that the Father hears us. As our Altar, our Sacrifice, and our Priest, He makes our prayers audible to the Father.

He shall never have to be replaced. He needs no substitute. He needs no relief. He is capable for all time to serve us. We know His sacrifice was once for all time, because it was perfect and complete. Everything He did for our sakes continues forever.

The suffering, praying, ministering, obeying, believing, and trusting that were the hallmarks of the life of our Priest continue to our benefit. He retains the love and sympathy He felt for men as He walked among them. He still shows the mercy and compassion that brought Him to the cross. As He then looked out upon men with great tenderness, so He looks out upon the world now.

Because our Lord is "able to save to the uttermost," we do well to "draw near to God through Him." We are confident that He is eager to make intercession for us. We are assured that the Father will hear Him to our benefit.

Heavenly Father, draw us to Yourself through Him who is able to save for all time. Amen.

—ᴠ—

March 8, 1971

March 9

—∞—

Read Hebrews 3:7–19
Psalm 26
"Behold, the days are coming," declares the Lord GOD, "when I will
send a famine on the land—not a famine of bread ... but of hearing
the words of the LORD." *Amos 8:11*

A THREAT OF FAMINE

Most of us do not understand how devastating a famine can be. Millions of people today live their short lives in hunger and die miserably of starvation. If we could understand their tragedy, we would do more to share our bread with them.

Our text refers to another kind of famine. It is a word of judgment. The day would come to the disobedient Israelites when they would no longer have God's Word. It always is a spiritually dangerous practice for people who have God's Word to grow indifferent to it, to ignore and despise it, to reject it in unbelief. Spiritual starvation is a dreadful judgment of God on people who harden their hearts against His Word.

This is a serious warning for our generation, when it appears that many people reared as Christians no longer have time or interest for the reading of the Holy Scriptures or for participation in worship services. Many are approaching a famine of hearing God's Word. Spiritual death is setting in, and they do not realize it. We must guard against this trend of tuning out God. Let us listen to the Good Shepherd. Let us pray that God's Word may reach our world today and that spiritual famine be averted among us.

Speak to us, Lord, and help us to believe Your Word. Amen.

—∞—

March 9, 1972

March 10

—⁂—

Read Romans 10:8–17
Blessed rather are those who hear the word of God and keep it!
Luke 11:28

THE BLESSED

The Spirit of God, who alone can make us beneficiaries of all that Christ has done on our behalf, does so by means of the Gospel. When He tells us the wonderful story of God's love, He takes us by the hand, as it were, leads us to the foot of Calvary's cross, and then explains to us who Jesus is and that He died and rose again for us. When you and I become so persuaded of this that we cry out, "That is my Lord and my Savior," then we personally receive the benefit of what Jesus did for us. That is why it is so important for us to hear the Word.

Our Lord also makes plain that hearing and knowing the Gospel can be without value unless we take the whole matter seriously and do something about it. If you and I say, "Jesus died for me," then this puts us under a great debt of love and gratitude toward Him and requires of us that we express this by "keeping" His Word. All our hearing will be useless unless we believe what we hear and sincerely express our faith in Christian living. Humble faith and grateful love go hand in hand. That is why the life of a Christian should bear the mark of Christian love.

O Holy Spirit of God, be with us in mercy when we hear or read Thy Word, that we might be enabled both to "hear and keep" it. For Jesus' sake. Amen.

—⁂—

March 10, 1961

March 11

—∞—

Read Hebrews 11:1–6
We walk by faith, not by sight. *2 Corinthians 5:7*

Living by Faith

The apostle Paul is here reminding us of a truth that we Christians dare not forget. To forget it, to misunderstand it, will constitute a serious loss for all of us.

Christians do not live by sight. This fact does not mean we are to close our eyes to the world about us or to shut ourselves off from the world. We cannot blind ourselves to the realities of life. But it does mean that we cannot judge life by what we see around us. Life is something more than what is apparent only to our sight. Therefore, the apostle says: "We walk by faith."

What is this faith by which we live? Faith is accepting God at His word, believing even though we cannot see or understand. Faith is conviction, the conviction created within us by the Holy Spirit that what God has spoken cannot but be true.

It is this faith that makes life worthwhile. Are we troubled about sin? God has told us we are forgiven through faith in His Son. Are we facing problems in life? Are we fearful of tomorrow? Is there some great worry in our lives? God has said that no power shall pluck us out of His hand. Living by faith, we need have no fears. As we live by this faith, life is beautiful. Each day we live, we live to the glory of God. The truly happy, successful life is lived by faith.

Lord, give us such a faith as this. Amen.

—∞—

March 11, 1954

March 12

—w—

If we say we have no sin, we deceive ourselves. *I John 1:8*

You Have What I Need

None is to be pitied more than the man who deceives himself. And no one deceives himself more than he who says he has not sinned. Strange to say, the saintly never deny their sins. Job confesses: "Behold, I am of small account" (Job 40:4). David admits: "Against You, You only, have I sinned" (Psalm 51:4). Upon the tender conscience of saints every transgression is registered and burns as a consuming fire.

We, too, have sinned. "Why confess if God knows all our sins?" He wants us to admit them. He wants us to search our hearts that we may discover our sinfulness. Otherwise, we shall want no Savior. The man who is well wants no physician. The man who has finished his meal wants no more food. And the man who thinks he has done no wrong wants no Savior.

At times, we even boast of our sins and call them trifling errors. We deceive ourselves if we do not admit the sinfulness of our sin. We must admit that our sins are so great that we cannot save our own souls. Our sins, no matter how small they seem to us, are so great that they damn us. We are lost creatures and therefore condemned creatures. That we must know. But if this were all that we knew, then we would despair. But, praise God, from the Gospel we learn that Christ has redeemed us. Confessing and admitting our sins, they are blotted out. Personally I am forgiven. That is what the cross means to me. I have peace and salvation because by God's grace I can say by faith: "[He] has redeemed me, a lost and condemned creature, purchased and won me from all sins . . . with His holy, precious blood."

Wash me and take away each stain; let nothing of my sin remain. Amen.

—w—

March 12, 1938
On this date in 1938, German troops occupy Austria (the *Anschluss*)

MARCH 13

—⟋⟍—

Read Matthew 27:29–32

SIMON OF CYRENE

Simon of Cyrene has become the symbol of all the cross-bearers of the world. A visitor in Jerusalem for the Passover, he was suddenly taken from the crowd and compelled to carry the cross of the One who had stumbled and fallen under its weight on the Way of Sorrows.

That is always God's way of doing things. The road of life may wind along smoothly for many days. Then something happens—sickness, the sudden loss of a loved one, a broken plan—and the way becomes rough and hard. Our hopes and plans must get out of the way for the plans of God.

It is a hard lesson to learn, but we must learn it. For the Christian heart, the heart that rests securely in God, the lesson is not as dark as we sometimes think it is. Simon lost his own way and found the way of Christ. So also do we. Simon lost control of his own plans, only to find that he was permitted by the grace of God to play a small role in greater plans than his. So also do we. It is never easy to carry a cross, but it is always blessed—blessed because it is God's way of bringing us closer to Him.

This is true also of the crosses of others. There is a strange truth at the very heart of the Christian life: bearing the burdens of others makes the weight of our own as nothing. As we carry them, Jesus joins us on the road, places the arm of His mercy and strength around us, and tells us: "Truly, I say to you, as you did it to one of the least of these My brothers, you did it to Me" (Matthew 25:40).

Graciously my faith renew; Help me bear my crosses,
Learning humbleness from You, Peace mid pain and losses.
May I give You love for love! Hear me, O my Savior,
That I may in heav'n above Sing Your praise forever. (LSB 440:6)

—⟋⟍—

March 14, 1940

March 14

—ɯ—

Read 1 Peter 2:24
Psalm 6
He Himself bore our sins in His body on the tree, that we might die
to sin and live to righteousness. By His wounds you have been healed.
1 Peter 2:24

His Wounds Do What?

Antibiotics heal. Physicians heal. Hospitals heal. Rest heals. We understand those connections. Peter, however, quoting Isaiah 53:5, says that the wounds of Jesus heal us. That relationship doesn't register so easily. How can someone else's wounds heal our wounds or our sickness? Can someone else's abrasions bring wellness to my cut and scratches?

In a miraculous way, the injuries inflicted on Jesus become the very reason God heals our spiritual wounds, caused by our own sin or by other circumstances. Because Jesus' wounds and death paid the penalty for our sins, God brings wellness to our injured souls. In that sense, the wounds of Jesus heal our wounds. The wounds of Jesus result in God restoring wholeness in us. The blood of Christ means that we will not bleed to spiritual death. Without His wounds on the cross, we would never be healed of our terminal condition.

During Lent, we ponder on this great inversion. Because Jesus was injured, we are healed. Because Jesus died, we live. Because Jesus was rejected, we are accepted. Yes, the wounds of Jesus bring healing to us.

Lord, we can never fully understand the magnitude of Your grace. Help us today to grow in appreciation for all that Your Son, Jesus, did for us. Amen.

—ɯ—

March 14, 2011

MARCH 15

—∿—

Read Genesis 42:9–38
They said one to another, "In truth we are guilty." *Genesis 42:21*

CONFESS IT!

I t was not until his brothers had faced up to their wicked deeds that Joseph could show his love to them. Years later, David found the same to be true.

A guilty conscience can be a terrible thing. It leaves no peace within or without. Psychology and the Bible both advise, "Release it"; "Confess it." As a festering boil must be lanced to get relief, so a pent-up sense of guilt must be given an outlet.

But it is hard to say, "I was wrong. I have sinned. I am sorry." In vain, we try to forget or cover up. The only way to peace and happiness is in facing the issue and asking for forgiveness.

The Bible suggests, "Confess your sins to one another" (James 5:16). This does not mean advertising our weaknesses and failures to the curious. It *does* mean that we should discuss the troublesome matter with a trustworthy friend. This can be one of the surest steps toward spiritual restoration.

Most important it is to confess our sins to *God*. Like the brothers of old, we can have no commerce with our heavenly Joseph until we have first confessed our sins. Only God can understand us completely. Only He through Jesus can bury our sins so that they return no more to haunt us and curse us.

Lord, there is mercy now,
As ever was, with Thee.
Before Thy throne of grace I bow;
Be merciful to me. Amen. (TLH 327:4)

—∿—

March 15, 1963

—⟋⟍—

For He will save His people from their sins. *Matthew 1:21*

BECAUSE OF SIN

Is sin really so terrible? Many things that the Bible tells me to be sin seemingly bring pleasure and delight. But the Scriptures, as well as human experience throughout the ages, prove that "sin when it is fully grown brings forth death" (James 1:15). Sin has brought on our natural death. God told Adam, "In the day that you eat of it you shall surely die" (Genesis 2:17). Adam and Eve transgressed God's command, and so "sin came into the world through one man, and death through sin" (Romans 5:12). We are a dying race because of sin.

Sin brings on spiritual death. "You were dead in the trespasses and sins" (Ephesians 2:1). Therefore by nature we are outside of the Kingdom. Thousands are going through life spiritually dead, rejecting Jesus Christ as their Savior and Redeemer.

Sin leads to eternal death. "Whoever does not believe will be condemned" (Mark 16:16). Sin sends man to hell. That's what sin does when it is finished. Is there no escape? Jesus went to the cross and died that we might live. But do we not all die? Do not men and women die all around us? But not all die spiritually. Through the Holy Spirit, we Christians are "born again, not of perishable seed but of imperishable" (1 Peter 1:23). Therefore, Jesus says to all believers, "Because I live, you also will live" (John 14:19).

Yet we believers die, do we not? But the sting of death is removed. We can depart in peace, unafraid, knowing that eternal life is ours in the world to come through Christ Jesus. The fear of death is removed. All this is possible only because Jesus went to the cross as my Redeemer to save me from sin and from death and from the power of the devil.

Redeeming love has been my theme And shall be till I die. **(TLH 157:4b)**

—⟋⟍—

March 16, 1938

—ᴀᴦᴧ—

Read John 8:31–59
Psalm 105
Your father Abraham rejoiced that he would see My day. *John 8:56*

THE JOY OF ABRAHAM

M any people gathered in the temple area of Jerusalem to hear the teaching of Jesus. To those who believed in Him, Jesus promised freedom from the guilt of sin and the fear of eternal death: "If you abide in My Word, you are truly My disciples, and you will know the truth, and the truth will set you free" (John 8:31–32).

Our Lord was very blunt in His condemnation of those who tried to discredit His identity and teaching. They dishonored God the Father when they spurned His Son. Instead, they should be like Abraham, who rejoiced in God's plan of redemption through His Son. But when Jesus professed to exist before Abraham, they wanted to stone Him, accusing Him of blasphemy.

During this Lenten period, we recall how our Lord was rejected and abused. May we always eagerly listen to His teaching and boldly proclaim Him as our Redeemer, even if we, too, suffer. The Word of Jesus is the truth that sets us free from the power of sin and eternal death. May we be ever faithful to Him as we worship Him with song and prayer during this sacred season!

We give thanks to You, Lord Jesus, and call on Your name. Grant us opportunities to make known among the nations what You have done. Amen.

—ᴀᴦᴧ—

March 17, 1991

March 18

—◊—

Read Matthew 26:6–16
Psalm 118:1–7
She has done a beautiful thing to Me. *Matthew 26:10*

A Beautiful Thing

I t happened in a house in Bethany. A woman anointed Jesus with a costly ointment. The disciples criticized her. It should have been sold and the money given to the poor. It sent Judas over the top; his covetousness matured into betrayal and, ultimately, his suicide. Sin always takes us on a downward road, and life becomes ugly, not beautiful. When the attitude of Judas gets the upper hand in our lives, it leads to spiritual suicide.

The ugliness of sin unto eternal death can be changed by something beautiful. The Gospel is truly something beautiful. It's a love story. "God so loved the world, that He gave His only Son, that whoever believes in Him should not perish but have eternal life. For God did not send His Son into the world to condemn the world, but in order that the world might be saved through Him" (John 3:16–17). The suffering and death of Jesus is not pretty, but it is beautiful. In that sacrifice is our forgiveness and our peace with God.

This woman anointed Jesus for His burial and was criticized for it. Jesus defended her and said it was a beautiful thing. We know His love. How beautiful are those things we keep doing for Him, through faith!

Jesus comfort me in Your forgiveness, and strengthen me in faith, that my life may be beautiful for You. Amen.

—◊—

March 18, 2008

March 19

—∿—

Read 2 Corinthians 5:14–21
Psalm 6

From now on, therefore, we regard no one according to the flesh.
2 Corinthians 5:16

A Matter of Perspective

Most airline passengers read, nap, or work during the flight. A few of us, however, keep our faces plastered to the window, mesmerized by the view. A sea of clouds viewed from above contains fascinating sculptures. A huge city overwhelms with its mass of homes, streets, and businesses. Such views captivate because they give a new perspective on the ordinary.

God's Word also gives us a new perspective on the ordinary. The devil, the world, and our flesh tempt us to view our lives from a totally human perspective. But when we view our goals and values, our decisions and relationships through God's Word, the view changes. We discover God's perspective through our daily private times with Him, in weekly worship, and in study with other believers. When seen from God's perspective, familiar things and people are different. Every human is someone for whom the Son of God died. His death redeems us from sin and eternal death. Jobs and possessions become tools to advance the kingdom of God. Relationships in every walk of life are opportunities to reflect God's love. How we view everything around us determines our attitude and our actions. What a blessing is God Word, the window through which we see with His eyes.

Lord God, help me see this world as You do—a world of sinners redeemed by Your Son. In His name. Amen.

—∿—

March 19, 2003
On this date in 2003, Operation Iraqi Freedom begins

—〰—

Read Matthew 26:59–68
Tell us if You are the Christ, the Son of God. *Matthew 26:63*

THE TRUTH ABOUT CHRIST

The world does not hesitate to express admiration for Jesus of Nazareth. Great educators bow before the superior teaching methods of Jesus. Philosophers delight to discern support for their systems in His teachings. Scientists reverence His persistent pursuit of truth. All this is not enough.

The high priest demanded: "Tell us if You are the Christ, the Son of God." Jesus answered firmly: "You have said so" (vv. 63–64).

Jesus is our Savior. He lived and labored, suffered and died, for our sins. He triumphed over every form of evil and gained the conquest over the grave. His victory over the tomb delivers us from the fear of death. This means liberty and security.

Jesus is our Redeemer. He freed us not only from the penalty of sin, but also from its power. He supports us when we are faced with our besetting sins and makes it possible for us to live His way of life in a hostile world. This means victorious living.

Jesus is an ever-present personality, our abiding Friend. He is Immanuel, God with us. Wherever we are, whatever we are doing, He is standing by. We need only to reach out the hand of faith and find the warmth of His handclasp. He says: "Behold, I am with you always" (Matthew 28:20). This means courage and comfort for us in heart and life.

Jesus is the pattern for all social relationships. If all people lived after His pattern, thought as He thought, and loved as He loved—there would be no more war, no more hatred, no more injustice, no more of man's humanity to man.

Thou Christ of God, we praise Thee for our redemption. Help us to follow Thy example of service. Amen.

—〰—

MARCH 21

—ɱ—

Read Luke 5:1–11
Psalm 137
[Jesus] said to Simon, "Put out into the deep and let down your nets
for a catch." *Luke 5:4*

UNREASONABLE DEMANDS?

I t is only natural that Peter and the other fishermen-
disciples following Jesus should question His odd request
about making an unscheduled fishing trip. The time, the
place, the depth—all seemed wrong! It seemed to be an unreasonable request. But the end result was an abundance of fish, and it
revealed their newly found leader as the promised Messiah.

Jesus makes seemingly unreasonable demands on His followers today. We are asked to accept Bible facts in simple faith. We
are urged to take up our cross and follow Him. We are to make
a definite commitment, to be either for Him or against Him. Our
lives in modern society grow more difficult as new philosophies
and "isms" emerge. We face ridicule in the schools and market-
places.

Yet as faithful Christians we follow Christ's seemingly unreasonable demands. Like Peter, we submit to His higher authority.
We trust the certain promises of God. And then, what a multitude
of blessings we receive! Peace, joy in Christ, and the assurance
of eternal life offset all negative pressures and provide a firm
foundation on which to build our lives and find true contentment.

Holy Spirit, strengthen our faith, that we may follow Jesus,
our Lord and Savior, and serve Him faithfully. Amen.

—ɱ—

March 21, 1983

MARCH 22

—◁◁—

Read Isaiah 55:1–13
He feeds on ashes. *Isaiah 44:20*

ASHES FOR BREAD

Wherefore do ye spend money for that which is not bread? asks Isaiah. But where do we find living bread for our soul? "I am the bread of life," says Jesus (John 6:35). He satisfies every need. Are we weeping? Jesus comforts. Are we wounded by sin? Jesus heals. Are we troubled? Jesus promises to be with us. Are we in distress? Come to Jesus, and find rest for your souls. Oh, what peace we often forfeit because we do not come!

To seek spiritual satisfaction anywhere else is feeding on ashes. Even the tiniest weed cannot grow in burnt-out coal. Yet how many are satisfying themselves with the husks of cults and isms of the day and are despising the Gospel of Jesus!

We must get back to God, back to that old glorious message that He so loved the world that He gave His only-begotten Son. No greater news release has ever been given to the world. This Gospel fills us with peace, gives us an eternal hope, and makes us sure and certain of our salvation. Yet how often are we absent from the house of the Lord!

Nothing will fatten the soul but the good old Gospel of the cross. "I am the bread of life," Jesus says. He satisfies, and He alone.

Redeemer and Lord, awaken in me a greater hunger for Thy Gospel, where Thou dost offer forgiveness and peace. Allow no other interest nor bewitching pleasure to lure me away from Thy saving Word. And give us all faithful ministers to proclaim it at all times. Amen.

—◁◁—

March 23, 1952

MARCH 23

—◊—

Read Luke 23:34–38

FATHER, FORGIVE THEM

These words, according to Dr. Luther, "clearly show that our Lord was attending to His true priestly office even while suspended in the air upon the cross. . . . He prayed thus that all might know why He was brought to the cross and that they might receive comfort from this knowledge."

It is indeed significant that our Savior's first word from the cross was a prayer for His enemies. Prayer as well as sacrifice belonged to the office of a priest. While He was sacrificing Himself on the altar of the cross for the sins of the world, He prayed for those who crucified Him.

This is a great comfort for us. For we, too, in truth are among the number of His crucifiers. If He died for our sins, as the Scriptures assure us, we must share in the guilt of those who nailed Him to the cross. When He prayed for His crucifiers, He prayed for us, and the prayer of the dying Son of God was not in vain.

The memory of His prayer should give Christians strength to "pray for those who persecute you" (Matthew 5:44). It is only when we thus pray for our enemies that we can be called the children of God and have fellowship with Jesus, who blessed His enemies even in death.

O Thou Prince of Peace, who on the cross didst pray for Thy crucifiers, implant in our hearts the virtues of faith and love, that we also may overcome evil with good. Amen.

—◊—

March 24, 1945

March 24

—✦—

Read Psalm 28
But Jesus remained silent. *Matthew 26:63*

The Silence of Jesus

When false witnesses arose in the court of Caiaphas and accused Jesus of many things, Jesus answered nothing. For their absurd, foolish lies, silence was His only answer. He who had patiently answered the often foolish questions of His disciples; He who had been ready to stay up late with Nicodemus to open to him new vistas of God's love; He who paused often to comfort those who labored and were heavy laden—now remains silent. It is a sad and awesome judgment of God when God no longer speaks.

The person who says, "It doesn't bother me when I do what God forbids or fail to do what He asks," should be afraid, not proud. God has become silent and is no longer speaking. Often when people have refused to hear God when He speaks—in His Word, in His house, or through the voice of conscience—God punishes by silence. The silence will be broken only when God speaks again on the Last Day: "Depart from Me." We join the psalmist in the prayer: "Be not deaf to me, lest, if You be silent to me, I become like those who go down to the pit" (Psalm 28:1). "Speak, Lord, for Your servant hears" (1 Samuel 3:9). "Blessed . . . are those who hear the word of God and keep it" (Luke 11:28).

Amid the noise of this earth may I hear Thee speak, O God. Keep me from saying or doing anything to bring Thy silence upon me. Amen.

—✦—

March 24, 1962

MARCH 25

—◎—

Read Genesis 50:15–20
Psalm 115
Our God is in the heavens; He does all that He pleases. *Psalm 115:3*

GOD HAS HIS PURPOSE

There are plenty of things going on nowadays that seem to be the devil's handiwork—things that make our times look like the "hour, and the power of darkness" (Luke 22:53). Yet even in the hour of darkness, God has His purpose.

Often it is precisely in the hour and the power of darkness that God has His moment. It was so at Calvary. In the very moment when Satan was making his most powerful impact there on that awful hill, God was fulfilling His most glorious purpose and plan for our salvation. God took hold of Satan's finest hour and used it to crush him forever.

What this means is that our desperate moments, when terribly crushing things keep happening to us, are not out of control but are being turned by the all-powerful One Himself into the great benedictions of our lives.

Maybe we can't see that at the moment. Maybe we can't see it in our lives. But surely we can see it in the life of Christ, and that is quite enough. God has His purpose. He had His purpose in what happened to Christ. He has His purpose in what keeps happening to us.

God of Abraham, Isaac, and Jacob, even in the hour and the power of darkness, with our hand firmly in Yours, we will walk with confidence.
Amen.

—◎—

March 24, 1974

March 26

—⚬—

Read Ephesians 3:16–21
Restore to me the joy of Your salvation. *Psalm 51:12*

Saved, but Unhappy

We sing this once a week, and we need to. Notice that we do not pray, "Restore to me salvation that I have lost," but, "Restore to me the joy of Your salvation." We know Christ became man. We know that He did much good, that He finally suffered and died for our sins, that He then rose from the dead. We know all this, but the thrill and excitement are often absent. Helmut Thielicke once said, "Too many of us Christians walk about as though we had gallstones." Some are like the older brother in Jesus' parable of the prodigal son. They stay at home. They are faithful in their work, in churchgoing, in Holy Communion attendance. They go to committee meetings. But they do all this without joy.

Why does this happen? We are inclined to forget who we are, who God is, what His Son has done, what His Holy Spirit does as the Lord and Giver of life. Quite often we remember our sins but forget that for the sake of Christ, God has forgiven them.

So we ask God to restore the joy of salvation. We ask Him to show us His salvation clearly once again so that we can taste its sweet savor and be joyful. God hears this prayer.

Heavenly Father, we ask You now to restore to us the joy of Your salvation; for Jesus' sake. Amen.

—⚬—

March 26, 1973

MARCH 27

—⁓—

Read Luke 24:36–48
Jesus said to them again, "Peace be with you." *John 20:21*

THE PEACE-GIVING CHRIST

I t was the risen, victorious Christ who spoke these words.
When He spoke them, He bestowed what He said. We can
wish others peace, but we cannot give it to them.

The risen Christ gives peace of conscience because sins have
been atoned for. The guilt of sin has been taken away, and the
power of sin has been broken. Now we have a full and complete
forgiveness. "In Him we have redemption through His blood, the
forgiveness of our trespasses" (Ephesians 1:7). And "though your
sins are like scarlet, they shall be as white as snow; though they
are red like crimson, they shall become like wool" (Isaiah 1:18).

The peace that the risen Christ bestows dispels fears. The disciples were very much afraid of the enemies. But not for long.
With the conviction that Jesus was alive, they faced the enemy
with superb courage and were willing to endure whatever had
to be faced for the sake of Christ.

The risen Christ bestows a peace that arms us with courage to
live for Him. In many respects, it takes as much courage to live
for Christ today as it did in the early centuries. We may not be in
danger of wild beasts in the arena, but we are faced by ridicule,
ostracism, non-promotion, or being discharged because we stand
for the principles of Christ and His Word. And God's people are
willing to face these things because they have a peace that the
world cannot know or take from them.

The peace of God, which passeth all understanding, shall keep
your hearts and minds through Christ Jesus. Amen.

—⁓—

March 28, 1951

MARCH 28

—ᴧᴧᴧ—

Read John 12:44–50
Psalm 135
In Him was life, and the life was the light of men. *John 1:4*

LIFE THAT IS LIGHT

T he fact that human life is subdued by death is enough to put the whole world in darkness. Unless death can be overcome, we are all captive to the gloomy night of sin and despair.

In his Gospel, John pointed to Jesus as the light that shines in the darkness. In Him was the life of God. By His death, He made this life available to people through faith. He was not overcome by the resistance and unbelief of His opponents. Rather, He was the light that enlightens everyone.

When Simeon saw the baby Jesus, he was ready to depart in peace because his eyes had seen God's salvation, "a light for revelation to the Gentiles" (Luke 2:32). Peter called Jesus "the Author of life, whom God raised from the dead" (Acts 3:15).

Because He is the life of the world, Jesus could raise dead Lazarus to life again. Because He is the light of the world, Jesus could make the man who was born blind see again.

Jesus is our life, our light. By the forgiveness of our sins, He gives us life to replace death. In that life, we now have the light that enables us to see how God does His work in the world. For our despair, He substitutes hope.

We confess that sometimes we even love the night of our sin, O God.
Forgive us. Enlighten us so that we live for You. Amen.

—ᴧᴧᴧ—

March 28, 1980

—ɱ—

Read John 5:21–26
Psalm 150
Now if we have died with Christ, we believe that we will
also live with Him. *Romans 6:8*

WE LIVE WITH HIM

Our life in Christ is like a coin with two sides. Side one shows that Christ died and we died with Him. This is our acquittal through the death of Jesus, our Substitute. It is the forgiveness of sins that it provides. It is the freeing from the guilt and punishment of sin. That is the one side. Side two means that Christ now lives and we live with Him. The two sides belong together.

To live with Christ means to walk with Him, to go where His feet lead us. It means to work with Christ, doing the kind of deeds He did and still does. It means to speak with Him and for Him, expressing the kind of thoughts He expressed. It means loving as He loved.

Dying comes first in Jesus' plan; He died, and we died with Him. But then comes living; He lives, and we live with Him. Jesus carries us through death to life. If we with our sins are dead with Christ, then we also live with Him, our risen Lord, in the newness of life. Thus the leading facts in Jesus' history become the principle facts in our biographies too. Our feet follow in His footsteps through death into a life that reflects His own life, both now and in eternity.

May we Thy precepts, Lord, fulfill
And do on earth our Father's will. Amen.

—ɱ—

March 29, 1978

MARCH 30

—⚬⚬—

Read 2 Timothy 4:6–18
Psalm 127
I have fought the good fight, I have finished the race, I have kept the faith.
2 Timothy 4:7

I HAVE KEPT THE FAITH

There comes a time when even the most faithful of God's workers must lay down the pen. The work is over. God has other plans. In his Second Letter to Timothy, St. Paul reveals that he realizes his work is nearly finished. One does not sense regret or sorrow in his words. Paul simply says that the time of his departure is at hand. He has done his best to be faithful to his calling. The race is over. Now it is his turn to be fully comforted by the fullness of Christ's promises. He will receive the crown of righteousness. One almost sees Paul reaching out for it in joyful anticipation.

Paul wrote these words not to boast, as though he were about to be repaid for all his hard work and great suffering. Rather, Paul wrote them because Christ would soon fulfill for him the very promises Paul had preached to others. Paul wrote these words to boast in the Lord Jesus, who had done such great things for him.

There is much comfort in Paul's words for any departing saint. A time comes for all of us when God calls us into His glory. What a joy to meet it with the certainty of the apostle. "There is laid up for me the crown of righteousness . . . and not only to me but also to all who have loved His appearing" (v. 8).

*Dear God, who calls and keeps us in Christ Jesus, be with us
and hold us in the true and saving faith. Amen.*

—⚬⚬—

March 30, 2006

March 31

—∿—

Read Romans 15:7
Psalms 19:14

[Jesus said,] "For John the Baptist has come eating no bread and drinking no wine, and you say, 'He has a demon.' The Son of Man has come eating and drinking, and you say, 'Look at Him! A glutton and a drunkard, a friend of tax collectors and sinners!'" *Luke 7:33–34*

Gospel Acceptance

Someone once said that the Church is not a hotel for saints, but a hospital for sinners. It's a catchy little saying, but is it true for Christians today? Just like those in Jesus' day who thought they were better than others and who rejected the social outcasts of their day, many Christians today avoid social outcasts.

Jesus ate and drank with the despised tax collectors and the outcast sinners in the society. He touched the untouchable lepers. He did not condone their sin. Rather, he accepted people as they were so that He might forgive their sin and transform their lives. He loves sinners. That's the good news of Gospel acceptance.

We ask the Spirit to install in us the acceptance our Savior showed, and still shows, of those who are different, those who are outcasts, those who annoy or harm us. By grace, we now are able to love the unlovely as Christ did. That's Gospel acceptance.

Thank You, gracious Lord, for accepting me as I am and for loving me so that I may show Your love in accepting others. Amen.

—∿—

March 31, 2004

April

Empower us with
Your Spirit, Lord Jesus,
that we may be Your
prophets, speaking
Your saving words
of forgiveness. Amen.

APRIL 1

—ᴍᴍ—

Read Acts 10:34–43
Psalm 119:105–112
This is the message we have heard from Him and proclaim to you,
that God is light, and in Him is no darkness at all. *1 John 1:5*

APRIL FOOLS?

Have you ever done something "foolish"? We all have! But to act foolishly at one time or another does not automatically make one a fool. That would imply that you cannot help yourself: "I am a fool, and therefore I act foolishly." None of us would want to say that of ourselves!

In fact, our "acting foolishly" may not always be in us at all, but in the eye of the beholder! St. Paul said that "the word of the cross is folly *to those who are perishing,* but to us who are being saved it is the power of God" (1 Corinthians 1:18, emphasis added). Imagine being labeled foolish by the world because you walk in what they consider the "dark ages" of a God they cannot see.

But you do see! You see God with the faith He has given you. You see the death and resurrection of His Son for the sins of the world. You see the love of Christ even for those who walk in darkness, and you begin to love them too. In the "foolishness" of faith, we are made wise in the wisdom, grace, and love of God!

Merciful God, give us the faith of those who walk in the light of Your salvation—the faith that walks within the shadow of the cross of Jesus. In His name we pray. Amen.

—ᴍᴍ—

April 1, 2003

April 2

—⟪⟫—

Read Philippians 2:5–11
Psalm 5
He is the radiance of the glory of God and the exact imprint
of His nature. *Hebrews 1:3*

JESUS, GOD WITH US

I saiah had said with prophetic vision: "Behold, the virgin shall conceive and bear a son, and shall call His name Immanuel" (7:14). When Matthew reports that the prophecy came true in the birth of Jesus Christ, he comments that Immanuel means "God with us" (1:23). The writer to the Hebrews also reminds us of this great mystery: God was in Christ, and in Jesus, a real man on our earth, God is with us.

We cannot understand this mystery of God becoming man. Only with the insight of faith do we see that in some unique and wonderful manner, Jesus embodies the fullness of God.

When Jesus touched a sensitive conscience with a gentle rebuke or made a scathing attack on the pride of a Pharisee, when He risked the contempt of respectable people by sitting down to eat with known sinners or laying His healing hand on the bodily disabled, then God Himself was present in the word and act of Jesus.

As we ponder the cross in the light of this mystery, a meaningless tragedy becomes a purposeful and loving act of God for us. As our Lord dies, God is there in Him, reconciling the world to Himself.

Lord Jesus, God with us, abide with us this day and always. Amen.

—⟪⟫—

April 2, 1969

—ᴍ—

Read Hebrews 12:12–24
Psalm 119:97–104
Father, the hour has come; glorify Your Son that the Son may glorify You.
John 17:1

THE GLORY OF THE CROSS

In the opening words of Jesus' prayer before He went out to the Garden of Gethsemane, He stated that an hour of glory was at hand.

Glory has to do with importance. What glorifies God is anything that displays His unique attributes—any of those qualities that command respect and awe. Scriptures record many instances in which God afforded an insight into what He is really like. Often, there was dazzling light. Often, great miracles of deliverance allowed people to see God's wonderful works on their behalf. Jesus' miracles belong to this category because they showed God's power and concern. All of this has to do with the glory of God.

But Jesus used the term *glory* to talk about His death. Death hardly suggests glory, especially death as a criminal on a cross. But what more clearly shows God for what He really is? He is gracious. He did not spare His only Son but delivered Him up for us all. God's mercy is boundless. Nowhere is this more clearly seen than in the death of His Son, Jesus Christ.

We glory in the cross of Christ. It is our salvation. Standing before the cross, we come to know God as He is. We praise Him for His glory.

We thank You, Father, that Your mercy knows no bounds. Amen.

—ᴍ—

April 3, 1985

APRIL 4

—ɱ—

Read John 14:12–17
Psalm 53
I do not pray for these only, but also for those who will believe
in Me through their word. John 17:20

WE HAVE A LORD WHO PRAYS FOR US

We have a Lord who is infinitely more able than any earthly sovereign to grant our petitions. That same Lord also prays for us. He has promised that whatever we ask the Father in His name, the Father, according to His will, will grant.

Christians customarily end their prayers to God by saying, "I ask this in Jesus' name" or "I pray for Jesus' sake." This is how our Lord has asked us to pray. But since we say it often, we can forget the tremendous meaning and result of this great privilege that our Lord has given us.

When we pray in the name of our Lord, we are admitting that we are worthy of none of the things for which we pray, that in our own name we have not even the right to ask. But we have a Lord who has granted us the right to pray. We have a Lord who has told us, "Sign My name to your prayers." Because He paid for our sins on Calvary, His Father and ours will grant every petition of ours that He deems in His wisdom to be for our good.

But there is more. Our Lord prays *for* us. He personally presents our petitions to our Father in heaven. He intercedes for us. We can be certain that our prayers are indeed heard and answered in the best possible way.

Jesus, our Lord, do Thou ever keep us before the throne of grace
and mercy, where Thou dost intercede for us. Amen.

—ɱ—

April 4, 1968
On this date in 1968,
Martin Luther King Jr. is assassinated

Read Matthew 26:40–41
Psalm 102:16–28
The spirit indeed is willing, but the flesh is weak. *Matthew 26:41*

TALKING IS EASIER THAN WALKING

How many projects do we start and never finish? How many "good ideas" are forgotten in the morning light? How many impulses to write notes of appreciation never find their way to paper?

We tend to talk about accomplishing much more than we do. We can have the best of intentions, but any number of reasons can cause us not to do what we say we want to do. Most of us learn to accept some of that as part of our fallen human nature, but it generates anxiety when we experience it because our best intentions are not always backed up with action.

One of the great truths of Scripture is that in God's relationship with us, His words and actions are consistent. God doesn't say He cares and then absent Himself when we need Him most. He doesn't say He loves us and then ignore or hurt us. His purpose is to free us from the power of sin. His action is to accomplish this even at the cost of His Son. His purpose is to release us from the curse of death. His action was to raise His Son from death and attach us to Him in Baptism so that we would live with Him forever.

Lord, thank You for following Your words with action. Help me to be more like You in so doing. In Jesus' name. Amen.

—ᴎᴎ—

April 5, 2001

APRIL 6

—⟋⟍—

Read I Corinthians 1:18–25
Psalm 18:1–7, 17–20
For the word of the cross is folly to those who are perishing, but to us
who are being saved it is the power of God. *I Corinthians 1:18*

TWO PIECES OF WOOD

Everything stands or falls on two pieces of wood. Take away the cross, and there is no reason for Holy Week. Take away the cross, and you might as well never again bring up the subject of sin. Denial will be the only way to "survive." But there is no survival without those two pieces of wood and the Savior who was nailed to them. On that cross were the sins of the world—yes, even your sins! Take away the cross, and you are left on a futile quest to settle matters with your Creator on your own. A sinful life against the backdrop of His perfect Law will always bring hopelessness.

Imagine the quests on which some mistakenly embark—quests to conciliate God somehow before life comes to a close. These never-ending pursuits always fail to bring peace.

So, it all stands or falls on those two pieces of wood fashioned into a cross. If Christ had avoided Calvary, we would still be in our sins. The end would be too frightening to ponder. Instead, we meet death knowing full well that one sacrifice on those two pieces of wood was enough. One sacrifice, once and for all!

*Dear Jesus, thank You for making it clear in my heart that the way
to the Father is by You and Your cross. Amen.*

—⟋⟍—

April 6, 2004

Read Luke 6:27–36
Psalm 129
Be kind to one another. *Ephesians 4:32*

REFLECTING GOD

The Bible says many things about God. It says God is all-knowing, all-powerful, present everywhere, eternal. Most important and very comforting to us is the fact that the Scriptures say that "God is love." Men may know that the deity is all-knowing and all-powerful. But until they know that God is love, as Lent resounds with that love in the dying of the Son of God, they cannot really know God.

God has put us, His children, into the world to learn, first of all for ourselves, this all-surpassing and eternal love. But God loves the world too, and He loves it with the same love with which He loves us. So He has put us here not only to know His love, but also to show His love. He wants us not just to absorb that love, but to reflect it in our daily lives as well. This the people of Christ have done through the centuries in their concern for the miserable ones of the world. Into a heathen world two thousand years ago, a world that was loveless and callous, they brought the amazing Gospel of the mercy of love.

We should be kind especially to the unkind. Who knows what shadows of fear, despair, cruelty, or tragedy may lie upon them? Therefore, they need God's love the more. We must tell them.

Father of love, help us to show Thy love by our love. Amen.

—ɯ—

April 7, 1965

APRIL 8

—w—

Read John 8:12–20
Psalm 112

Jesus spoke to them, saying, "I am the light of the world. Whoever follows Me will not walk in darkness, but will have the light of life." *John 8:12*

THE LIGHT OF LIFE

Remember the long moments when, during a storm or a sudden failure of electrical power, your home was plunged into darkness? Only after someone found a light, such as a candle, would you attempt to move about the house or to accomplish what had been so abruptly interrupted by the darkness.

One day on the temple grounds of Jerusalem, Jesus suggested to a well-informed group of Pharisees that they, too, were experiencing a form of darkness. He advised them to follow Him as the "light of the world" so that they would not have to grope about in the darkness of their own sinful ignorance. They were to recognize Him as the light of life by His crucifixion as well as by His identification with the heavenly Father: "When you have lifted up the Son of Man, then you will know that I am He, and that I do nothing on My own authority, but speak just as the Father taught Me" (John 8:28).

We know so well that the power of sin can overcome us with the darkness of shame and despair. Only Jesus can provide the light of life for our salvation.

"In Him was life, and the life was the light of men. The light shines in the darkness, and the darkness has not overcome it" (John 1:4–5).

Lord, You are my light and my salvation; whom shall I fear?
You are the stronghold of my life. Amen.

—w—

April 8, 1984

April 9

—⚬—

Read Ephesians 5:1–14
Psalm 119:137–144

Whatever is pure ... if there is anything worthy of praise, think about these things. *Philippians 4:8*

THINKING ABOUT THINGS PURE

Some people have trouble controlling their evil desires. A part of their problem is that they let their minds dwell on illicit pleasures. St. Paul urges us to turn away from every impurity and think about "whatever is pure."

In doing this, Christians have the help of the Holy Spirit, who dwells in their hearts. He directs their thoughts to Christ, who by His blood made them clean. The Spirit leads them to focus their minds on the person, redeeming work, and holy life of their Savior. He leads them deeper into all truth revealed in the Word. This makes for a pure heart and mind, as our Lord said, "You are clean because of the word that I have spoken to you" (John 15:3).

To achieve purity and grow in it, we need to search the Scriptures daily, for there we find strength and guidance. We need to pray that God might create a clean heart in us and renew a right spirit. Then a clean life can follow—a life of industry and temperance, of "all holy desires, all good counsels, and all just works" (Collect for Peace, *LSB*, p. 233).There is nothing automatic about this: we need to think hard about pure things.

Lord Jesus, help us to be good and gentle, pure and clean, in every respect more like You. Amen.

—⚬—

April 9, 1981

April 10

—⦙—

Read 1 Corinthians 10:23–33
Do all to the glory of God. *1 Corinthians 10:31*

CONCERNING EATING AND DRINKING

The pagan people of St. Paul's day often ate and drank to the glory of their false gods. In fact, elaborate banquets, which usually ended in indescribable debauchery, were a part of the routine of idol worship. Perhaps St. Paul was thinking of these heathen feasts when he wrote about eating and drinking to the glory of God.

Eating and drinking are part of the necessary routine of daily living. Christian and unbeliever alike must have food and drink to live, but there is a difference in their eating and drinking. The unthinking worldling eats and drinks solely for his own benefit and pleasure; the believer eats and drinks to the glory of God. How? By remembering God's providence, by acknowledging His goodness, by praising His mercy. When the believer folds his hands before each meal and prays, "The eyes of all look to You, and You give them their food in due season" (Psalm 145:15), he is glorifying God in his eating and drinking. When a child of God prays after each meal, "Oh give thanks to the LORD, for He is good; for His steadfast love endures forever!" (1 Chronicles 16:34), he again is magnifying God's glory. When he employs the energy and strength gained through food in the service of God and neighbor, the Christian is doing it "all to the glory of God." To do this is part and parcel of the abundant life the believer is living in Christ Jesus.

Dear Lord, enlighten us, we beseech Thee, by Thy Holy Spirit, and consecrate us wholly unto Thy service, that whatever we do may be done to Thy glory, through Jesus Christ, our Lord. Amen.

—⦙—

April 10, 1948

APRIL 11

—⁂—

Read Matthew 17:22–23
Psalm 120
Jesus said to them, "The Son of Man is about to be delivered
into the hands of men, and they will kill Him, and He will be raised
on the third day." And they were greatly distressed. *Matthew 17:22–23*

DELIVERED INTO MAN'S HANDS

L ent is a season given over to Christ's suffering and death. Some complain that this is depressing or melancholy and say we should think of happy things instead: "Less cross, more resurrection; less Good Friday, more Easter." But we learn from the Lord Jesus Himself the importance of His cross.

Three times He takes His disciples aside to tell them what is coming, to warn and prepare them, and to let them know that He has come to suffer and die. We learn with the disciples that the cross always must be on our hearts and minds.

Paul reflects the centrality of the cross, saying that he came preaching nothing but Christ crucified (1 Corinthians 2:2). Martin Luther said, "The cross alone is our theology." Does this mean that we are melancholy and sad? By no means! The opposite is true. There is no better news than the cross, no happier event than the Lord's death. Good Friday is the best Friday! In His cross and death, our Jesus opened the way for us to enter eternal life. Minds fixed on the cross are full of the joy of forgiveness.

Lord, grant that the preaching of Your cross will bring Your people
joy and peace. Amen.

—⁂—

April 3, 2009

Read John 11:38–44
The last enemy to be destroyed is death. *1 Corinthians 15:26*

WHY LAZARUS COULD LAUGH

D r. C. F. W. Walther, pioneer Lutheran leader in the middle of the last century, once began an Easter sermon with this startling claim: "Today I shall preach a funeral sermon for Death." A dead tyrant cannot destroy or terrorize. "Death is swallowed up in victory . . . through our Lord Jesus Christ" (1 Corinthians 15:54–57).

In his play *Lazarus Laughed*, Eugene O'Neill pictures this faith in victory over death. A few weeks before His own death and resurrection, Jesus had called Lazarus from his four-day rest in the grave. In the play, the brother of Mary and Martha confronts the cruel and crazy Caligula, who is to be the successor to Tiberius Caesar, emperor of Rome. He threatens Lazarus with execution. But Lazarus looks into his face, laughs softly "like a man in love with God," and answers, "Death is dead, Caligula!"

Lazarus had experienced the death-destroying power of the Prince of Life. He could laugh at death because Jesus had conquered it and removed its "sting."

Death might as well be dead as far as the believer is concerned; it has no power to destroy us. We who belong to Christ can join the seventeenth-century man of faith John Donne as we face "the last enemy," and say,

Death, be not proud. . . .
Death, thou shalt die.

Thanks be to God, who gives us the victory through our Lord Jesus Christ. Amen.

—w—

April 12, 1961
On this date in 1961, Russian Yuri Gagarin
is first man in space

—ᴍ—

Read Revelation 7:9–17; Ephesians 2:6–7
Psalm 71
[God] raised us up with [Christ] and seated us with Him
in the heavenly places in Christ Jesus. *Ephesians 2:6*

SEATED WITH JESUS

How often it feels as though we are sitting in the back row—of the balcony, no less—when it comes to honor! Few of us are numbered among the great, the noble, and the mighty. Most of us Christians are just ordinary folk, doing what our hands find to do and trying to be faithful in our daily work.

This is not bad unless we also fail to realize and appreciate the status we have with Christ Jesus and the truth of our union with Him. He does not want us to think poorly of ourselves; after all, He felt we were worth dying for. Therefore, as Christians we are not confined to any backseats of life. We are seated with Christ in the heavenly realms. We participate as members of His Body in the grand reign of Christ over His enemies. We are a part of His design to unite the whole universe under His lordship.

Maybe this sounds a bit removed from the nitty-gritty of life's struggles, because we do at times experience discouragements. But God cannot lie; He says you are seated with Christ in heavenly places. It is more than enough to cause our spirits to soar!

*When I am down, Lord Jesus, help me to recall that my union
with You assures me of ultimate victory. Amen.*

—ᴍ—

April 13, 1989

April 14

—∽—

Read Colossians 3:1–10
Work out your own salvation with fear and trembling. Philippians 2:12

Trembling

This statement from Paul seems at first blush to contradict the central truth of Christianity, which is to the effect that a man is saved wholly and solely by grace, through faith in Christ Jesus. The Bible even says, "The one who does not work but believes in Him who justifies the ungodly, his faith is counted as righteousness" (Romans 4:5).

Despite this fact, the apostle writes by divine inspiration: "Work out your own salvation with fear and trembling." What is more, the apostle means precisely what he says. If one would be a Christian, he must take his Christianity seriously. Too many think that they can live as they please and yet be Christians because they are saved by the grace of God alone and not by what they do.

This attitude is not new in our time. It showed itself already in the days of Paul. That explains why he so often writes on just this subject.

If we actually do believe in Jesus as our Savior and trust in His atoning sacrifice, we must respond to His love by living a God-fearing life. For Holy Writ expressly states that "faith by itself, if it does not have works, is dead" (James 2:17).

Since this is so, we must ever strive, with the help of God's Holy Spirit, to show by our whole lives that we are followers of Jesus. To be a Christian demands more than just this, that we memorize our catechism or subscribe to certain creedal statements. We must express our faith in life.

—∽—

April 14, 1940

—ᘯᘯ—

Read John 13:1–17
Then He poured water into a basin and began to wash the disciples' feet.
John 13:5

BEYOND SELF

Our blessed Savior sat down with His disciples on Maundy Thursday evening for the sacred meal of the Passover. For fifteen hundred years, the meal had reminded God's people of the blood of the Lamb of God to be shed one day for them and their sins. Now on this evening, when He was to be betrayed into the hands of His murderous foes, the time had come to which the ages had looked forward.

Presently, He arose from the Passover table. He laid aside His long, flowing outer garment. As His wondering disciples watched, Jesus took a towel and girded Himself with it, poured water into a basin, and began to wash their feet, passing from one amazed disciple to the next.

Thus our divine Master showed Himself by this symbolic act as the great Servant of God and of man. His mission was to serve as no other could—by laying down His holy life in pain and death to cleanse humankind from sin. His whole life was of necessity a life beyond self.

On the morrow, the Lamb of God would die on the altar of the cross. This evening, He would institute the Lord's Supper of bread and wine and of His body and blood. But in this symbolic act of the foot washing, He summed up all of His existence as a life beyond self. Then He said: "I have given you an example. . . . A servant is not greater than his master" (vv. 15–16).

O holy Savior, heal our lives by Thine atoning service, and help us
to follow Thine example. Amen.

—ᘯᘯ—

April 15, 1954

April 16

—⚬—

Read John 16:16–23
Psalm 75
You have sorrow now, but I will see you again, and your hearts will rejoice. John 16:22

SORROW TURNED TO JOY

The Christian life is movement. We move on, always in anticipation of what our Lord will do for us. We know He has completed the work of our salvation for us. But we also know that He has not yet completed His work in us. We will experience the totality of His saving work when we enter His eternity.

Our Lord's disciples experienced this sense of anticipation when they stood with Him this side of His death. Jesus prepared them for His death, resurrection, and ascension by announcing His departure.

The interval during which they experienced His absence was a picture of the Church as it waits to see Him again. And as the disciples saw the Lord again in resurrection appearances, we see Him in Word and Sacrament.

Yet the waiting to see Him in eternity is not without its pain and sorrow. As our Lord endured the agony of Gethsemane and the cross, so the Church suffers as it waits. But as the mother forgets the anguish of childbirth, so our sorrow and pain will be turned to joy when we see Him again in eternal glory.

Heavenly Father, give us Your Spirit, that we may live in anticipation of joy in Christ. Amen.

—⚬—

April 16, 1967

—⚏—

WHAT'S IT TO YOU?

The Church is no place for pride, jealousy, and rivalry. James and John tried to exalt themselves when they mistakenly asked for favored positions in the Messiah's kingdom. We find this jealous rivalry again beside the Sea of Galilee. The timing is only a few weeks after the resurrection, after Jesus had restored Peter to apostleship.

The risen Savior had revealed to Peter that he would die as a martyr. Because he had sincerely affirmed three times, "You know that I love You" (John 21:17), Peter willingly accepted the sad news. Then he pointed to John, of whom Jesus was especially fond: "Lord, what about this man?" (v. 21). There is a hint of resentment: "Is he going to get something I won't get? Will he be ahead of me, so that I get second-best treatment?" Jesus rebukes him sharply: "What is that to you?" We practice sinful rivalry when we measure our performance for Christ by someone else's, when we will not be outdone by another. "Will George go? Then I will go too." "Martin doesn't tithe, so why should I?" The Savior humbled Himself to serve all mankind, bearing all our guilt. Now, exalted by the Father, He challenges *each* of us, *one by one*: "Follow Me—even to a cross. Follow Me, regardless of the calling and task of another."

Savior, I follow on, Guided by Thee....
Only to meet Thy will My will shall be. Amen. (TLH 422:1)

—⚏—

April 17, 1961
On this date in 1961, Bay of Pigs invasion
of Cuba begins; fails by April 19

April 18

—✦—

Read John 1:26–34
Psalm 16

There is one mediator between God and men, the man Christ Jesus, who gave Himself as a ransom for all, which is the testimony given at the proper time. *I Timothy 2:5–6*

JESUS IS THE ONE

I n these verses, John points to Jesus as "the testimony given at the proper time." This is what all of the saints rightly do. They point to the One who can save, the only One who takes away sin. The people were looking to John for help. And he did baptize them with water for repentance. But John's task was not to bring attention to himself. His most important task was to point to, and bring attention to, the Savior.

Why is it God's will for the focus to be on Jesus? It is not because Jesus is eager for adoration from the fawning crowds. As a matter of fact, He often shied away from the crowds, seeking to do His work quietly.

Rather, we fix our eyes on Jesus because He is the key—the only One who can reconcile us to the Father and take away God's angry wrath. In and of ourselves, we are lost in sin and in desperate need of salvation. Christ, the sacrifice for our sin, brings us back to that perfect relationship with God for this life and in the life to come.

Dear Father in heaven, we thank You for sending those in our lives who point us to Your Son, our Savior. Please help us to fix our eyes on Him and point others to the cross. In Your name we pray. Amen.

—✦—

April 18, 2010

—ᘰᒳ—

Read Matthew 12:38–42

DECLARED TO BE THE SON OF GOD

Is Jesus God's only-begotten Son? The answer to that momentous question hung in the balance when our Savior died on Golgotha's cross. Because Christ had taught: "I am the living bread that came down from heaven" (John 6:51), many of His hearers left Him. When He said, "I and the Father are one," they even took up stones to stone Him (John 10:30–31). The high priest Caiaphas had placed Him under oath, saying: "I adjure You by the living God, tell us if You are the Christ, the Son of God" (Matthew 26:63). When Christ answered that He was, some members of the Council said, "He deserves death" (Matthew 26:66). They did not want to hear Him say that He was true God. They wanted to silence Him forever and therefore demanded His crucifixion.

Everything depends on the truth of Christ's claim. If He is not true God, He is not even a great prophet, for then He would have told an untruth. Then we would have reason to doubt all of His teachings. Then our redemption, our forgiveness, our salvation, our resurrection, yes, everything would be uncertain. Then we would be without hope.

Thank God, the empty tomb, the message of the angel, and the many appearances of the risen Christ convince us that He is true God. This greatest of miracles is the strongest proof of all. Therefore, St. Paul states: He is "declared to be the Son of God *in power* . . . by His resurrection" (Romans 1:4, emphasis added). Oh, how we should rejoice! Christ is true God. Regardless of what others may say, I have a divine Savior who has redeemed me and all mankind. I must tell others of this glad news.

—ᘰᒳ—

April 19, 1938

And when He had said this, He breathed on them and said to them,
"Receive the Holy Spirit. If you forgive the sins of any, they are forgiven
them; if you withhold forgiveness from any, it is withheld." *John 20:22–23*

ABSOLUTION

The disciples, whom the risen Lord was sending out in His name to declare that peace had been made between rebellious man and God, were given authority to say in His stead and by His command, "Your sins are forgiven."

When a penitent sinner, by the grace of God, is led to confess his sins, our Lord has given to His servants here on earth the power to say, even as Nathan said to David, "The LORD also has put away your sin" (2 Samuel 12:13). Even as the Lord Jesus said to the sick of the palsy, "My son; your sins are forgiven" (Matthew 9:2), so does He say it to us through His appointed spokesmen.

The woman in Simon's house, the Samaritan woman at the well, Zacchaeus the publican, Simon Peter after the denial, and many others have heard these gracious words: "Your sins are forgiven." And so the Lord's disciples in all ages, as messengers from a benevolent King, announce to certain rebellious subjects who have laid down their arms that pardon has been given them. God is our King, and we have been rebels. Jesus Christ has made this pardon available to us, and absolution, or the forgiveness of sins, is declared to us by the Lord's messengers in His name and by His command. This declaration comes to us in the form of words to encourage and to comfort us.

We confess unto Thee, almighty God, that we have sinned grievously against Thee in thought, word, and deed; and we humbly beseech Thee to pardon our iniquities, to look with grace and mercy upon us, and to declare unto us the entire remission of all our sins; through Jesus Christ, who alone can take away the sin of the world. Amen.

—⁕—

April 20, 1939

April 21

—꘧—

Read Luke 15:11–32
Restore to me the joy of Your salvation. *Psalm 51:12*

A Treasure Regained

David occupied a throne. He was an outstanding statesman and was endowed with great ability as a musician and a poet. He was wealthy. But he was unhappy. He had lost something without which his many other blessings were empty. He calls it the joy of God's salvation. He had once had it. It had enriched his youth. It had sustained him through the years when he carried heavy responsibilities. But grievous sins, which had driven him into the depths, had robbed him of it. Pathetically, he pleads that it may be given back to him.

We need to offer the same prayer. Our sins tarnish the joy of God's salvation. Our work and our pleasures tend to crowd it into an obscure corner of our hearts.

We may still retain the form of godliness. But its radiance has been dimmed. We attend services, but we sing listlessly. We listen halfheartedly to the Word of God. We may begin to wonder whether it pays to go to church. Little or nothing has happened within us to equip us for the tasks and experiences ahead.

There is a way back to the joy that once was ours. The first step is to reexamine our life in the light of God's Law. The next is to look to God's salvation. It is a salvation to inspire joy, born of love in the heart of God. God's own Son died for it. This assures us of God's unfailing care here and eternal life beyond.

My Jesus is my treasure,
My life, my health, my wealth,
My friend, my love, my pleasure,
My joy, my crown, my all,
My bliss eternally. Amen. (LSB 730:4)

—꘧—

April 21, 1955

Read Philippians 2:5–7
John 14:15–26

Have this mind among yourselves, which is yours in Christ Jesus, who, though He was in the form of God, did not count equality with God a thing to be grasped, but made Himself nothing, taking the form of a servant, being born in the likeness of men. *Philippians 2:5–7*

CHRIST-MINDEDNESS

These words are full of pure gold. Here is the secret of joy in hard times. Here is the solution of all our tragic mistakes, our false ideas, and what is wrong in the world. It is the mind of Christ.

The mind of Christ was to do the will of God. In Gethsemane, He prayed to His Father, "As You will" (Matthew 26:39). "Christ did not please Himself," said Paul (Romans 15:3). Voluntarily, He submitted to the death of the cross because He knew man was lost and could not be saved without His sacrifice. Humbly, though He possessed all majesty, He minded this task until it was finished and the sinner saved.

It is most important that this mind of Christ be in us. The Spirit of God calls us to this mind of Christ by the Gospel, enlightens, and keeps us in the knowledge of this mind of Christ. He creates faith in our hearts to see Christ as He is in truth, and thus He awakens us to a new life, so that we serve and humbly trust in God's love toward the fallen sinner.

Let us keep this mind of Christ with us always.

Lord, that we may live to Thee and serve Thee, and may Thy mind dwell in us until it grow to be our mind as well. Amen.

—⟋∿⟍—

April 22, 1942

April 23

—ᔈ—

Read Luke 10:1–12
Psalm 74
The one who hears you hears Me. *Luke 10:16*

WE ARE PROPHETS

Jesus completed His instructions to the seventy-two. He sent them out to towns and villages. Their message was "The kingdom of God is near" (Luke 21:31).

These disciples, in a sense, were prophets. Jesus commissioned them, giving them the words to speak. They were His mouthpieces. When people listened to them, they were hearing Jesus Himself, for it was His message that the seventy-two proclaimed.

Jesus' commission applies to us. Today we are His prophets, His witnesses, His mouthpieces. Our commission is to speak His words. We share His saving message in the power of the Gospel. This is our role as His redeemed people.

Our prophetic message is the message Jesus has given to us. Sinners need to hear this message: "Whoever believes and is baptized will be saved, but whoever does not believe will be condemned" (Mark 16:16). People need to hear that God laid all their sins on Jesus, that He died on the cross so that they could be fully and freely forgiven. We are to tell the words of Jesus. "Whoever believes in [God's only Son] should not perish but have eternal life" (John 3:16).

As modern-day prophets, we are privileged. We represent Christ Himself. We can direct our friends to their friend, Jesus.

Empower us with Your Spirit, Lord Jesus, that we may be Your prophets, speaking Your saving words of forgiveness. Amen.

—ᔈ—

April 23, 1990

April 24

—⟋⟍—

Read 2 Corinthians 4
One thing I do: forgetting what lies behind and straining forward to what
lies ahead, I press on toward the goal for the prize of the upward call
of God in Christ Jesus. *Philippians 3:13–14*

GOAL-CONSCIOUS

Here we have the secrets of a great life. It is, first of all, one of concentration. "One thing I do." As a man of culture, the apostle Paul had varied interests. But all were centered on one goal.

In this, the apostle did not allow himself to be handicapped by the past. He did not carry its burden—the hurts inflicted on him by others, the sins that God had forgiven, the mistakes from which he had profited—into the future.

He looked forward. Ahead was a destiny of such supreme importance that he did not dare allow anything to deflect his attention from it.

If we once see what St. Paul saw in faith, our life cannot be one of scattered, aimless energies, of bitter regrets, of accumulating worries and hatreds. Nor can we with advancing years say, "Memory is the only friend that grief can call its own."

We look forward, upward. The best is ahead. There is a prize of grace at the end of the course. All of our activities will converge on that one point. All that we have and all that we do will be evaluated in the light of that prize.

Then, worldly pomp, begone!
To heav'n I now press on. (LSB 716:6)

—⟋⟍—

April 24, 1946

APRIL 25

—m—

Read James 3
Set a guard, O LORD, over my mouth; keep watch over the door
of my lips! *Psalm 141:3*

SMALL, BUT MIGHTY

When God gave to man the power of speech, He entrusted him with something that may bring life or death. An angry word may kill a friendship. An uncharitable remark may send someone into the depths of depression. A bit of gossip may ruin a promising career.

The psalmist, therefore, prays that God may set a sentinel at his mouth who will carefully examine every word before allowing it to pass over his lips. Conscious of his sinfulness, he feels that he cannot master the tongue without God's watchful care.

But more is needed. The poet William Cowper calls the tongue "the interpreter of thought." It reveals what is in the heart. We, therefore, need to add another prayer of the same psalmist: "Create in me a clean heart, O God, and renew a right spirit within me" (51:10).

What a blessing the tongue may then be! The prophet writes: "The Lord GOD has given me the tongue of those who are taught, that I may know how to sustain with a word him who is weary" (Isaiah 50:4). A word telling of the Savior who died for us may bring spiritual life to one who is living in the shadows of death. Andrew said to his brother Peter: "'We have found the Messiah' (which means Christ)" (John 1:41). He thus, by the grace of God, set into motion a chain reaction of conversions that have continued to the present day.

But when within my place I must and ought to speak,
*Then to my words give grace Lest I offend the weak. (**LSB 696:3b**)*

—m—

April 25, 1952

April 26

—⟶⟶—

Read 2 Timothy 2:8–19
Psalm 70
Remember Jesus Christ, risen from the dead, the offspring of David,
as preached in my gospel. *2 Timothy 2:8*

REMEMBER!

There is a friendly word we often treat as an enemy, an excellent word that we often resent and tend to despise because it admonishes. It is the word *remember*.

"Remember to wear your boots." "Remember to take your umbrella." "Remember to pick up the groceries." How often *remember* becomes a word of dreary obligation!

But we must make friends with this word *remember*. It is often used in the Bible. When God gave the Ten Commandments, He wove this word into its very texture. Through the writer of Ecclesiastes, God said: "Remember also your Creator in the days of your youth" (12:1). God asks that we remember His commands and His blessings.

Still another of God's reminders comes to us through St. Paul: "Remember Jesus Christ." We need this reminder if we are to grow each day as Christians. Indeed, this is what constitutes a true education. We must be delivered from self-centered thinking. We need to forget ourselves in order that we may remember Jesus Christ and turn our minds to Him.

Heavenly Father, let us now remember Your redeeming work in Jesus Christ, our Savior. Amen.

—⟶⟶—

April 26, 1987

—ɯ—

Read Mark 5:24–34
Psalm 62
[Jesus] turned about in the crowd and said, "Who touched
My garments?" *Mark 5:30*

THE TOUCH OF FAITH

Amazing! A throng of people presses toward Jesus, and a woman in pathetic physical condition makes her way through the packed crowd to touch our Savior's garment. For her, nothing had worked. She had spent everything on cures. But she had heard about Jesus. Impelled by what she heard, she touched Jesus' robe and, wonder of wonders, she was cured.

Faith distinguished the woman's touch from others in that crowd. The woman touched Him intentionally, with the touch of faith. The woman touched Him because she knew her need and was convinced of His power and willingness to heal. She was right. But it was not Christ's garment that healed her, nor her touch. Jesus did it in response to faith. And even that faith was His gift to her (Ephesians 2:8–9), created by the Word concerning Christ (Romans 10:17). The healing power was not in the robe, but in the One who wore it. The healing power was not in the faith of the one who believed, but in the One who creates and gives faith.

Our Savior still comes to sin-sick souls offering His healing gifts. Through Word and Sacrament, He creates and nourishes faith and trust, even as He gives the fullness of His grace and the sweetness of His love. By His grace we reach out to Him with the touch of faith.

Savior, You have said, "Your faith has made you well; go in peace"
(Mark 5:34). Let us hear and believe. Amen.

—ɯ—

April 27, 2005

April 28

—꿈—

Read Matthew 21:1–9
Psalm 124
Jesus Christ is Lord, to the glory of God the Father. *Philippians 2:11*

From Cross to Crown

S hortly before His death and resurrection, Jesus was honored by the multitude in Jerusalem that sang: "Hosanna to the Son of David! Blessed is He who comes in the name of the Lord! Hosanna in the highest!" (Matthew 21:9). We today have even more reason to give honor to the exalted Christ, acknowledging His glory and hailing Him as our King.

When we honor our King, let us make sure that we know how He attained His glory and honor. For Him, the way led to the cross, to death for our sins. The only way He could be glorified was through self-giving, and that meant death on the accursed tree. It was a difficult way, but since it was the Father's will, Jesus accepted it. He knew this way alone would lead to His and the Father's glory. He saw the cross as His crowning. He knew He would be glorified when He was lifted up from the earth.

Jesus made clear that true honor in His kingdom comes through self-giving service. Therefore, He served as no man has ever served before or since, for He served even unto death so that we might enter His kingdom. For us, too, there can be no honor except it come through service. Also our crown comes through a cross—the cross of Christ.

Dear Father, let the mind of Jesus Christ dwell in us. Amen.

—꿈—

April 28, 1976

APRIL 29

—m—

Read Genesis 3:1–24
There is no fear in love, but perfect love casts out fear.
For fear has to do with punishment. *I John 4:18*

AFRAID? WHY?

What a pathetic sight to see Adam and Eve trying to escape from the presence of God by hiding in some bushes in the Garden of Eden! Why were they hiding? What had God done to make them afraid of Him? God had done nothing, but Adam and Eve had. They had eaten of the forbidden fruit; they had sinned. They were no longer perfect in love; hence, they were in torment.

We look at ourselves. Maybe we do not attempt to hide from God in a bush, but do we ever find ourselves trying to hide from Him behind a cluster of good works or reasonable excuses? How often we are tempted to do this! Why? Because we are guilty and afraid. For this we have no one to blame but ourselves. God is doing nothing today to make us afraid of Him. Look at those beautiful flowers in your garden. Who sent the rain and the sunshine to make the glories of spring possible? Who is it that still opens His hands and satisfies the desires of every living thing? Who is it that is still the merciful and forgiving Father in Christ?

It is our God. Do these things cause us to fear? Never! Our own guilt indicts us; God's grace in Christ forgives us. His perfect love for us draws us to Him. Then our love will increase and cast fear aside. For there is no fear in love.

—m—

April 29, 1953

April 30

—⟋∿⟍—

Read 2 Thessalonians 2:13–15
Psalm 84
The God of peace will soon crush Satan under your feet. *Romans 16:20*

Victory over Satan

Christ is Lord. Raised from the dead by the Father's power, He stands as supreme Head of the world. Death has lost its sting and sin its stranglehold on us. We ourselves have been crucified with Him. Now Christ lives in us, and we live to God. "The old has passed away; . . . the new has come" (2 Corinthians 5:17).

Jesus Christ is Lord, but His rival and opponent Satan does not want to admit His lordship. The old evil foe himself is judged. The time until he, too, is finally handed over to the Father is short, but he is making the most of it. Even though he has a standing reservation to live forever in the nether gloom of darkness (Jude 13), he continues working unceasingly to take with him as many as he can get.

The modern world for the most part discounts Satan as unreal and therefore as no threat. It is his chief accomplishment to make people think so. Even in believers' lives he works unnoticed too often. But he will not succeed! God who announced peace to the world in His Son will give lasting peace. Soon on the Day of Judgment, the former lord of this world will lie crushed under our feet. The Kingdom is ours!

Living Lord, give us of Your wisdom and power to make us victorious over Satan. Amen.

—⟋∿⟍—

April 30, 1975

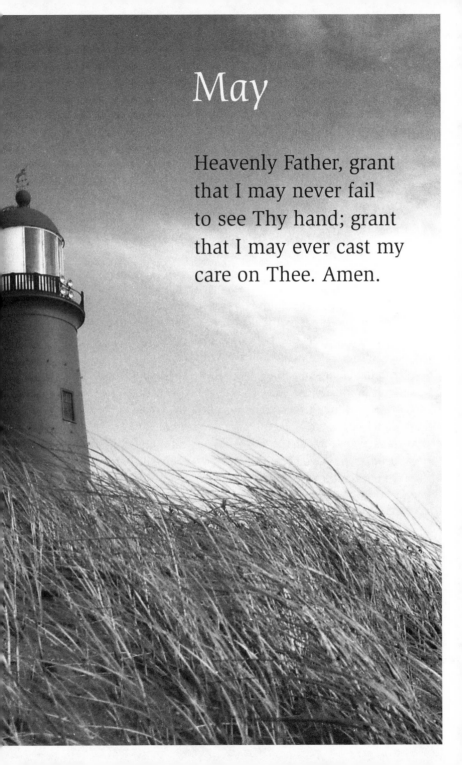

May

Heavenly Father, grant
that I may never fail
to see Thy hand; grant
that I may ever cast my
care on Thee. Amen.

MAY 1

—⁓—

Read Romans 6:3–8
Psalm 66
But you are ... a people for [God's] own possession. *I Peter 2:9*

GOD'S OWN PEOPLE

We often hear the Christian religion spoken of as a great mystery. The word *mystery* is used in many ways in our day. We sometimes speak of a "murder mystery," or we say something is a "mystery" if it cannot be explained easily.

At the heart of the Christian faith lies the greatest mystery of all, the truth that cannot be grasped by the human mind, that the Son of God became a real man in a real world, that He lived and died and rose again, and that in some way we cannot understand, He took our human nature to heaven with Him. Although we cannot understand this, we believe it through faith, which the Holy Spirit has created in our hearts.

Even though we do not know how the great God of all the earth could become a human being, we have the proof of it before our eyes every day. That proof is the fact that there are in this world people who have become God's own people by being joined to the Son of God through faith and have become the sons and daughters of God. They have been baptized into Christ and now share in His life. They are a mystery, but only to those who do not know the God of love. These Christians know whom they have believed.

*Give me eyes of faith, O heavenly Father, to know who I am
and to live in this world as belonging to Thee. Amen.*

—⁓—

May 1, 1966

MAY 2

—⟪⟫—

Read 2 Corinthians 7:5–13
Psalm 51
For godly grief produces a repentance that leads to salvation
without regret, whereas worldly grief produces death. *2 Corinthians 7:10*

FIRST GRIEF, THEN JOY

R epent!" was the clarion call of John the Baptist. "Repent!" was the stringent note sounded by Jesus in
His first public utterance. The first step to God is through
the dust of repentance. Without repentance, there is no faith; without faith, there is no love; without love, nothing is worth having.

"The whole life of the Christian is to be an ongoing repentance," Martin Luther wrote in the first of his Ninety-five Theses.

To repent means to confess our sins, to recognize that sin is our
number one problem. To repent means to turn away from sin to
Christ and to resolve not to sin at all.

"Blessed are those who hunger and thirst for righteousness,"
Jesus said (Matthew 5:6). We hunger and thirst for righteousness
when we realize how far we are from God's standard: "You therefore must be perfect, as your heavenly Father is perfect" (Matthew
5:48). First, the Holy Spirit convicts us of our sin. Then He leads
us to the righteousness of Christ. In that righteousness, we are
righteous in God's sight.

Jesus, Thy blood and righteousness
My beauty are, my glorious dress. Amen. (LSB 563:1)

—⟪⟫—

May 2, 1983

May 3

—ⁿⁿⁿ—

Exodus 20:1–17
Psalm 11
I am the LORD your God. *Exodus 20:2*

WATCH THE DETOURS

God says, in effect: "I am the LORD your God. . . . You shall have no other gods before Me" (vv. 2–3). Is that an easy commandment to follow? We don't worship idols made of wood or stone, but maybe other "gods" are lurking about, calling for our attention. The person or thing we love more than God is an idol.

"I am your beautiful lawn. Cut me, trim me, fertilize me, weed me, keep me green, and you can worship me on Sunday with great satisfaction."

"I am your comfortable home. Paint me, fix me, keep me in good repair, buy me new furnishings, and you can worship me with great pride."

"I am your family. Feed me, clothe me, educate me, and shower attention on me, and you can worship me with adoration."

It is easy to be distracted by the calls of these "gods." Much of what they demand is good and necessary. However, the Lord our God reminds us that He is a jealous God, and He tolerates no rivals. What to do?

Jesus had the answer. "Love the Lord your God with all your heart and with all your soul and with all your strength and with all your mind, and your neighbor as yourself" (Luke 10:27). He loved God so much that He went to the cross. He loved His neighbors so much that He died for their sins. Faith in the Savior enables us to worship God and serve others.

Lord, grant us true faith and love. Lead us to true worship of You and true service to others. Amen.

—ⁿⁿⁿ—

May 3, 1985

MAY 4

—◊—

Read John 1:1–12
Psalm 87
He is actually not far from each one of us, for "In Him we live and move
and have our being"; as even some of your own poets have said,
"For we are indeed His offspring." *Acts 17:27–28*

HIS OFFSPRING

Paschal said, "Man is a God-shaped hole," incomplete by himself. St. Augustine has said, "O God, Thou has created us for Thyself, and our hearts are restless until they find their rest in Thee."

Who has not experienced that strangely restless feeling that comes when least expected? It can come when we are at the "top of our game"—often right at the apex of tremendous achievements in life. Then, suddenly, there is restlessness and dissatisfaction. We yearn for more fulfillment than the world can ever give us. We yearn for more satisfaction than people can give us. We try to find peace, but always it seems that we don't quite belong, relationships don't live up to our expectations, and human institutions fail us.

Our yearning is for God. It is interesting that God's Word tells us that He is also yearning for us—and searching for us. What a blessing we find when through His Word we hear the message of His love and concern as demonstrated in the cross of His Son! For we belong to Him. We are God's offspring in Christ. And we shall be happy only when we acknowledge and live according to this fact.

O God, I thank You for creating and loving me. Amen.

—◊—

May 4, 1986

MAY 5

—⟋⟍—

Read Ephesians 6:10–18
We do not wrestle against flesh and blood, but against the rulers, against the authorities, against the cosmic powers over this present darkness, against the spiritual forces of evil in the heavenly places. *Ephesians 6:12*

WISDOM REQUIRED

A high school wrestling coach discovered to his amazement that the majority of his wrestlers were also members of the chess team!

Wrestling and chess? Despite the absence of physical exertion in the latter, both require a high degree of intelligence. This counters the popular notion that wrestling requires all brawn and no brain.

Christians are wrestlers. We combat the devil and all his princes, powers, and rulers of darkness. Satan's cunning and wiles are thoroughly described in Scripture. He is a terrifying, able foe.

It will never do for Christians to be unintelligent wrestlers. The unbelieving world often regards Christians as docile, unthinking people who accept what they are told, exist in blind faith, and rarely exercise a brain cell. We dare not accept this description. Else we shall lose the fight.

Our sanctified common sense must be used extensively in wrestling against Satan. Wisdom is available through Christ, who fought and defeated the devil for us. "If any of you lacks wisdom, let him ask God" (James 1:5). He provides it in His Word. But let us apply it and so put on the whole armor of God!

Lord Jesus, make me a wise wrestler, that I may fight a good fight of faith and win. Amen.

—⟋⟍—

May 5, 1961
On this date in 1961, Alan Shepard
is first American in space

MAY 6

—〰—

Read Isaiah 53:4–7
Behold, the Lamb of God, who takes away the sin of the world! *John 1:29*

OUR LAMB

When Pharaoh persisted in his refusal to let the children of Israel leave the land of Egypt, the Lord God told the Israelites that He was going to destroy the firstborn of the Egyptians. He instructed His people to select, for each household, a lamb without blemish, to slay it, daub its blood on the doorposts, and eat it while dressed for travel. At midnight, the angel of death moved throughout the land, killing the firstborn of the Egyptians but passing over the houses that bore the blood of the lamb. Thus those families that took God at His word were saved.

The Passover lamb was a shadow of things to come. John the Baptist, pointing to the Lord Jesus Christ, said, "Behold, the Lamb of God, who takes away the sin of the world!" Jesus is the Lamb of God without blemish and without spot. But He who knew no sin was made sin for us. Silent, oppressed, afflicted, He was led to the slaughter. Christ, our Passover Lamb, was sacrificed for the sin of the world, and that means our sin also. He was wounded for our transgressions. He takes away what is offensive to the holiness of God and destructive to the happiness of man. He has redeemed us to God by His blood, out of every kindred and tongue and people and nation. Let us take God at His word. Behold the Lamb of God, and be saved by His blood.

O Lamb of God, who takes away the sin of the world,
have mercy on us. Grant us Thy peace. Amen.

—〰—

May 6, 1960
On this date in 1960, Civil Rights Act
of 1960 is signed into law

Read Philippians 2:5–11
Psalm 30
Do nothing from rivalry or conceit, but in humility count others more
significant than yourselves. *Philippians 2:3*

THE TELLTALE MARK OF MATURITY

Note the day when you stopped thinking of yourself first and foremost. For that was the beginning of your maturity.

For the first years of life, we are almost completely concerned about our own needs. We are insecure. We worry that we will not be taken care of. So we grasp every chance to insure our own rights. When the pie is divided, we want the biggest piece, or at least as much as the next person.

It takes a long time before our attitude changes. But gradually it does, when someone captures our heart. Soon that other person—the beloved—assumes first place in our attentions. We begin to make sacrifices for the loved one. We value the person more than his or her possessions. This turning point is reached at different times with each person. Some may reach it at age 10; others not till 25; others, tragically, never.

With Christians, it is the love of Jesus and their love for Him that triggers the turnaround. "He must increase, but I must decrease" (John 3:30) becomes the Christian's way of life. At that moment, maturity sets in—and a useful life begins.

Loving Savior, give me the mind that was in You, that I may serve You and those whom You have redeemed. Amen.

—⧗—

May 7, 1977

MAY 8

—⟋ᨠ⟍—

Read Luke 17:5–10
The apostles said to the Lord, "Increase our faith!" *Luke 17:5*

MORE FAITH

O ne of the first gifts we are to pray for is faith, a faith that will be constantly increased despite all the storms and stresses of life. The disciples recognized the need for such a faith after our Lord had told them that they must forgive whenever wrong had been done them. Realizing this would require superhuman strength, they ask that their faith be increased.

If we had no faith, then almost everything in the world would be worthless. We must have a faith that will recognize our own sinfulness. We do not want a faith that will lead to despair. We want a faith that will turn us to the Savior on Calvary.

In praying for faith, let us not make the mistake Dwight L. Moody says he made. "I prayed for faith and thought that someday faith would come down and strike me like lightning. But faith did not seem to come. One day I read in the tenth chapter of Romans, 'Now faith comes by hearing, and hearing by the Word of God.' I had closed my Bible and prayed for faith. I now opened my Bible and began to study, and faith has been growing ever since."

Praying plus reading and studying will, with God's grace, increase our faith.

O Lord, heavenly Father, in whom is the fullness of light and wisdom, enlighten our minds by Thy Holy Spirit, and give us grace to receive Thy Word with reverence and humility, without which no man can understand Thy truth. For Christ's sake. Amen.

—⟋ᨠ⟍—

May 8, 1945
On this date in 1945,
V-E (Victory in Europe) Day

Read Romans 5:12–21

May the God of hope fill you with all joy and peace in believing, so that by the power of the Holy Spirit you may abound in hope. *Romans 15:13*

ABUNDANTLY FILLED, PURPOSEFULLY SPILLED

The overflowing cup in Psalm 23 is a familiar image to Christians. Paul's Letter to the Romans reminds us, "Much more have the grace of God and the free gift by the grace of that one man Jesus Christ abounded for many" (5:15). Yes, God's "abundance of grace" (v. 17) so fills us up that we "shall not want" (Psalm 23:1).

So now what? Anything so abundantly filled up has a natural upshot. Picture a cup full of water. When more water is added, that cup spills over—naturally.

So it is with us. God fills us up with joy and peace through His gift of grace so that we overflow with hope and joy and peace in our dealings with others. Abundant outpouring from God should produce thankful overflow in us. Unfortunately, we do not always respond that way. We fail sometimes to spill over to others with God's gifts. But over and over again, God sends His Holy Spirit into our hearts to make us new creatures, filling our hearts so they overflow with joy and peace. God has so abundantly filled us with hope, joy, and peace that we spill the overflow into our relationships and daily life.

O God of hope, thank You for filling us with Your grace and gifts. Help us to overflow with them before those with whom we live and work. Amen.

—ᴎᴠ—

May 9, 1996

Read I Peter 3:13–22
Psalm 64
Even if you should suffer for righteousness' sake, you will be blessed.
I Peter 3:14

EVEN IF . . .

I t is unthinkable that anyone should suffer because he loves, forgives, has mercy, and aids those who need help, including those who do not deserve it. It is unthinkable that anyone who follows the way of love and righteousness should be maligned, mocked, and even manhandled. What reason is there for violating one whose love runs that strongly and that deeply? It is insanity.

But we must reckon with that kind of insanity. That kind of insanity nailed Jesus to the cross. That kind of insanity also caused Peter to share his Lord's lot. That kind of insanity still rears its ugly head today.

Yet even if it is there and tries to squash and even slay that man or woman or youth who is bound and determined to be and do what is right, that insanity will also be swallowed up. Righteousness will prevail. The righteous one will rise as the victor in the end. How do we know? Through Baptism, he partakes of Christ's victory. Peter says, "Baptism . . . now saves you . . . through the resurrection of Jesus Christ, who has gone into heaven and is at the right hand of God, with angels, authorities, and powers having been subjected to Him" (1 Peter 3:21–22).

Father, thank You for showing me in Christ that even if the righteous suffer, they are blessed. Amen.

—⚶—

May 10, 1976

MAY 11

—ᴍᴍ—

Read Galatians 6:1–10
Psalm 55
Bear one another's burdens, and so fulfill the law of Christ.
Galatians 6:2

HELP WITH YOUR BURDENS

Despite the scores of people we may encounter each day during our hectic lives, many of us remain lonely. Research shows that, more than anything else, people today long for meaningful relationship. People are searching for more than superficial friendships. As the line from the theme song of the TV show *Cheers* said, people want to go "where everybody knows your name." We want to be able to express ourselves and to be accepted.

God did not create us to be alone. We need God, and we need one another. We Christians are called to support and build up one another in the faith. As God loves us and establishes a personal relationship with us through His Son, Jesus Christ, so we love others and are loved by them.

We are called to mutually strengthen those whom God has placed in our lives. We value open and honest communication. We practice patience with others, knowing God is not yet finished with them or us. Because Jesus gave His life for us, we are able to give support, strength, and friendship to people in need. Whether it be in the home, at work, in church, or with others in the bowling league, the love of Christ enables us to carry one another's burdens.

**Loving God, as You have loved me, for Jesus' sake, so help me
to love others. Amen.**

—ᴍᴍ—

May 11, 1994

MAY 12

—ɯ—

Read Matthew 9:35–38
Psalm 72
And you also will bear witness, because you have been with Me
from the beginning. *John 15:27*

CHRIST'S WITNESSES

After Jesus had said that He would send His Spirit to testify of Him, He added: "You also will bear witness." It is our joy to give personal witness to others about our Savior because, by the experience of our faith, we have been with the Lord. We know Him as our God and Savior. By faith, we have been with Him in His journeys. We have been with Him at Calvary and at the open tomb. We have heard His words and seen His miracles. Therefore, we bear witness. This is an obligation to Christ in our life. It is part of Christ's ministry on earth through us. It is our personal responsibility and privilege. No one else can do it for us.

Paul was a mighty witness for Jesus. Before him, John the Baptist "came to bear witness about the light" (John 1:8), to point men to the "Lamb of God, who takes away the sin of the world!" (John 1:29). John said, after he had baptized Jesus: "I have seen and have borne witness that this is the Son of God" (John 1:34). Jesus Himself "before Pontius Pilate made the good confession" (1 Timothy 6:13).

Now we bear witness to bring souls to Christ. To us, Jesus says as He said to Paul: "Do not be afraid, but go on speaking and do not be silent" (Acts 18:9). Peter urges believers to be ready "to make a defense to anyone who asks you for a reason for the hope that is in you" (1 Peter 3:15).

Lord, strengthen us to be faithful witnesses for Thee. Amen.

—ɯ—

May 12, 1970

May 13

—∿—

Read 1 Corinthians 10:1–13
Proverbs 13
By insolence comes nothing but strife, but with those who take advice
is wisdom. *Proverbs 13:10*

BE HUMBLE ENOUGH TO LISTEN

Taking advice is not always easy. Within each of us is the voice of pride that likes to believe "I can do it alone. I don't need the help of others." The Book of Proverbs tells us insolence breeds strife. This is true because, in insolence and pride, each of us thinks he or she has all the answers. Then, when our answers contradict those of someone else, conflict results.

The wisdom of Scripture encourages us to put pride aside and be willing to listen to the advice of others. It's not easy to be humble enough to listen, yet to do so can spare us from many painful experiences.

That's what 1 Corinthians tells God's people. Recounting many of the events Israel experienced during the wilderness wanderings, Paul concludes, "These things happened to them as an example, but they were written down for our instruction, on whom the end of the ages has come" (v. 11). We would do well to put pride aside and listen to the advice of God's Holy Word. It is advice that calls us to repentance and saving faith. It points us to Jesus, God's own Son, in whom our sins are forgiven and by whom we become the heirs of God's eternal kingdom. It is advice that is imparted by the Holy Spirit, our Counselor, who leads us to all truth.

Father of all wisdom, open our hearts and minds to the perfect guidance of Your Word. In Jesus' name. Amen.

—∿—

May 13, 1995

Read Judges 6:11–24
Psalm 13

Gideon said to Him, "Please, sir, if the LORD is with us, why then
has all this happened to us?" *Judges 6:13*

GOD WITH US

What do you answer someone like Gideon? "Why does God allow this? If He is with us, why doesn't He do something about it?" Notice that the Lord doesn't get into an argument. He directs Gideon's energies toward leadership instead of debate. He encourages him to use God's strength to help Israel. How can Gideon do that? The Lord answers, "I will be with you" (v. 16).

That's the point: The Lord is with His people. Jesus promised the power of the Holy Spirit to those who believe in Him and are baptized. That power is to be used for God's people. Jesus offered His life for our eternal benefit. In thankfulness, we dedicate our lives to serve Him and His people.

Gideon was not brave or even optimistic. He'd rather debate God's justice than fight. Yet God chose him for this work and pushed him forward.

God still acts that way today. He chooses us to help others against the enemies of sin and Satan. If we whine, "How can I do it?" we hear God's answer to Gideon: "I will be with you."

That is the key that unlocks the courage within us, pushes us forward, and ends all debate.

Lord Jesus, show us how to serve You today. Give us the courage to face Your enemies, trusting firmly in Your power to prevail. Amen.

—⚡—

May 14, 1988

MAY 15

—᠁—

Read Philippians 4:10–13
Psalm 138
I have learned in whatever situation I am to be content. *Philippians 4:11*

BE CONTENT

Y ou have an easy life," a woman said to her friend. "All you do is press a button to wash your dishes, do your laundry, cook your food." The other woman replied, "Oh, yeah? My finger hurts."

How can we deal with an unhealthy discontent? We believe what Jesus said: "One's life does not consist in the abundance of his possessions" (Luke 12:15). Contentment is not dependent on things. Let us be grateful for what we have. We don't need everything we think we do. God is a wise parent. He does not believe in giving us more than we can handle. If we have much, let us thank God and share our bounty. If we have little, let us find reason to give thanks and not complain.

The apostle Paul learned that the secret of contentment is a Person. He explained, "I can do all things through Him who strengthens me" (v. 13). Paul turned to the Lord for power to cope with much or little, good times or bad times. The Son of God loved Paul, and He loves us so much that He gave His life for us. Now we who trust in Him will live forever. He who spared not His own Son but gave Him up for us all, will He not give us all that is good for us?

Jesus, help us develop a closer relationship to You and be content with our present circumstances. Amen.

—᠁—

May 15, 1990

May 16

Read Luke 24:50–53
Psalm 47
He led them out as far as Bethany, and lifting up His hands
He blessed them. *Luke 24:50*

THE UPLIFTED HANDS

The departure of friends is a sad occasion. But when Jesus was parted from His disciples, the occasion was one of joy. The leave-taking of loved ones often causes heaviness of heart. But when Jesus took His visible leave of His disciples, they returned to Jerusalem singing praise to God.

Why? Because the last view they had of their crucified and risen Lord showed Him going up into heaven with His hands uplifted in blessing. What an impression this final scene must have made on the hearts and minds of the disciples! What promise those uplifted hands must have held forth to them! And what promise they hold forth to us!

The hands of the ascended Christ are still uplifted in blessing. He blesses us with His divine presence even as He promised, "Behold, I am with you always" (Matthew 28:20). He blesses us with His divine intercession, for "if anyone does sin, we have an advocate with the Father, Jesus Christ the righteous" (1 John 2:1). He blesses us through His indwelling Spirit, who sheds His love abroad in our hearts, comforts us with the assurance of His forgiveness, and establishes in us His peace.

We are beneath the uplifted hands of Jesus. And we are blessed.

Lord Jesus, extend Thy gracious hands over us and shower us
with Thy blessings. Amen.

—ᴍ—

May 16, 1969

MAY 17

—⚹—

Read Matthew 18:8–14

WHITHER?

We come from God, and God wants us to return to Him and be with Him in all eternity. Man has been created for eternity. The song of the gypsy, "The dewdrop vanishes, and so do I," ignores man's eternal destiny. The grave is not the goal of man's life. "It is appointed for man to die once, and after that comes judgment" (Hebrews 9:27). This life is but a preparation for eternity. Since man's fall into sin, not all are journeying toward a blessed eternity. Christ speaks of a place where there shall be weeping and gnashing of teeth, a place of hell-fire and of torments so great that Dives exclaimed with the heart-rending cry: "I am tormented in this flame" (Luke 16:19–31). But because of God's redeeming grace in Christ Jesus, there is found in eternity also a place of unmarred and never-ending joys for all believers. "In [God's] presence there is fullness of joy; at [His] right hand there are pleasures forevermore" (Psalm 16:11).

According to God's will, everyone should journey heavenward. God wants all to be saved. His plan of salvation embraces all sinners. Christ died for all. And by the Gospel, the Holy Spirit offers the bliss of heaven to all.

In view of man's eternal destiny, our supreme task on earth consists in preparing for a blessed eternity. Christ says, "Seek first the kingdom of God" (Matthew 6:33). Our hands and feet, our eyes, our earning capacity, our honor and reputation among men—all seem very important to us. Yet Christ tells us that the loss of all these things is less serious than the loss of eternal life. "What will it profit a man if he gains the whole world and forfeits his soul?" (Matthew 16:26). Today and every day I must keep my eternal destiny in mind and avoid everything that might weaken or stifle my saving faith in Jesus.

—⚹—

May 18, 1937

MAY 18

—⟋⟍—

Read Matthew 10:21–39
Psalm 106
Whoever loses his life for My sake will find it. *Matthew 10:39*

LOSING LIFE TO FIND IT

To know Jesus is to know true peace of mind and joy in our hearts through the forgiveness He earned for us on the cross. No greater treasure could come to us, for in Christ's forgiveness we have also the assurance of eternal life.

However, to know Jesus Christ and to follow Him means to know the bitter opposition of those who hate the Savior and His followers. These enemies are commonly summed up as the devil, the world, and our flesh. These make the going hard for the Christian. As Christians, we must fight them off every bit of the way to heaven. At times, we may grow weary of the struggle. We see others taking the broad and easy way, and we are tempted to go that way also.

Christ encourages us to follow Him rather than to take the way to eternal destruction. If need be, we should be willing to lose, to spend, to devote totally our lives in the process of living for Him. Even if we do actually lose our lives for Him, we will have lost nothing that we will not lose anyway. What will we gain? We receive the fullness of life in Him and the satisfaction that goes with it; we receive the life eternal.

St. John writes, "God gave us eternal life, and this life is in His Son" (1 John 5:11).

Lord Jesus Christ, Thou hast given Thy life for me. Let me ever be willing to give my life for Thee. Amen.

—⟋⟍—

May 18, 1978

MAY 19

—⟋⟍—

Read Daniel 4:4–18
Psalm 15
His kingdom is an everlasting kingdom, and His dominion endures
from generation to generation. *Daniel 4:3*

FOR THINE IS THE KINGDOM

I n the above text, Daniel repeats the words of David in
Psalm 145:13: "Your kingdom is an everlasting kingdom,
and Your dominion endures throughout all generations."
God's dominion, or kingdom of power, extends over the whole
universe: trees, flowers, grass and weeds, money, knowledge, war
and peace, hungry children and well-fed kings, houses and huts,
Christians and dope addicts, crooks and criminals, astute busi-
nessmen and common laborers, palaces and prisons, hopes and
happiness, tragedies and hurts, the strong and powerful as well
as the weak and helpless, farms and cities, hills and rivers, mountains and seas, rockets and missiles, trips to the moon, sunshine
and floods, good times and bad, the blind and lame, the vigorous
athletes. All this is under God's dominion, and in all of this He
gives us a share. We are to be good stewards.

God's dominion extends also over His kingdom of grace; we
are shareholders in it also. This is the Holy Christian Church, the
communion of saints, which Jesus Christ purchased with His own
blood. And God rules also over the kingdom of glory, which is
heaven. It, too, is an everlasting kingdom. May we always yield to
God's total rule!

Father, help us recognize Your kingdom and further it. Amen.

—⟋⟍—

May 13, 1980

Read John 1:3–5
Psalm 67
In the same way, let your light shine before others, so that they may
see your good works and give glory to your Father who is in heaven.
Matthew 5:16

LET YOUR LIGHT SHINE

How are you at sharing your faith in Jesus Christ? As we think about sharing our personal faith, many images come to mind. In a *Peanuts* cartoon strip, Peppermint Patty tells Charlie Brown that she should have been an evangelist because she converted another kid at school by hitting him with her lunch box.

Unfortunately, that's the kind of attitude that runs rampant through our society with regards to witnessing our Christian faith. Right away, we think of knocking on doors, of coercing people, of shoving the message down someone's throat, something he may not want and certainly does not understand. But maybe we use those negative experiences as excuses for not making the most of opportunities to witness to Jesus.

Christ tells us in the Sermon on the Mount to let our light shine. As the light of Jesus and His mercy shines, His light also shines through us. Rather than a "have to" motivation about sharing our faith, Christ produces in us an attitude of joy in living and speaking that is the most effective witness for Him.

Gracious Lord, may the light of Your mercy shine in me and through me this day. In Jesus' name. Amen.

—ᴫᴫ—

May 20, 2010

May 21

—m—

Read Psalm 40:1–11
And they sang a new song, saying, "Worthy are You to take the scroll
and to open its seals, for You were slain, and by Your blood
You ransomed people for God." *Revelation 5:9*

CELESTIAL MUSIC

Music, like a genuine smile, is the same in all languages. It exalts the soul. It allays the ruffled spirit. It makes the heart gentler, tender, discreet. "Music is one of the fairest and most glorious gifts of God, to which Satan is a bitter enemy; for it removes from the heart the weight of sorrow and fascination of evil thoughts. . . . I would have all arts, especially music, placed in the service of Him who gave and created them," said Luther.

Handel, composer of *Messiah*, exclaimed: "But what is all this compared to the grandest of all makers of harmony above?" Music is the speech of angels, an art of heaven given to earth and returning in perfected measure with us to heaven. One picture of the saints above is that they sing and that they love.

Out on Bethlehem's fields that first glad Christmas night, angels from the realms of glory thrilled the shepherds, wide-eyed with wonder, with their celestial melodies. "Glad songs of salvation are in the tents of the righteous" (Psalm 118:15) as we join in the theme song of the Lamb who was slain and who redeemed us to God by His blood!

Unnumbered choirs before the shining throne
Their joyful anthems raise,
Till heaven's glad halls re-echo with the tone
Of that great hymn of praise.

—m—

May 21, 1950

MAY 22

—⚹—

Read Hebrews 4:11–16
Since then we have a great high priest who has passed through
the heavens, Jesus, the Son of God, let us hold fast our confession.
Hebrews 4:14

REMAINING FAITHFUL

A small boy was greatly pleased with his picture card and its text, received at Sunday school. The text read: "Have faith in God." On his way home, however, the precious possession slipped from his fingers and fluttered from the open streetcar window. Immediately, a cry of distress arose: "I have lost my 'Faith in God'! Stop the car!" The good-natured conductor signaled, and the card was recovered amid the smiles of the passengers. One of them said something about the "blessed innocence of childhood," but a more thoughtful voice answered: "There would be many happier lives if only we older ones were wise enough to call a halt when we find ourselves rushing ahead on some road where we are in danger of leaving our faith in God behind us."

Having considered what our great High Priest, Jesus, the Son of God, has done for us, how He suffered, died, rose from the dead, and ascended into heaven to be our everlasting Savior, we have every reason to "hold fast the confession of our hope without wavering, for He who promised is faithful" (Hebrews 10:23). Judas lost the faith and went "to his own place" (Acts 1:25). Perhaps you can recall someone who once believed but is now a backslider and a renegade. Oh, how many there are who "believe for a while, and in time of testing fall away" (Luke 8:13). Losing the faith means losing our soul.

Help us, O Lord, to endure unto the end, that we may be saved. Amen.

—⚹—

May 22, 1947
On this date in 1947, Cold War begins

MAY 23

—⚊⚊—

Read Acts 23:1–11
Psalm 24

For consider your calling, brothers: not many of you were wise according
to worldly standards, not many were powerful, not many were
of noble birth. *1 Corinthians 1:26*

GOD BLESS SUPPORTING ACTORS

People tend to admire the stars who appear on stage and on the large and small screens. Even the church has its stars—those folks whose God-given talent and dedication have brought them a measure of attention not given to us average church members.

God doesn't use only stars to accomplish His will. He also calls on "supporting actors" to point us to Christ. Prince Jonathan set aside his own chance to inherit a throne and saved the life of his friend David, the future king (1 Samuel 20). Jehosheba hid the royal baby Joash from his murderous grandmother Athaliah, making possible the continuation of David's line, which included Jesus, our Savior (2 Kings 11).

It is easy to admire Paul for his courage before the powerful and mighty. But that courage was not his own. The Lord Himself supported him, encouraged him, and kept him faithful. Christ strengthened Paul with the strength He Himself demonstrated as He stood before the Sanhedrin, Herod, and Pilate on the way to the cross. This is the strength He promises to give to all who bear His name, for He will remain faithful, even unto death. He is our supporting actor. By His acts, He supports us.

Lord, grant us faith to believe that, because You are faithful, You will support us in every trouble.

—⚊⚊—

May 23, 2006

MAY 24

—ᴍᴍ—

Read 2 Thessalonians 3:6–18
Psalm 37:1–9
Now may the Lord of peace Himself give you peace at all times
in every way. The Lord be with you all. *2 Thessalonians 3:16*

BLESSED ARE THE PEACEMAKERS

Nations seek peace with one another so the world does not erupt into war. Families strive to keep siblings and spouses living in harmony to achieve happiness. Businesses labor to settle grievances with employees to ease production woes.

Regardless of all the efforts put forth to gain it, peace is elusive. Although we seek peace, we don't often find it. Both sides have to be willing to talk, to make concessions and compromises. Clashes of wills must end before peaceful solutions are found.

To us, peace usually means an absence of conflict and fighting. But Jesus, through the cross, gives a deeper, more abiding peace. He is our peace, the Prince of Peace. His peace gives us quiet rest and serene comfort, even in the midst of conflict, stress, trial, and war.

Jesus gives us the peace that surpasses all understanding. Peace comes into our hearts as He leads us to believe and trust His saving grace. He gives us His own peace—not a worldly peace— but the peace of sin forgiven, the peace of reconciliation with God, the peace bestowed on those who dine at the marriage feast of the Lamb in His kingdom, which has no end.

Give us, who share this wondrous food,
Your body broken and Your blood,
The grateful peace of sins forgiv'n,
The certain joys of heirs of heav'n. (LSB 623:2)

—ᴍᴍ—

May 24, 2005

May 25

—⚬—

Read Psalm 90
Remember how short my time is! *Psalm 89:47*

REMEMBER THAT THE SANDS RUN OUT

I n pleading with God to remember the shortness of his days, the psalmist actually stirs our memory to a very sober fact. Life expectancy has been lengthened considerably in the past decades; nevertheless, our threescore years and ten are still but a dot on the line of time.

But it is enough. God gives us these days to learn of Him and His Son, Jesus Christ. He who is in a living relationship with his Savior, though his total time on earth be numbered by minutes, has fulfilled his purpose. Most of us, however, are granted many useful years in service to God and man. Even if our life seems extremely short, it is the seed of life everlasting if we have received the engrafted Word and are children of God's grace.

As we remember the shortness of our time on earth with all its suffering and endless problems, we are grateful as we recall that our life with Christ in glory is eternal. If we remember this, we can with courage look forward and with confidence look upward. God has given us a lively hope that makes the close of our earthly days the threshold to heaven.

We know this to be certain because God sent Jesus into the world to redeem us from sin and death, that by faith in Him we may live forever in His presence. Remembering this puts our mind at ease.

Our God, our Help in ages past,
Our Hope for years to come,
Be Thou our Guard while troubles last
And our eternal Home! Amen. (TLH 123:1)

—⚬—

May 25, 1959

MAY 26

—∿—

Read 1 Corinthians 1:18–31
Psalm 26
For since, in the wisdom of God, the world did not know God through
wisdom, it pleased God through the folly of what we preach
to save those who believe. *1 Corinthians 1:21*

WISDOM—FOLLY

A blind man will never fully appreciate great art and a deaf person great music, for we learn of these things through means they do not possess. The way to God is not through our intellect, but through faith created by the Holy Spirit through the Gospel. We do not "discover" God by our own reason and thinking power. The Holy Spirit reveals God through the Gospel and receives us through the water of Baptism. The Holy Spirit uses believers as witnesses who tell us the message of God's love and mercy, which God revealed in sending Christ Jesus into our world to take our sins upon Himself and die for them and thus to make peace with God. All this is foolishness to natural man, and he seeks to destroy Him. But this is not possible, because God is God. And through the resurrection of Jesus Christ, we are assured that He is God of very God and has conquered, lives, and rules forever.

The word of the cross is folly to those who are perishing, but to us who are saved it is the power of God. We believe that it is not through our own intellectual power that we believe in Jesus Christ, our Lord, but by insights supplied by the Holy Spirit. We are thankful that by His persuasion we believe.

Give us grace, O precious Light, to walk by faith and not by sight. Amen.

—∿—

May 26, 1965

May 27

—m—

Read Matthew 10:1–15
And I heard the voice of the Lord saying, "Whom shall I send,
and who will go for us?" Then I said, "Here am I! Send me." *Isaiah 6:8*

SEND ME

The call to arms has been heard in almost every generation of men. With such calls hearts become anxious, and the enthusiasm of soldiers is dampened by the tears of a beloved mother or devoted wife.

Isaiah also heard the call to march forward. It came from the Holy of Holies, from God.

The enemies of the Lord, the prince of darkness with his mighty host, are out to destroy the kingdom of the Lord. Thousands, yea millions, are enslaved and in bondage to sin. Who shall proclaim to them the Gospel of deliverance? The Son of Man went forth to war and crushed the serpent's head and destroyed the works of the devil. But we must know that we are free, lest, blinded by sin, we go on in our evil ways and to eternal death.

Whom shall I send? Who will go for us? asks the Lord. He calls to arms the children of His grace, who have been delivered from their bondage and are citizens of His kingdom. But how can we go? We have no weapons, no atomic energy. "Not by might, nor by power, but by My Spirit, says the LORD of hosts" (Zechariah 4:6). Not with battleships, superbombers, and atomic energy. With such weapons naught can be done in His kingdom.

How, then, shall we deliver man from the old evil foe? Preach the Gospel. This Gospel of Calvary delivers the souls of men from sin, death, and the bondage of Satan. In this Gospel we have a weapon that blasts sin and Satan out of the hearts of men and makes their souls temples of the Holy Spirit.

—m—

May 24, 1948

MAY 28

—␣—

Read Isaiah 49:7–18
Psalm 121
He who keeps you will not slumber. Behold, He who keeps Israel will
neither slumber nor sleep. *Psalm 121:3–4*

ALWAYS ON THE JOB

One of the common characteristics of our human nature is our inconsistency. We have our ups and downs, our good days and our bad days. And because we continue to be both saint and sinner, we are not consistent in our love and in our response to God's grace. No matter how hard we try, we must at times admit with the apostle Paul: "For I do not do the good I want, but the evil I do not want is what I keep on doing" (Romans 7:19).

But one of the characteristics of God is that He is perfectly consistent. He does not have His ups and downs. Jesus Christ is the same yesterday and today and forever. The psalmist reminds us that God's steadfast love endures forever. In the giving of His Son, God made a commitment, a covenant He will never break. He has declared an everlasting and unchanging love, and He sealed His promise with the blood of Jesus.

We "fall asleep on the job" at times. Love cools, and attention wavers. Not so with God! There is no moment or situation when we are beyond His care—not because we are strong in holding on to Him, but because He is strong in holding us. He who keeps us will neither slumber nor sleep.

Change and decay in all around I see;
O Thou who changest not, abide with me. Amen. **(LSB 878:4b)**

—␣—

May 28, 1984

May 29

—ᴍ—

Read Romans 11:33–36
The Almighty—we cannot find Him; He is great in power. *Job 37:23*

I BELIEVE IN GOD

A pastor tells the story of a little girl who knelt to say her evening prayers. She prayed as usual for her parents and her brothers and sisters, asking that God would take care of them. Then she added a new request: "And, dear God, take good care of Yourself, for I don't know what would become of us down here if anything should happen to You."

Isn't it true that we sometimes act as though God could not take care of Himself and His problems? Luther, the great reformer, at one time became utterly despondent. His wife, Katie, anxious to teach him a lesson in trust, dressed in mourning clothes. When he inquired, "Who died?" she answered, "God." Quickly the lesson came home to him.

"The Almighty . . . is great in power." Committing ourselves into His care and keeping, we can rest assured that everything is being properly controlled and carried out.

We confess, "I believe in God." Some people use that expression merely to indicate that they believe in the existence of God. But the Christian thereby declares: I have confidence in God; I trust in His wisdom and in His judgment; I have not the least doubt that He can and will control my life in such a way that all things will work out for my ultimate good.

Heavenly Father, grant that I may never fail to see Thy hand; grant that I may ever cast my care on Thee. Amen.

—ᴍ—

May 29, 1947

MAY 30

—∽∞∼—

Read John 16:20–33
Psalm 33

So also you have sorrow now, but I will see you again, and your hearts
will rejoice, and no one will take your joy from you. *John 16:22*

SORROW TURNED TO JOY

Our days are full of sin and sorrow, temptations and tragedy. We suffer because of wars and violence, abuse
and deception, neglect and abandonment. Some of this
has been brought upon us by our own actions; some things we
suffer because of the actions of our neighbors, which we cannot
control. We are restless. We know this life is not our true home.
We, the baptized, are sojourners in this land, anxiously awaiting
the time for us to go home. As God's children, we long to be with
our Father.

Our Lord knows this. He promises that our sorrow will end and
we will rejoice. We will have no needs or wants. We will be satisfied. On that day, we will no longer sorrow. Our hearts will rejoice.
The joy we will have will not be taken from us.

Until then, we wait amid tribulation, yet in hope. For the Father
sent His Son to die for us because He loves us and wants us to
live with Him. Christ knows our heartaches and hurts because He
took them upon Himself. Our sorrows will come to an end. God
loves us. He promised to take us to Himself in heaven, so we wait
in faith.

*Lord Jesus, thank You for promising to take us to Yourself in heaven
and to turn our sorrow into joy. Amen.*

—∽∞∼—

May 30, 2009

MAY 31

—ᴍᴍ—

Read Job 38:1–11
Psalm 8
What is man that You are mindful of him? *Psalm 8:4*

IMPORTANT TO GOD

What tiny speaks of humanity we are! We travel the highways, see thousands of vehicles on our journey, and realize that they are just a few of the many on the face of the earth. The masses of people in large cities astound us. Although the earth seems large, we are told that the earth is part of the Milky Way galaxy, which may have billions of suns and planets. How important am I anyway?

Not only do we feel insignificant because of our microscopic position in the universe that God created, but we also feel isolated when we consider our failure to live up to God's standards. We know we ought to be separated from God forever because of our failure to love Him and one another as we should.

The concern of our heavenly Father is amazing. He gave His Son into death for us. "This is love, not that we have loved God but that He loved us and sent His Son to be the propitiation for our sins" (1 John 4:10). In addition, our Lord Jesus informs us that not one sparrow "will fall to the ground apart from your Father" (Matthew 10:29).

God's love is constantly focused on us. We are important to Him. Am I insignificant? Not to God!

Heavenly Father, thank You for Your loving concern for every detail of my life. In Jesus' name. Amen.

—ᴍᴍ—

May 31, 2000

June

Help me remember,
Lord Jesus, that by the
grace of God I am what
I am, a forgiven sinner,
now privileged to serve
You. Amen.

JUNE 1

—∼∼—

Read Jonah 2
Call upon Me in the day of trouble; I will deliver you,
and you shall glorify Me. *Psalm 50:15*

PRIVILEGED TO PRAY

One of the grandest privileges we Christians enjoy in this world is that of prayer to our heavenly Father. Think of the manifold troubles we meet on life's rough way: sickness, sorrow, suffering, want, privation, and, oh, the sins that so easily beset us! Truly, we are engulfed in a sea of troubles. And must we endure these troubles in sullen silence, in mute resignation?

By no means. We have the privilege of taking every one of our troubles to the Lord in prayer. God even commands us to do so: "Call upon Me in the day of trouble." And He hastens to add: "I will deliver you." What a precious, precious promise: "I will deliver you"! No matter how great the troubles nor of how long-standing, "I will deliver you," says God. No trouble is so great or so firmly rooted but God is able to deliver us, and He assures us that He will do so. He may not do it today. He may not do it tomorrow. But He will certainly do so in His own good time. Meanwhile, let us avail ourselves of our glorious privilege and pray. We have God's command to call upon Him. We have His promise to hear us. We have troubles without number. What more and better inducement to pray could we possibly have? Then let us take our troubles to Him who says: "Call upon Me in the day of trouble; I will deliver you, and you shall glorify Me."

Oh, what peace we often forfeit;
Oh, what needless pain we bear,—
All because we do not carry
Ev'rything to God in prayer! (LSB 770:1b)

—∼∼—

June 1, 1939

June 2

—ɱ—

Read Romans 8:28–29
Psalm 91
God is our refuge and strength. *Psalm 46:1*

Our Strength

From some evils, we can flee. Some difficult situations we must face. We work, and often our daily calling presents serious problems that tax our inner resources. Family living brings heavy demands on our capacity to understand, to show patience, to love, and to make needed decisions. There are always the temptations to be like the world and to permit ourselves to be squeezed into the mold of conformity with that which has no part in God. High pressures of life seem to allow only the fittest to survive, and we wonder whether we are that fit.

But God knows us, as He did the Church of Philadelphia, that "you have but little power" (Revelation 3:8). Our weakness does not move Him to contempt. Rather, He is able to "sympathize with our weaknesses" (Hebrews 4:15). He not only knows how to help and cares enough to help, but He is also our Strength. Victory or success does not depend on how much power we have in ourselves but on God our strength. "Our God whom we serve is able" (Daniel 3:17), we say as we see Him bring deliverance. With Paul, we triumph: "I can do all things through Him who strengthens me" (Philippians 4:13).

Lord, give me the faith to say, "My help comes from the Lord." Amen.
(Psalm 121:2)

—ɱ—

June 2, 1967

JUNE 3

—⧈—

Read Luke 15:11–24
Psalm 92
When he came to himself. *Luke 15:17*

HOW DO WE FIND OURSELVES?

The Germans have a greeting that, translated literally, means "How do you find yourself?" The question concerns itself with the general well-being of people. It is an interesting question for every human being. Just how does a person find himself?

The prodigal son in Christ's parable found himself when he was sitting in a pigsty. He had gone through all his money. The companions he had picked up with his free spending had abandoned him. He was debating whether he should attempt to satisfy his hunger with the husks the pigs were eating. Then "he came to himself." Like the prodigal, we wander off to a far country when we sin. We leave the Father's house and table. We try to satisfy our spiritual hunger with the empty husks of do-it-yourself religion. We need to come to ourselves.

After the prodigal son had found himself, he resolved to go home to his father and say, "I have sinned." We must go home with him and admit that we, too, have sinned. The wonderful thing about this is that when we return, we find that the Father is waiting. He opens His loving arms. He forgives our sins. He restores us to sonship. He celebrates our return. We truly find ourselves in the Father's house.

Father, apart from You, we are lost. Help us to find ourselves and abide in Your presence forever. Amen.

—⧈—

June 3, 1972

Read Romans 6:1–4
Psalm 65

The Spirit immediately drove Him out into the wilderness. And He was
in the wilderness forty days, being tempted by Satan. And He was with
the wild animals, and the angels were ministering to Him. *Mark 1:12–13*

FROM WATER TO WILDERNESS

I f at all possible, avoid the wilderness. Why did the Spirit
send Jesus into the desert? Jesus had just come from a re-
markable event. At the Jordan River, He was baptized by
John, the forerunner of Christ. There, a voice from heaven said,
"You are My beloved Son; with You I am well pleased" (Mark
1:11). At that point, the Spirit sent Jesus out into the desert. "He
was in the wilderness forty days."

These words bring to mind Israel's forty-year wilderness trek,
as they emerged from the waters of the Red Sea. Commissioned by
God to be "a kingdom of priests and a holy nation" (Exodus 19:6),
they failed their mission. So God sent them on their wilderness
way. His purpose was to strengthen them for further endeavors.
But in the end, they always failed.

Jesus picks up God's mission. Now Jesus must meet the same
trials and tests as Israel and not fail. Therefore, "the Spirit immediately drove [Jesus] out into the wilderness" and on to the
cross, where as the Lamb of God He was sacrificed for the sins of
the world. Even though tempted by Satan himself, Jesus met and
mastered the test of the wilderness.

*God, make us strong to carry out Your will. In Your beloved Son's name
we pray. Amen.*

—☁—

June 4, 1997

JUNE 5

—ᴍ—

Read John 1:10–13
Psalm 84
Truly, truly, I say to you, unless one is born again he cannot see
the kingdom of God. *John 3:3*

BORN A SECOND TIME

We *have* been born anew! The first time we were born we came into the world as children of human parents. But we were born a second time. Through God's life-giving Spirit working in the water of Holy Baptism, we received new life as God's children and entered the kingdom of God.

Think of it! We have God's life within us. We are offspring not just of human parents but also of God. "That which is born of the flesh is flesh, and that which is born of the Spirit is spirit" (John 3:6). We are spirit as God is Spirit. At our first birth, our human parents shared their earthly life with us. Through our second birth, God shared His life with us. All this has been made possible through Christ, who redeemed us on the cross.

Because we have been born a second time, we can live as God lives. We can think His good thoughts, feel His good emotions, do His good deeds. We can love. We can help. We can serve.

Children usually look like their parents. We can look like God. "Be imitators of God, as beloved children" (Ephesians 5:1). We can! For we are God's children.

God's life is eternal, and we share in it. We follow Jesus to resurrection.

*Praise to Thee, life-giving Spirit, for the new life that is mine
now and forever. Amen.*

—ᴍ—

June 5, 1968
On this date in 1968, Robert F. Kennedy
is assassinated in Los Angeles

JUNE 6

—ɷ—

Read Romans 12:10–17
For we are His workmanship, created in Christ Jesus for good works,
which God prepared beforehand, that we should walk in them.
Ephesians 2:10

GOD'S WORKMANSHIP

S aved by grace, through faith in Christ, not by works
of our own. That is the only Gospel found in the New
Testament. "A person is . . . justified by faith in Christ
and not by works of the law" (Galatians 2:16). This central truth
of the Christian religion needs again and again to be emphasized.

But there is also another side that must be equally emphasized.
And that is this: the faith that justifies, the faith by which we are
saved, is not a dead knowledge in the head, but a living thing in
the heart. "Faith working through love" (Galatians 5:6). Saving
faith, as Luther so often points out, is an active, busy thing that
performs good works without questioning.

Here God tells us that we are His workmanship. Even as He
has given us our body and soul, so He has now given us spiritual
life and power, "created in Christ Jesus" for the express purpose
that we should perform good works. We are saved not only for the
life hereafter, but equally so for this life on earth. We are saved
to serve! Yes, the apostle goes so far as to tell us that God has
ordained, or determined, the very works in which we should walk.
The Christian life is a walking, or serving, in good works according
to God's will and plan. How far we daily come short of that! How
can we improve? By daily searching out God's will in His Word, by
daily seeking God's guidance in sincere prayer, and by frequently
seeking spiritual strength in the Sacrament.

**Thou God of grace, make me to abound in love and good works,
for the sake of Jesus Christ. Amen.**

—ɷ—

June 6, 1944

JUNE 7

—ᴍ—

Finally, be strong in the Lord and in the strength of His might.
Ephesians 6:10

STRONG IN THE LORD

I n the fight of faith we must look to our omnipotent God
for strength. Through Christ, we are "more than conquerors" (Romans 8:37). "I can do all things through Him who
strengthens me" (Philippians 4:13).

Paul had been summing up the duties of children and parents,
servants and masters. When all is said and done and you are en-
deavoring with the help of God to be the children and parents,
servants and masters that you ought to be, then finally be strong
in the Lord.

Our strength to be as we ought, whatever our relationship to
our fellow man, our strength to fight the fight of faith, whatever
our place or position in life, is in the Lord.

With might of ours can naught be done,
Soon were our loss effected;
But for us fights the valiant One,
Whom God Himself elected. (*LSB* 656:2)

Our strength for the warfare of faith is not to be found in ourselves nor in our fellow man. The psalmist cries out: "My flesh
and my heart may fail, but God is the strength of my heart and my
portion forever" (Psalm 73:26).

We must draw close to the great Champion of our soul, Christ
Jesus. He alone can help us in this spiritual conflict. He knows
what the battle is like. He has been through the thick of it. He has
met our enemies and conquered them for us.

Strong in the Lord of hosts And in His mighty pow'r;
*Who in the strength of Jesus trusts Is more than conqueror. (**TLH 450:2**)*

—ᴍ—

June 7, 1938

JUNE 8

—ɷ—

Read 2 Kings 4:1–7
Psalm 12
Better is a neighbor who is near than a brother who is far away.
Proverbs 27:10

FRIENDS AND NEIGHBORS

Some believe that one of life's most powerful driving forces is the desire for approval. In fact, the desire for approval is so strong that it leads some to violate their own sense of right and wrong in an attempt to gain the acceptance of others. So, when you hear someone say, "I don't need anybody. I'd rather be alone," you can take it with a grain of salt. Probably such people have felt rebuffed so often that they are now afraid to reach out and touch someone.

In God, we live and move and have our being. For reasons not always clear to us, He is always letting other people cut in and out and across our path of life. Some may be our neighbors and some may become our intimate friends. This is good.

God says, "Love your neighbor as yourself" (Leviticus 19:18). First, love yourself! It is surprising how many people fail to do this. They do not recognize their own worth. They must be miserable. With proper self-regard goes love for the neighbor, a potential friend.

Jesus is the Friend of sinners. He loved us, died for us, and chose us to be His friends—all this without merit or worthiness on our part. And He tells us: "Love one another."

O God, if I have to live alone, let there be a friend within calling distance to help me; for Jesus' sake. Amen.

—ɷ—

June 8, 1982

Read Hebrews 10:18–24
Psalm 115
By a single offering He has perfected for all time those who are
being sanctified. *Hebrews 10:14*

ONCE FOR ALL

Some kinds of damage can be made good. If I break a piece of glassware in a store, I can pay the purchase price. If I dent a fender, I can have it restored to its original shape. The more serious the damage, the more I must pay.

Other kinds of damage are beyond restitution. How could one replace a human life? Or the affection alienated from one to whom it rightfully belongs? Or the life stolen away from God and given over to His enemy? Such damage I did to myself in my relationship to God. I did it when I withheld from God the total loving obedience and the perfect trust I owe to Him. I cannot make it up to God.

But Christ could and did make perfect restitution. He replaced my failures with His perfect righteousness. For the cancellation of all my guilt and penalty, He went to His cross for me. By His action, I am restored to what I was meant to be. I have been stamped with the sign of the cross of Christ, who made good for all the damage. Covered by His perfection and sacrifice, I am so perfectly restored that I pass my Maker's inspection and He accepts me into His service.

Thank You, Lord Jesus, for clothing me in the robe of Your righteousness. Amen.

—ɯ—

June 9, 1977

JUNE 10

—ɯ—

Read Luke 4:16–32
All spoke well of Him and marveled at the gracious words that were
coming from His mouth. *Luke 4:22*

GRACIOUS WORDS

S hortly after His Baptism and temptation, Jesus returned
to His hometown, Nazareth. The rabbi gave Him the
privilege of addressing the people in the synagogue on
the Sabbath. Jesus took Isaiah 61:1–2 as His text and explained it
as referring to Himself and then applied it to the people. They were
deeply impressed. First, they marveled at His gracious words. No
one had spoken so kindly, so winsomely to them. He brought new
life into the Scriptures and new meaning into their humble lives.
They were uplifted and comforted. They felt drawn closer to God.

But as Jesus spoke on, their sentiment changed. He told them
of the bad record of their forebears and revealed to them the wickedness of their own hearts. Then they turned against Him. In their
wrath they drove Him out of town. A sad story!

But this story continues to repeat itself in our day and in our
congregations. When our pastor speaks to us about the love of
God in Christ (as in John 3:16) and extends Christ's invitation (as
in Matthew 11:28), the hearers think of these as gracious words.
But when the preacher corrects, rebukes, warns, and threatens,
many close their hearts and say, "The minister should stick to the
Gospel!" Thus Christ Himself is rejected! The gracious words of
Christ's Gospel can lodge only in hearts that have been humbled
and made conscious of their need of a Savior from sin.

*Lord God, we pray that Thy Holy Spirit may open our hearts to receive
the full truth of Thy Holy Word. Amen.*

—ɯ—

June 10, 1951

June 11

—⁂—

Read James 4:3–17
You ought to say, "If the Lord wills, we will live and do this or that."
James 4:15

CONSIDER GOD IN YOUR PLANNING

A foolish rich man had laid up money and goods that he thought would last a lifetime. Feeling secure, he said boastfully, "Soul, you have ample goods laid up for many years; relax, eat, drink, be merry" (Luke 12:19). He did not give thanks to God for his blessings, and he had no thought of ordering his life according to God's wishes. He felt he had earned what he had and that he could do as he pleased. That night, he died. "Man proposes; God disposes."

Our text not only reminds us that God orders our lives, but it also encourages us to say so as we do our planning. Many Christians in the past had the custom of saying, "If the Lord wills, we will go here or there, we will do this or that," as the text suggests. This good custom deserves to be revived. But the attitude of the heart is more important than use of the words. Our hearts are to be grateful and humble, and they are to respond to the will of God in all things.

James does not, of course, discourage planning and careful forethought. Scripture nowhere condemns planning as such, but only planning that does not take God into account. God gave us intelligence that we might plan with care. But all our plans should be made in view of the uncertainty of life, in view of our dependence on God for life and health, and in view of our need for His guidance and blessing. In acknowledging his dependence on God, David said, "My times are in Your hand" (Psalm 31:15).

Lord, help us to acknowledge Thy rule and to commit our lives to Thee; in Jesus' name. Amen.

—⁂—

June 11, 1955

JUNE 12

—ɷ—

Read Acts 2:22–28
Psalm 119:153–160
The fruit of the Spirit is . . . joy, peace. *Galatians 5:22*

JOY AND PEACE

A problem that plagues the human mind and spirit is the continuing presence of illness, tragedies, wars, and other evils. Why can these not stop? Can God not exercise a preventive power or, at least, guarantee His followers an exemption from their effects?

God's express Word to us, along with our own observations, tells us that we are not exempt. Days of pain and affliction may come.

Such days, however, are not signs of God's disinterest or absence. They are the times when He gives us the power to persevere and overcome. His Spirit bestows the gifts of joy and peace.

Strange as it may seem, the joy given by God is there right in the midst of our unhappiness. His peace, as a further fruit of the Spirit, comes in the presence of monumental affliction.

Jesus said, "Peace I leave with you; My peace I give to you. Not as the world gives do I give to you. Let not your hearts be troubled, neither let them be afraid" (John 14:27). It is the peace He gained for us.

God calls us to faith in the face of troubles. His Spirit gives us the power to respond with joy and peace.

Father, when we are disheartened, give us joy; when we are troubled,
give us peace; when we are dispirited, give us Your Spirit. Amen.

—ɷ—

June 12, 1984

June 13

⁓

Read Romans 5:20–6:15
Psalm 15

Do you not know that all of us who have been baptized into Christ Jesus
were baptized into His death? *Romans 6:3*

WORK TO BE DONE

C heap grace" describes an attitude that views salvation
like a "Get out of jail free" card—we can do whatever
we want because we are forgiven. Every time we con-
sciously sin, we are giving in to this attitude.

We have been freed from sin in order to live an abundant life.
The Law of God guides us in that life. The Commandments are
not God's way of keeping us from doing fun things; they make our
life better. A parent tells a child to avoid the red burners on top of
the stove not to be a spoilsport, but to keep the child from getting
burned. Likewise, God gives us the Commandments to keep us
from harm. Violating them leads to broken relationships, injured
bodies, and devastated souls.

Our salvation was not cheap; it cost Jesus His life. Being saved
means the Holy Spirit now dwells in us. He gives us the ability to
willingly keep the Law, though we still contend with our sinful
nature. We are not saved by keeping the Law, but we endeavor to
avoid sin out of thanksgiving for Jesus' love and knowing His Law
is His plan for an amazing life.

*Lord, thank You for saving me from my sins. Help me to live a life
pleasing to You. Amen.*

⁓

June 15, 2011

JUNE 14

—⟡—

Read Hebrews 7:11–19
Psalm 115
So Jonah arose and went to Nineveh, according to the word of the LORD.
Jonah 3:3

JONAH'S RESPONSE

J onah and many others suffered much as a result of his disobedience to God's first call to service. But this time, Jonah arose and went to do what his Lord had commanded.

Obedience to the Word and will of God is a wonderful thing and produces nothing but happiness. Many examples of this are found in the Bible. Noah did all that God commanded him. Abraham, when the Lord called him to leave home to go to an undisclosed land—to become the father of the Lord's chosen people— "went, as the LORD had told him" (Genesis 12:4). Our Lord Himself, "although He was a Son, He learned obedience through what He suffered" (Hebrews 5:8).

Why did Jonah insist on learning obedience to God the hard way? For the same reason that we react similarly to God's Word: We know better! We find it so difficult to submit to authority; we want to do things our own way. Jonah learned by bitter experience that God's way is the only way. May we be as fortunate in learning this fact! In the meantime, let us be grateful that Jesus, who learned to be obedient, took our sins of disobedience with Him to the cross, so that now we are forgiven for all our sins.

Blessed Lord Jesus, give us the grace of obedience to You
and all rightful authority. Amen.

—⟡—

June 14, 1974

June 15

—◊—

Read Matthew 6:25–34
Whatever your hand finds to do, do it with your might. Ecclesiastes 9:10

HERE

There is a tendency in our day to be concerned unduly about world problems to the point of ignoring the duties and responsibilities that lie close at hand. We feel also that our thinking has to be in terms of eras if it is to win any respect. The difficulties our world faces today are overwhelming. There is no doubt about that. In floundering fashion, we are trying to gain a foothold in a new and soberingly different world. And we are so fearfully small and weak.

God has a word for us that cuts the problem down to our size. "Whatever your hand finds to do, do it with your might." Here is a refreshing antidote for the agony of the world that keeps interfering with our small life. It is so easy to neglect the tasks that surround us by concentrating on world affairs about which we can do little.

When we see only the great difficulties that confront us, we easily fall into a mood in which we complain with the French philosopher Renan, "O God, when will it be worthwhile to live?" There is enough in our restricted environment to tax our abilities and strength. If we set ourselves to the work at hand and cheerfully go about it, we shall learn to sing with the English poet Coleridge, "O God, how glorious it is to live."

Be with us, O God, and help us see and do the task at hand, that we despair not of the problems of our times. In the name of Christ we ask it. Amen.

—◊—

June 15, 1946

June 16

—∞—

Read Revelation 3:1–6
Psalm 46

Behold, I have engraved you on the palms of My hands; your walls are continually before Me. *Isaiah 49:16*

Unfailing Security

I saiah, God's spokesman, asks, "Can a woman forget her nursing child, that she should have no compassion?" (49:15). Yes, she may forget, he declares, and many have. "Yet I will not forget you," God promised us (49:15). "I will never leave you nor forsake you" (Hebrews 13:5). "I am with you always, to the end of the age" (Matthew 28:20).

The Lord uses strong contrasts: "The mountains may depart and the hills be removed, but My steadfast love shall not depart from you" (Isaiah 54:10). God's kindness appears in His creation, His providence; it comes to its climax in Christ's sacrifice of redemption. That kindness is as lasting as eternity itself.

No one shall pluck us out of the Savior's hands—this bespeaks our unfailing security. God has engraved us on the palms of His hands—not on the sides of the mountains, for they shall depart; not on the face of the sun, for it shall lose its light; not on the surface of heaven, for it shall roll up like a scroll. No, "I have engraved you on the palms of My hands," the hands that control the world; the hands that gave us Christ, the Savior; the hands extended in blessing. No corroding power will ever erase our names from God's hands.

Precious Lord Jesus, be our refuge in trial, our comfort in sorrow, our security in death, and our joy in eternity. Amen.

—∞—

June 16, 1983

June 17

—m—

Read Philippians 2:19–24
But you know Timothy's proven worth, how as a son with a father
he has served with me in the gospel. *Philippians 2:22*

JOY IN DEDICATED CO-WORKERS

The joy of Christian love is expressed in trusting our co-workers. St. Paul had full confidence in young Timothy. As a son with a father, Timothy had labored with Paul on many missions. Because Timothy knew the love of Christ, he had a loving concern for people.

Paul also trusted Epaphroditus as a brother and fellow soldier in the army of Christ.

Disheartened by the weakness of some, Paul says, "They all seek their own interests, not those of Jesus Christ" (v. 21). He does not lose heart by thinking only of the insincere people. He rejoices that God in His grace touched Timothy and Epaphroditus with the true love of Jesus and made them trustworthy co-workers.

When people are wrapped up in their own affairs, we are inclined to be discouraged. Satan tempts us to suspect every professing Christian. A careful look around will show us true co-workers, concerned for our welfare and ready to serve. The one true friend or the faithful partner is enough to bring us joy.

Are we ready to trust our co-workers? Paul could give Timothy full confidence on his missions. We can depend on the power of Christ in our co-workers. We know that joy of pastors and fellow servants in the work of Christ.

We thank Thee, Lord, for the joy of co-workers. Amen.

—m—

June 17, 1961

JUNE 18

—꠸—

Read Proverbs 12:9–28
Psalm 107
Aspire to live quietly, and to mind your own affairs, and to work
with your hands, as we instructed you. *1 Thessalonians 4:11*

THE VALUE OF WORK

Christians in Thessalonica and in our world today need
to understand the value of work. Our Lord holds us ac-
countable to support ourselves and our families, to earn
our own living. I know Paul isn't telling us that we ought to be
driven by our work. In fact, he's not really making a statement at
all about work attitudes beyond simply telling us that God created
us to take responsibility for our own welfare in this world—to earn
our own way.

Some big questions remain: In modern society, do we make it
possible for everyone to earn his or her own way in life? How do
we best provide every human being the dignity of a job? What are
we prepared to do to provide for those who can't work or can't
find work?

Paul worked in Thessalonica, probably making tents, to earn
his own way. Jesus learned the carpenter's trade, and then He left
that work to carry another piece of wood—the cross—to Calvary
for us. He dignified our lives by granting us forgiveness and eternal
life. He asks us to dignify everyone's life by providing the opportunity for all to work.

**Lord Jesus, thanks for Your work that gave us our salvation. Bless us in
our daily work. Use us to provide the dignity of work for everyone. Amen.**

—꠸—

June 18, 1988

Read Luke 12:16–21
Give us each day our daily bread. *Luke 11:3*

THE TRUE SECURITY

W hat shall we eat?" or "What shall we drink?" or "Wherewithal shall we be clothed?" These questions are asked in genuine earnestness by those who seek security in an abundance of things. When the gifts of God are allowed to occupy the throne of our heart, anxiety is likely to occupy our mind.

When a person seeks his security in the creation rather than in the Creator, the abundance of things does not still this anxiety. The wealthy materialist worries just as much as the penniless pauper, perhaps more. Having much in possessions does not give a man more security than having few things. The reason is simple. All things are transitory. No thing or combination of things, no matter how precious, is secure. The material gifts of God are as shifting sand; they make a poor foundation on which to rest one's hope. In the Gospel of Luke, we find a man who felt secure in the many things he had laid in store. Jesus characterizes the man as a "fool."

The material was never meant to take the place of the Maker. The only true security we have in this changing world is this knowledge: "Your heavenly Father knows that you need them all" (Matthew 6:32). "If you then . . . know how to give good gifts to your children, how much more will your Father who is in heaven give good things to those who ask Him!" (Matthew 7:11).

Our Father, help us find our peace in Thee through the heavenly Bread,
Christ Jesus, our Savior. Amen.

—⁓—

June 19, 1964

June 20

—⧖—

Read John 14:1–6
Psalm 20
Let not your hearts be troubled. Believe in God; believe also in Me.
John 14:1

TRUST IN GOD

Many things trouble our hearts: a drug-addicted loved one, an aging parent, a dangerous intersection, the future of our country. Much trouble is in our world, and we take it all to heart.

Of course, the world has attempted to respond. It has prompted us to *Say No to Drugs*. It has incorporated safe-sex programs into public school curricula. It has declared war on terrorism. Yet our troubles are always with us. They knock at the doors of our hearts.

The good news for us today is that the Lord is concerned about what is happening in your heart. Jesus comforts us with His promises of salvation through the cross. Christ's promises melt away the crushing weight of this world's troubles and replace them with trust in Him.

So do not measure who and what you are by what is happening in your heart. Do not look to the world to salve your pain. Jesus has come. He has gone the way of the cross and death for you and in your place. He has won life and salvation; He brings forgiveness and healing. He sets your heart at rest, healing you with His forgiveness and love. The Lord of Life has brought you peace. Amen.

Lord Jesus, set aside the weight of those things that trouble my heart.
Heal me, make me whole, and give me Your peace. Amen.

—⧖—

June 20, 2006

JUNE 21

—∿—

Read Romans 13:1–7
Psalm 77:13–20
Be subject for the Lord's sake to every human institution. *1 Peter 2:13*

RESPECTING HUMAN AUTHORITY

Rebellion against authority is everywhere, and it's no stranger among Christians either. A bumper sticker advises, "Question Authority," as if the human race needs any encouragement to do so. Satan told Adam and Eve to question authority: "Did God actually say . . . ?" (Genesis 3:1). Ever since, a rebellious spirit has plagued the human spirit, and generation after generation follows in the steps of our first parents. In our time, we see an alarming erosion of respect for authority in government, school, home, and church.

People need to recognize God's authority in human institutions. Many of these are God's agents for promoting peace, order, and progress. We have the right and duty to question human authority when it conflicts with God's Word, but where God has chosen to work through human institutions, we are to treat them with respect and obedience.

We respect authority "for the Lord's sake." Jesus modeled obedience at home and over against the government, and when He became "obedient to the point of death, even death on a cross" (Philippians 2:8), He forgave and renewed us to follow in His way—to submit to government and those who exercise authority over us. He motivates and empowers us to do so.

Keep us faithful, Lord, and obedient to the authorities You have given us. In Jesus' name. Amen.

—∿—

June 21, 1998

JUNE 22

—ɱ—

Read John 7:53–8:11
Psalm 130
Let him who is without sin among you be the first to throw a stone
at her. John 8:7

THROWING STONES

A woman had been caught in an adulterous act. Jewish law prescribed death by stoning. The scribes and Pharisees dragged her before Jesus and asked what He thought should be done. Their purpose was either to trap Him into siding with her or to side with them. Either way, His ministry of mercy among sinners would be jeopardized. Jesus exposed their cruel self-righteousness by saying, "Let him who is without sin among you be the first to throw a stone at her." One by one, they dropped their stones and left.

We have the saying "Those who live in glass houses ought not throw stones." When we hear of the moral failings of others, it is so easy to condemn. Upon seeing a criminal on the way to the gallows, George Whitefield remarked, "There, but for the grace of God, go I." In the sight of God, we are all guilty sinners who stand condemned. Not one of us is without sin.

In Jesus Christ, there is forgiveness and the opportunity to live a new life, a life of love and one that lifts others up instead of throwing stones at them. As God in Christ loved us despite our failings, so we love those around us.

Help me remember, Lord Jesus, that by the grace of God I am what I am, a forgiven sinner, now privileged to serve You. Amen.

—ɱ—

June 22, 1980

JUNE 23

—〰—

Read James 3:1–12
Psalm 49
From the same mouth come blessing and cursing. My brothers, these
things ought not be so. James 3:10

SANCTIFIED SPEECH

There is a tremendous power in words. This power can either be for good and a blessing, or it can be for evil and a curse.

God does not want us to use our tongues in a bad way. He doesn't want us—and others—to be destroyed by the evil that is in our hearts and that can come out through our mouths.

That is why God Himself has spoken. He has spoken out of His heart of love. He has spoken redemptively through Jesus Christ, His Son. He has spoken and acted out His Word to us in a manger, on a cross, and from an empty tomb. He speaks to us in a special way in Holy Baptism and Holy Communion.

Jesus' silence under suffering atoned for our sins of speaking too hastily and too much. Jesus' words atoned for our cowardly silence when we should have witnessed boldly. Jesus is God's Good News, the Word made flesh, who communicates to us His love, mercy, grace, and forgiveness.

Our tongues can be a great power for healing and good among people. God's Spirit unlocks our tongues and moves us to a level of conversation and speech that glorifies God and wins over souls to Christ.

*O Jesus, Word of God Incarnate, help us to be Your living words
here and now. Amen.*

—〰—

June 23, 1993

June 24

Read Galatians 2:17–21
Psalm 22:12–22

I have been crucified with Christ. It is no longer I who live, but Christ who lives in me. *Galatians 2:20*

SEEING OURSELVES ON THE CROSS

Were you there when they crucified my Lord?" These words and their melody are charged with emotion. Jesus' mother and some disciples were there in person. We were there because our sins helped nail Him to the tree. St. Paul goes a step further and suggests that we were not only at the foot of the cross but on it! Can we see ourselves on a cross beside Jesus? More correctly, can we see our sins borne in His body on Calvary? We should be able to see ourselves on every crucifix we view in faith.

This is strange but powerful imagery. We are crucified with Christ—dead to sin and alive to righteousness. The hymn "Rock of Ages, Cleft for Me" reminds us that Jesus' death provides the "double cure: Cleanse me from its guilt and pow'r" (*LSB* 761:1). Trusting in Jesus, our sins are forgiven, and God declares us not guilty. At the same time, the power of His Spirit enables us to live a more godly life. Truly a double cure!

If ever we doubt the full forgiveness of our sins, if ever we feel powerless to avoid committing certain sins, we should see ourselves crucified with Christ. His Spirit will come to our rescue with full and free forgiveness.

Gracious God, help us live as believers dead to sin and alive to righteousness because of Christ, our Savior. Amen.

June 24, 2002

June 25

—∭—

Read Matthew 13:18–23
Martha welcomed Him into her house. And she had a sister called Mary,
who sat at the Lord's feet and listened to His teaching. *Luke 10:38–39*

Too Flustered about Serving

The two Bethany sisters present an interesting picture. Martha, it seems, has been much maligned. Some have depicted her as a worldly minded person, with scarcely a thought about spiritual matters. But Martha was a lovely character. We should not forget that it was she who provided for Jesus' comfort; and all that hurrying to and fro was done out of love for Him. Nor should we forget that it is mentioned in the Bible that "Jesus loved Martha and her sister and Lazarus" (John 11:5).

However, Martha made a big mistake at the time when Jesus was a guest in her home and was proclaiming words of heavenly wisdom. She was all bothered about cooking and serving. When Jesus, the Teacher come from God, addressed Himself to her and her sister about eternal values, that was no time to be flustered about preparing a dinner or serving refreshments.

It is good to remember that any service, even though it is rendered in love to Christ, dare not interfere with the hearing of His Word. Any service that causes distraction and disturbs the quietness and composure so essential when the Word of God is proclaimed, merits from the divine Teacher no commendation, but rather words of kindly reproof.

Distracting thoughts and cares remove,
And fix our hearts and hopes above. Amen. (John Fawcett)

—∭—

June 25, 1950
On this date in 1950, Korean War begins

JUNE 26

—᳁—

Read Leviticus 25:11–23
Psalm 49
Now the full number of those who believed were of one heart and soul,
and no one said that any of the things that belonged to him was his own.
Acts 4:32

IT'S MINE!

Grandpa picks up the toy. "It's mine!" he says mischievously. "No, it's mine!" protests the child. They both know it's a game, but "It's mine" can be deadly serious.

The children of Israel were required to return property to its original owner every fifty years; every seven years the ground remained unsown—no crops were planted. The land was their livelihood, their way of amassing possessions for themselves. God wanted to remind them that nothing really belonged to them; it had all come from His generosity.

After Pentecost, the first Christians were filled with the Spirit and the wonder of salvation Jesus gives to all who believe in Him. They shared their possessions so generously that there was not a needy person among them.

To say that all we have comes from the Lord is easy, but "It's mine" is deeply entrenched in the human heart. To "put our money where our mouth is" does not come easily. Let's stop and take a look at what we value most—the furniture we've picked, the crop we've planted, our name on the office door. Whose are they really?

**O Lord, I will not trust in my wealth, for nothing is worth more
than Your ransom of my soul from death. Amen.**

—᳁—

June 26, 1994

JUNE 27

—ɯ—

Read Acts 15:13–21

GOD-PLEASING CHURCH MEETINGS

The first general Church meeting was held in Jerusalem. It was quite a meeting. There were some reports to be heard that were inspiring. Particular attention was devoted to the Church's mission program. Nothing was quite so vital as this program. After all, the Lord had said, "Go therefore and make disciples of all nations" (Matthew 28:19). Nothing had so filled all the delegates with joy as the wonderful reports of the Lord's blessing on this advance of His kingdom.

Of course, there were those who found some fault with the procedure. There were those who felt that the new converts should really conform to all the old laws of Moses as they had. Others felt that this should not be done. A real argument developed, which almost split the Church. No doubt the devil was rubbing his hands in unholy glee.

At this point, James settled the matter by using his God-given common sense. When he finished his speech, the Gospel was once more triumphant. Christian love and harmony prevailed. Things that were obnoxious were removed. Everyone was happy to carry on as before, in fact, with greater zeal than ever.

Herein we find a wonderful lesson for us all. Anything and everything is good in the Church so long as the progress of the Gospel in all its truth is not hindered. The Word of God decides all important issues. Otherwise, we use our good, sanctified common sense and show brotherly love. In that way, peace and harmony prevail. May God bless His business among us and thwart the attempts of the devil to disrupt and hinder the work. Then we shall go forward as a strong and united Church.

—ɯ—

June 27, 1954

June 28

—〜〜—

Read Philippians 4:4–13
We know that for those who love God all things work together for good,
for those who are called according to His purpose. *Romans 8:28*

CERTAINTY OF FAITH

Our sins, our mistakes, our poor and wrong decisions cannot limit or slow down God working for our ultimate good. Moses is an excellent example of this.

Moses killed a man one day while walking in his princely role in Egypt. Murder is a vicious sin, and Moses had to flee for his life to the barren, nomadic desert of Sinai. Life with Pharaoh's throne as high reward was suddenly dashed to the rocks by one horrible blow. God, however, who forgives, can make all things new, even the results of sin. So God worked this flight and the forty-year stay in Sinai into a discipline and training that Moses would need to bring thousands of Israelites out of Egypt. Moses with Paul could say, "All things work together for good, for those who are called according to [God's] purpose."

Our mistakes, our sins, the unfortunate place on life's road where we find ourselves because of the wrong turn we took years ago—none can be changed now, as much as we desire this. The past stands. However, God can weave all these failures into an ultimate good by His grace, which sent Jesus to the cross to blot out all our transgressions. God can make *everything* serve His purposes to lead us to repentance and faith, to test and strengthen our faith. And we find peace and hope at the foot of the cross.

*Jesus, turn all things to my ultimate good, as I come to Thee
for healing from sin. Amen.*

—〜〜—

June 28, 1962
On this date in 1962, the United Lutheran Church in America,
Finnish Evangelical Lutheran Church of America, American Evangelical
Lutheran Church, and Augustana Evangelical Lutheran Church merge to form
the Lutheran Church in America

JUNE 29

—ɷ—

Read Exodus 16:1–13
Psalm 16
Then the LORD said to Moses, "Behold, I am about to rain bread
from heaven for you, and the people shall go out and gather a day's
portion every day." *Exodus 16:4*

GOD PROVIDES

The desert where the Israelites marched from Egypt toward the Promised Land is totally barren. There is no vegetation to be seen, no water anywhere—nothing but boundless sand and rocks. No living being could sustain life there. Imagine the hopelessness of God's people as they faced this scene. As always, God heard their prayers. In miraculous fashion, He provided bread, quail, and water for them daily. There was always enough for the day, but only for that day.

I have a friend who is a worrier. No matter what the situation, she finds something to worry about. Yet one whole section of the Sermon on the Mount advises us not to worry. "Look at the birds of the air . . . your heavenly Father feeds them. Are you not of more value than they?" (Matthew 6:26). What assurance this is! God promises to provide our daily needs. Jesus taught us to pray, "Give us this day our daily bread" (Matthew 6:11). More important, He promises nourishment for our souls with the highlight of life eternal, thanks to Jesus' sacrifice for our sins. Nothing on earth can compare with this greatest provision of all.

Heavenly Father, thank You for our daily blessings of food, clothing, and especially for the promise of the robe of salvation. In Jesus' name. Amen.

—ɷ—

June 29, 2000

JUNE 30

—ᙡᙡ—

Read John 20:24–29
Unless I see in His hands the mark of the nails, and place my finger
into the mark of the nails, and place my hand into His side,
I will never believe. *John 20:25*

THOMAS

Thomas is more or less an obscure apostle. Because his name is generally linked with that of Matthew, some of the Church Fathers were of the opinion that he, too, was a publican. His name suggests that he was a twin, for the name *Thomas*, in Greek *Didymus*, means "twin."

Thomas was genuine in his courage. When at one time the disciples cautioned Jesus against going into Judea again, to Bethany where Lazarus was sick, Thomas said to his fellow disciples, "Let us also go, that we may die with Him" (John 11:16).

He was of a practical bent of mind. "You know the way to where I am going," said Jesus. Thomas answered Him, "Lord, we do not know where You are going. How can we know the way?" (John 14:4–5). His thoughts could not readily rise above the concept of a kingdom of power.

He was honest in his doubts. The disciples told him for the nth time that Jesus was seen of many on that bright Sunday after the dark Friday. But Thomas said, "Unless I see in His hands the mark of the nails . . . I will never believe." He did not say, "I am willing to believe if—" But he said, "Unless—, I won't believe."

Gently Jesus dealt with this honest doubter. Jesus always deals understandingly and kindly with those who have honest inquiries, who have real doubts and wish to be shown. Jesus permitted Thomas to examine the stigmata and then spoke to him: "Blessed are those who have not seen and yet have believed" (v. 29).

"My Lord and my God!"

—ᙡᙡ—

June 30, 1945

July

Grant us Your Holy
Spirit, O God, that our
minds and hearts may
be one in faith and
love for our Lord Jesus
Christ. Amen.

—w—

Read Matthew 20:20–28
Whoever would be great among you must be your servant.
Matthew 20:26

THE SECRET OF GREATNESS

Mrs. Zebedee, a lady of our Lord's day, had two sons, James and John. Like many other mothers, she had high ambitions for her sons. She wanted them to occupy positions of distinction without having to work or sacrifice to attain them. Hence, she one day boldly asked our Lord to give places of preference to her sons.

When the disciples of Jesus learned about this, they in real human fashion became irritated and jealous. Jesus noted their excitement and quickly put them at ease. He said, "Whoever would be great among you must be your servant."

Jesus is the greatest character in history, with a name that is above every other name, because He did infinitely more for the human family than any other person. He fulfilled God's Holy Law for us. He saved us from our sins by suffering and dying on the cross in our stead. He fully earned His place at the right hand of the Father.

You cannot inherit true greatness, buy it, or attain it through the influence of other people. The principle "whoever would be great among you must be your servant" applies in every area of life.

Dear God, for Jesus' sake, endow us with a rich measure of love toward Thee and toward our fellow people so that we might live lives of service that evidence a measure of true greatness. Amen.

—w—

July 1, 1959
On this date in 1959,
the St. Lawrence Seaway opens

JULY 2

—⚮—

Read Philippians 1:21–30
But these are written so that you may believe that Jesus is the Christ,
the Son of God, and that by believing you may have life in His name.
John 20:31

THE GIFT OF FAITH

The great gifts in life are those that we have so fully, so freely, that we rarely stop to think of their wonder and their worth. The gift of sight—can we put a monetary value on it? Our seeing eyes are the means by which we receive into our souls the glories of God in nature. What would we take in exchange for the gift of hearing beautiful music and the voices of friends, for the exuberance and joy of good health, for the very air we breathe? Life itself is a gift. Most people will give up all else, if need be, to preserve and prolong the span of life. Yet, inevitably, we die.

But unending life, life perfected and glorified, is given to us only by our Lord and Savior, Jesus Christ. This greatest of all gifts is ours through yet another gift, that of faith in Christ as our Redeemer. Our faith is the means whereby we receive from Him true life, in this world and in the world to come. Through faith in our risen Lord, death itself is conquered for us. For all eternity, we shall live and not die.

Surely, then, in all of life, we ought to guard and cherish this precious gift from our almighty God, the gift of faith, created in us by the Holy Spirit through the Gospel.

**O God, for the gift of faith in Christ we are humbly grateful.
Guard Thou and preserve this faith in us. Amen.**

—⚮—

July 2, 1964
On this date in 1964, Civil Rights Act
of 1964 is signed into law

July 3

Read Mark 2:13–22
Psalm 52
Blessed are those who mourn, for they shall be comforted. *Matthew 5:4*

FROM MOURNING TO JOY

In this vale of sorrows, many tears are shed. The world is full of people who weep. "For everything there is a season, and a time for every matter under heaven: . . . a time to weep, and a time to laugh," says the preacher (Ecclesiastes 3:1, 4). It is good to remember the order: first we cry, and then we will laugh again. "April showers bring May flowers," according to an Arabic saying. Also, "All sunshine makes a desert."

Jesus has a good word to say to those who mourn for their sins. He calls them blessed. Yes, blessed are those who repent—those who know what sin is and what it does—and sorrow over it. Sin is the transgression of God's Law. Sin destroys and kills. It separates us from God.

No Christian can ever delight in sin. He considers not only what it does to him but also what it did to Jesus Christ on the cross. Sin cost the heavenly Father the life of His own and only dear Son.

There is also great comfort in knowing and believing that Jesus was crucified for our sins. Indeed, blessed are all who put their confidence in what the Gospel proclaims: "The blood of Jesus His Son cleanses us from all sin" (1 John 1:7).

Dear Savior, "Now hear me while I pray; Take all my guilt away;
O, let me from this day Be wholly Thine!" Amen. (LSB 702:1)

—⟋⟍—

July 3, 1979

JULY 4

—ᴍ—

Read Romans 13:1–8
Psalm 33
Blessed is the nation whose God is the LORD, the people whom
He has chosen as His heritage! *Psalm 33:12*

LORD OF THE NATIONS

Government works best if leader and follower recognize the divine Giver of all power and authority. The psalmist declares, "Blessed is the nation whose God is the LORD." He is none other than Jesus Christ, the Son of God.

Paul wrote, "For by Him all things were created, in heaven and on earth, visible and invisible" (Colossians 1:16). Jesus Himself announced, "All authority in heaven and on earth has been given to Me" (Matthew 28:18).

The Holy Scriptures show this so well. Through the ages, leaders come and go. Nations rise and fall in spite of best-laid plans. History is clearly in the hands of God.

Through Jesus, our Lord, we know God as our heavenly Father who loves us. He rules the world and the destiny of nations in the best interest of His plan of salvation. Paul wrote, "All things work together for good, for those who are called according to His purpose" (Romans 8:28).

Let us thank God for the blessings of homeland and government, for freedom to worship, for the privilege to proclaim His love in word and deed, for the opportunity to live under Christ in His kingdom and to serve Him.

Lord God, be gracious and merciful unto us and bless us for Jesus' sake.
Amen.

—ᴍ—

July 4, 1974

JULY 5

—⁂—

Read Acts 15:13–29
These are a shadow of the things to come, but the substance belongs
to Christ. *Colossians 2:17*

SHADOW AND SUBSTANCE

The Colossians considered themselves very religious, for they observed carefully the laws pertaining to meat, drink, and holy days. Paul reminds them that such things are shadows. The body is of Christ. In a certain book, there is a chapter on religion. It has many references to altars, anthems, choirs, bells, bishops, deans, organs, and vestments. But one turns its pages in vain in the hope of finding some reference to the Word of God or the promise of salvation through Jesus Christ.

Some people look upon church music, the proper keeping of church festivals, and the correct form of a pastor's robe as very important, but, after all, these things are not needful for our salvation. Far more important is it to have the Word of God in its purity, so that the way of salvation may be clear to every Christian. Fine churches and good music are desirable, but they are not Means of Grace. Purity of doctrine is vastly more important. It is a fine thing to be able to read the church service beautifully, but it is infinitely better to "read [one's] title clear to mansions in the skies" (Isaac Watts).

Forbid, O Lord, that we shall put our trust in anything other than Thy gracious promises of everlasting life, but make us ever mindful of Him who died for us: Jesus Christ, our Lord. Amen.

—⁂—

July 5, 1949

July 6

—⚒—

Read Luke 17:1–10
Psalm 130
Whenever you stand praying, forgive, if you have anything against anyone, ·
so that your Father also who is in heaven may forgive you
your trespasses. *Mark 11:25*

FORGIVE AND BE FORGIVEN

God forgives us completely through faith in Jesus Christ. Yet it is equally true that if we refuse to forgive someone who has wronged us, we cannot expect to receive forgiveness from our heavenly Father. In Ephesians 4:32, Paul writes, "Be kind to one another, tenderhearted, forgiving one another, as God in Christ forgave you." And when Peter asked, "Lord, how often will my brother sin against me, and I forgive him?" the Lord's answer was clear: no less than "seventy times seven" times (Matthew 18:21–22).

True forgiveness is not a matter of human decision. If we try by our own strength to forgive one who has harmed us, that forgiveness will be incomplete or even impossible.

We must take Christ's work as our source of strength, remembering His substitutionary death on the cross for us even while we were enemies of God. When we ask God to enable us to forgive as He has forgiven us, we can then truly forgive others. Having been washed clean and forgiven all our sins, we are able to set aside our angry pride and forgive others.

Compassionate God, help us to remember always Your great mercy through Jesus' blood and merit, that we, too, may forgive. Amen.

—⚒—

July 6, 1993

July 7

—ᴀᴠᴠ—

Read John 5:19–27
Truly, truly, I say to you, unless a grain of wheat falls into the earth
and dies, it remains alone; but if it dies, it bears much fruit. *John 12:24*

A Grain of Wheat

A grain of wheat, or a seed of any kind, is a common object. But there is something wonderful and mysterious about it. We bury it in the ground, where it dies. Soon, new life bursts out of this seed. It sprouts, grows, and bears fruit.

To help us understand the meaning of His death and burial, Jesus used the picture of a seed. He had come into the world that men might have life and that they might have it more abundantly. What was difficult for the people of His day to understand, and what still baffles people today, is that He had to suffer and die to accomplish His earthly mission. As the little seed dies in the ground in order to produce more seeds and reproduce more life, so He would produce life in others by dying Himself.

His resurrection from the dead, after He had paid the penalty for our sins on the cross, now enables us to live in Him. The believers, who will live eternally with Him, are the fruit of His suffering and death. May we always believe in Him as the Savior, who was willing to die that we might live.

But if we are to bear fruit as Christians, we, too, must die to sin. Our old sinful nature must be crucified. Selfishness must die, and we must live our lives for Christ. Thus, we, too, shall find life, eternal life, the abundant life, and bear much fruit to the glory of God. He that loses His life for Christ's sake shall find it.

*O Holy Spirit, cause us to die unto self and sin, that we may love
and live for Christ now and in all eternity. Amen.*

—ᴀᴠᴠ—

July 7, 1956

July 8

—∽∽—

Read 1 Peter 3:8–22
Psalm 26
Live in harmony with one another. Do not be haughty, but associate
with the lowly. Never be wise in your own sight. *Romans 12:16*

Agreeing with One Another

Generally, we like to have things done our way. It is hard to listen to others. We like to think that our way is the best—the only—way. But our way may not be the best. Others could have a good idea, possibly a better idea. They may suggest the best way out of a situation, the most workable plan. To insist on one's way is not in agreement with the words of St. Paul: "Live in harmony with one another." Be willing to agree with one another!

The least we can do is listen to one another before we insist on our way. The other person may have an excellent idea. It is not belittling to listen and even to admit someone else has a good idea, even a better idea.

The apostle Paul urges unity in our living with one another—agreement with others, willingness to accept what they suggest, working together, and sharing.

God has worked out our salvation in Jesus Christ, and it is not belittling to let Christ's atoning work bear fruit in us. We do need Christ. As there is unity between us and Christ, so may we develop unity between ourselves and those with whom we live and work.

Lord Jesus, may we live together in the bond of unity. Amen.

—∽∽—

July 8, 1981

Read Ruth 2:1–13
Psalm 89

When you reap the harvest of your land, you shall not reap your field right up to its edge, nor shall you gather the gleanings after your harvest. You shall leave them for the poor and for the sojourner. *Leviticus 23:22*

CARE FOR THE NEEDY

How beautifully our God provides for all people! He was so caring that He gave instructions to the Israelites to provide the needy with an opportunity to secure food without cost. The law of gleanings was His care for the needy.

Ruth, the Moabite woman of our reading, provided for herself and her mother-in-law by gleaning the fields of Boaz. She met her basic needs while maintaining her dignity. Boaz acknowledged God's care and blessed Ruth, saying, "The LORD repay you for what you have done, and a full reward be given you by the LORD, the God of Israel, under whose wings you have come to take refuge!" (Ruth 2:12).

We may not be needy in the sense of lacking daily provisions. Perhaps we've never had to glean a field or live off the generosity of a relative or the community. Yet all of us are needy—needy for forgiveness and salvation.

God's provision for the needy with the law of gleaning surely should be comforting to us. For if He is so careful to provide for food, will He not even more readily provide forgiveness, life, and salvation to all who seek them in Christ? His giving of these will not be leftovers on the edges or in the corner, but bounty upon bounty. He cares so much for us.

Lord, we praise You for providing for all our needs. Amen.

—〰—

July 9, 1985

Read Matthew 7:21–27
Psalm 60
Whoever walks in integrity walks securely. *Proverbs 10:9*

PROMISE TO THE UPRIGHT

In the Old Testament, uprightness is an ethical concept. It is a form of behavior pleasing to God and considered praiseworthy among the righteous. The psalmist writes: "Light dawns in the darkness for the upright; He is gracious, merciful, and righteous" (112:4).

The upright are promised great blessings, to be enjoyed not only at some future time but also now. Enjoying divine protection, the upright says in faith: "My shield is with God, who saves the upright" (Psalm 7:10). God makes the upright feel the joy that belongs to such. God says: "Shout for joy, all you upright in heart!" (32:11).

The upright lives according to his faith. He knows and feels that, in Christ, God is pleased with his life. He knows that the psalmist has written: "Blessed is the man who walks not in the counsel of the wicked . . . but his delight is in the law of the LORD" (1:1–2).

She who is convinced that she is forgiven walks surely, for she knows where she is going, how she will get there, and that Christ goes with her. She is joyful in this knowledge and says with St. Paul: "I live by faith in the Son of God, who loved me and gave Himself for me" (Galatians 2:20).

Lord, walk with me so that I may walk uprightly. Amen.

—⚏—

July 10, 1978

JULY 11

Read Ephesians 2:1–10
Psalm 119:33–40
The life I now live in the flesh I live by faith in the Son of God,
who loved me and gave Himself for me. *Galatians 2:20*

THE POWER OF THE GOSPEL

David Brainerd, a pioneer missionary to the American Indians, gave this testimony to the practical value of the Gospel: "I never got away from Jesus and Him crucified. And I found that when my people were gripped by this great evangelical doctrine of Christ and Him crucified, I had no need to give them instructions about morality. I found that one followed as the sure and inevitable fruit of the other."

In the cross is found all there is of the grace of God. There is forgiveness for our guilt, peace for our turmoil, cleansing for our impurity, power for our weakness, courage for our fear, love for our bitterness, victory for our defeat. This is what many of us have experienced yonder on the mountain with Christ.

Holiness is not the way to Christ. Christ is the way to holiness. We are privileged channels of His grace. Every working Christian will joyfully say it: "I am just a channel, Christ the power; I am just a branch, Christ the vine; I am just the vessel, Christ the light; I am just the cup, Christ the water."

O Holy Spirit, grant that the power and glory of the cross
may be manifested in me. Amen.

July 11, 1971

JULY 12

—ᴍ—

Read Titus 2
We are His workmanship, created in Christ Jesus for good works.
Ephesians 2:10

SAVED TO SERVE

God has called us to His kingdom for a purpose. He has chosen us to be instruments for good. Jesus has redeemed us that we "may be His own and live under Him in His kingdom and serve Him in everlasting righteousness, innocence, and blessedness" (Small Catechism, explanation of the Second Article).

Faith is the root of Christian life, and good works are the fruit. Without faith, it is impossible to render any service pleasing to God. But faith must also bear fruit, for faith without good works is dead.

Jesus set us a pattern for life in His own life. He said: "The Son of Man came not to be served but to serve" (Mark 10:45). Similarly, service is the real test of Christian life today. By it, people determine the sincerity of our faith. "You will recognize them by their fruits," Jesus said (Matthew 7:20).

The Holy Spirit has created the new life in us by faith in Christ so that we might serve God by our good works. If our lives are adjusted to His will and purpose, we shall act as His lips to speak words of truth, comfort, and hope. We shall be His feet to run errands of mercy and love. We shall be His hands for deeds of kindness. We shall be His heart to win men back to God's favor and fellowship. We are saved to serve. Are we serving well?

O Christ, Thou didst die for me. Help me to be faithful in Thy service.
Amen.

—ᴍ—

July 12, 1952

JULY 13

—⁂—

Read Amos 6:1–7
Psalm 23
Woe to those who are at ease in Zion, and to those who feel secure
on the mountain of Samaria. *Amos 6:1*

COMPLACENT?

World Series champions often struggle to win again. So easy to rest on past accomplishments! Top management sometimes relaxes after climbing the corporate ladder. Confirmed Christians take it easy in worship attendance, Bible study, witness, and service. Their relationships with God and with other believers begin to slip. Complacency.

Amos writes to both Judah and Israel with a bold message against complacency. He describes their lives of ease—lying on beds inlaid with ivory, dining on choice lambs, strumming on harps, and drinking wine by the bowlful, while both countries are headed for destruction. He condemns their pride and self-satisfaction. He calls them to repentance and trust in the promised Messiah.

Amos's words rock our complacency as well. We drift away from God and His Word, filling our lives with trivialities. We forget about God's plan for the world and our key missionary role in that plan. Our complacency shattered by the reality of God's judgment, we turn to the One who came for us, always intent on His saving mission. Never complacent about His Father's plan or the opposition of Satan, Jesus went to the cross and finished the work of paying for our sins. Even now, He hears and forgives. And we, complacent no more, live for His purposes.

Lord, rouse us to live for You. Amen.

—⁂—

July 13, 1988

July 14

—w—

Read 1 John 3:1–3
Psalm 38
Creation waits with eager longing for the revealing of the sons of God.
Romans 8:19

Looking Ahead

Much of what we do today is for tomorrow: plant in spring for harvest in August; school today for a career tomorrow; work now for wages later; save in the present for spending in the future.

However, there is much that is discouraging about looking and planning ahead. The auto-salvage yards of our great cities and little towns are filled with twisted and broken wrecks cramped and piled together. Fifteen years ago—and even more recently—those cars were beautiful and gleaming in show windows, and people hoped to buy and own them.

What we look forward to and work for so often wears thin and wears out. Moth holes, mildew, rust, cobwebs, and ashes are the symbols of yesterday's hopes. Still, men set their eyes and hearts on the things that fade and wilt and pass.

One thing endures: the Word of God with God's promise of life. The Word was made flesh and dwelt among us. Men could see God's promise being kept. They could see His love in action as Jesus lived and loved and died and rose, emerging from the tomb with never-ending life for us. The Son of God makes us children of God. We are already His children. The completion and perfection of this gift awaits us in the glory that fades not away.

Raise our sights, Lord, and be our hope, our joy, our peace. Amen.

—w—

July 14, 1965

July 15

Read Isaiah 61
Psalm 147:1–13
He has sent me to bind up the brokenhearted. *Isaiah 61:1*

SHATTERED

Have you ever felt broken inside? And not just broken, but even shattered like a mirror? Outside you look fine; but inside, your life, your dreams, your aspirations are broken into a million pieces, and you don't know how to put them together again. And even if you were able to reassemble the pieces, your mirror would still be fractured and useless.

Christ came into our world in order to reorder and rebuild the "broken mirror" of our hearts and lives. Christ came to re-create our sinful and broken world in His own image, the image we lost when our first parents brought sin into the world. Christ broke the power of sin when He suffered on the cross. Christ broke the power of the devil when He remained faithful to the Father, even when He was forsaken on the cross. Christ broke the power of death when He died on the cross. And now Christ lives to apply His resurrection power, through the Gospel, to all our hurts, anger, grief, sorrow, and brokenness.

Through Christ, we first were made. He is the only one who can fix us. He declares us forgiven, clothing us in His holiness by grace. He makes the mirror of our lives shine like new. Having restored us to Himself, Christ gives us life through Word and Sacraments.

Merciful Father, create anew the sin-cracked mirror of my life to reflect Your love for me in Jesus Christ. Amen.

July 15, 2004

July 16

—⟋⟍—

Read Luke 15:11–24
Psalm 95
His father saw him and felt compassion, and ran and embraced him
and kissed him. *Luke 15:20*

MERCY WITHOUT MEASURE

We can imagine the thoughts that surged through the mind of the prodigal son as he trudged along the dusty road that led back to his father's house. Would the door be open—the door to his father's *home*, the door to his father's *heart*? How did his father feel toward him? What did he think? What would he say? What would he do?

The young man would never know unless he would throw himself completely on his father's mercy. And so he does just that! We need not repeat here the reception he received, as described in the passage above. There was love aplenty, even for the prodigal, in the tender father's heart.

And there is also love aplenty in the tender heart of our *heavenly* Father. There is mercy without measure. As the Scriptures tell us, "Where sin increased, grace [mercy] abounded all the more" (Romans 5:20). "In this is love, not that we have loved God but that *He loved us* and sent His Son to be the propitiation [the payment] for our sins" (1 John 4:10, emphasis added). Could we ever doubt the fullness of God's love, the wonder of His matchless mercy in Jesus Christ, our Lord and Savior? Indeed not! That is why we sing:

Just as I am; Thy love unknown
Has broken ev'ry barrier down;
Now to be Thine, yea, Thine alone,
O Lamb of God, I come, I come.
Amen. (LSB 570:6)

—⟋⟍—

July 16, 1976

JULY 17

—∿∿—

Read Hebrews 11:17–40

HOW FAITH COMES AND GROWS

I t is through the channel of Christian faith that all the riches of divine grace come to us. Faith is the questing, reaching, holding hand that claims all the blessings of God's infinite love and wisdom. We naturally ask, "How does faith come to us, and how can we grow in faith?"

The Bible answers, "Faith comes from hearing" (Romans 10:17). The faith God gives is something altogether different from what many people think it is. The only faith that pleases God is the faith He Himself gives. This faith comes to us only, but surely, when the heavenly Father gives us His Holy Spirit so that, by His grace, we believe His Holy Word and lead a godly life according to it. God-pleasing faith is not something we imagine, but it is taking God at His word. It is through the Word of God that the Holy Spirit engenders in us the new life of faith. Only when God's Word is the foundation of our faith does faith rest squarely upon truth. For this reason, we must gladly hear and learn God's Word. Serious Christians who are earnestly concerned about keeping the faith unto the end will eagerly seize every opportunity to grow in the knowledge of God's Holy Word.

But merely hearing the divine Word is not enough. "But be doers of the word, and not hearers only" (James 1:22). Faith grows stronger as we use the Word. If we are true to this Word, God opens a sure path to a larger faith. God always entrusts us with more gifts when we are faithful in the use of those He has already given.

Lord, increase our faith! Amen.

—∿∿—

July 17, 1942

July 18

—⊶—

Read John 15:14–21
You did not choose Me, but I chose you. *John 15:16*

Chosen of Him

We are the friends of Jesus. No greater honor can come to any man. We are on terms of intimacy with the Son of the Most High. Birth does not confer this distinction upon us; by nature, we are enemies of God and of His Son. We do not achieve this honor by our own merit or worthiness; what we do can never stand up under His searching gaze.

We are the friends of Jesus because He has chosen us. Grace prompted this choice. In us was only vileness and filth. We were dead in sins. But He took pity on us. He called us by the Gospel and enlightened us. He removed our blindness and obstinacy. His blood cleanses us from all sin. Everything needed to make us fit for His holy fellowship He did.

We try to talk about this love. But human language breaks down when it attempts to describe the love of Jesus for sinners. Our very thoughts, which otherwise roam the universe and daringly approach the deepest mysteries, become confused as we dwell on the love that chose us and made us God's friends.

But we do believe it. We must believe it. God has said so definitely and conclusively. We are the friends of Jesus. We are chosen of Him. Whether we can understand it or not, whether we can express it or not, the fact remains. The Gospel declares the glorious fact. By God's grace, we accept what the Gospel says. Friends of Jesus we are, let men, let conscience, let Satan himself protest and snicker. We look to Jesus. We know whom we have believed. He has chosen us.

Praise be to Thee, O God, for Thy choice of me, a poor sinner.
More and more, help me to value the friendship of Jesus. Amen.

—⊶—

July 18, 1939

July 19

—⁂—

Read Romans 7:18–25
Godly grief produces a repentance that leads to salvation without regret,
whereas worldly grief produces death. *2 Corinthians 7:10*

Sorrow over One's Proneness to Sin

It is the work of God that we sorrow at all over our sins and weaknesses. Millions indeed sorrow with "worldly grief." They know in their secret hearts that God is never mocked and that the wages of sin are always paid. But this produces no desire for godliness; it is secret terror, a "fearful expectation of judgment" (Hebrews 10:27). This is death at work in life until life is swallowed up in death.

But we sorrow because of the sorrow we cause the heart of God, who has made us, loved us, redeemed us, been patient with us far beyond our deserts. It bows us down that we should thus treat God. And still, perversely, we sin. We despise ourselves for yielding to sin; yet we yield. We look back in sorrow; we look forward in near despair: "Wretched man that I am! Who will deliver me?" (Romans 7:24).

But the very fact that we sorrow and struggle at all shows that we love God. Otherwise, there would be no struggle. Sin would reign in peace. Why, then, do we sin? We love God indeed, but because of our sinful flesh, we love ourselves still more. We need to love God much more, self much less.

The important thing is that we do sorrow and do battle. Though we fail again and yet again, still we must not lose heart. Victory lies ahead if we confess our sins, seek help again and again in Word and Sacrament to strengthen our faith, and, by the gracious aid of the Holy Spirit, keep on fighting sin. This battle is worth it.

Lord, give me the sorrow that works repentance not to be repented of.
Amen.

—⁂—

July 19, 1940

July 20

—҉—

Read Romans 8:18–25
No one looks on the light when it is bright in the skies. *Job 37:21*

The Light in the Clouds

Some days are radiant with light. The sun, which God created to rule the day, shines from a clear sky. Other days are dark and foreboding, even at noon. The light really is not gone. It just is not visible, though we know the sun is shining above the gloom. We have had these days. We know that, sooner or later, the wind will sweep away the clouds and restore light to our eyes and gladness to our hearts.

Our lives are often on the unilluminated side of the cloud. The light often seems indistinct. The fault lies with our limited minds. We cannot understand the fullness of God's being, nor the mystery of the Godhead. We cannot understand the mysteries connected with the divine plan of redemption.

But it matters little, since enough of the mystery is revealed in the Gospel to show us the way of salvation. We know that God loves us and sent His Son to save us. We have sufficient truth shining through the cloud in the Word of grace. The pure rays of the Gospel always filter through our darkness of sin, giving us strength to walk the path of faith. In heaven, we shall see behind the clouds the overwhelming light of God's glory.

Guide us while here we wander
Until we praise You yonder. Amen. (LSB 745:5)

—҉—

July 20, 1969
On this date in 1969, U.S. astronaut
Neil Armstrong takes first steps on the moon

July 21

—※—

Read Deuteronomy 26:1–11
Psalm 118

As in Adam all die, so also in Christ shall all be made alive. But each in his own order: Christ the firstfruits, then at His coming those who belong to Christ. *1 Corinthians 15:22–23*

FIRSTFRUITS

The first tomato from a new vine is very sweet, and I'm always grateful when the tomatoes start turning red in the summer. Like the ancient Israelites, I want to give thanks to God, offering Him the firstfruits of my garden.

The firstfruits are a promise of the good things to come. The first tomato is a sign and promise that more will follow. To offer up the firstfruit is to live in faith and confidence that its sign and promise will be fulfilled.

The Bible calls Jesus the firstfruits of the human race. He is the one who suffered and died on behalf of everyone, to free us from the power of death. He is also the one who rose from the dead, never to die again, to give us life. As our living Lord and Savior, He is the first to rise to life. But He will not be the last.

Jesus is the guarantee of our own resurrection. In Him, God has promised that He also will raise us from the dead, on the day Christ returns and death is finally destroyed. That will be the day of God's great harvest, and we will rejoice.

Father, send workers into Your harvest fields, that many people may be given faith, life, and salvation in Your Son, Jesus. Amen.

—※—

July 21, 2007

July 22

—⟶ww⟵—

Read Proverbs 31:10–31
Luke 7:36–50
Her sins, which are many, are forgiven—for she loved much. *Luke 7:47*

WHAT PRODUCES REPENTANCE

From the story of the sinful woman who anoints Jesus feet we may learn what produces true repentance. If you would go out into the open in below-zero weather and take a piece of ice and crush it, it would still remain ice. You may pound it into a thousand pieces, but as long as you stay in that cold atmosphere, every fragment will still remain frozen. But bring the ice into a warm house, and soon it will melt and turn into water.

Thus a man may try to crush his cold heart of sin. He may set his sins before himself and dwell on all their enormity and still not become penitent. There may be elaborate confession, a bowed humility, a voluntary reformation, but no godly sorrow.

But come to our Lord Jesus and His sweet Gospel. From the cold winter of duty, come into the warm summer of love. Let your frozen spirit bake in the warmth of the Sun of Righteousness. Listen to the Savior's words, which melted the woman's heart into penitence, which caused her eyes to flow with tears and her hands to pour out the precious ointment. Then we, too, will find that we have been forgiven much, and we will also love much.

*Almighty God, who hast given Thine only Son to be unto us both
a sacrifice for sin and also an example of godly life, give us grace
that we may always most thankfully receive His inestimable benefit and
also daily endeavor to follow the blessed steps of His most holy life
through the same Jesus Christ, our Lord. Amen.*

—⟶ww⟵—

July 22, 1947

JULY 23

—w—

Read Acts 4:23–31
Lord, look upon their threats and grant to Your servants to continue
to speak Your word with all boldness. *Acts 4:29*

NOT SAFETY BUT COURAGE TO SPEAK

The present emphasis on security and safety threatens to make its way into the Church. The Early Church was not looking for a "soft" Christianity but prayed that God might give them all the courage to tell the story of Christ, crucified for our sins that we might have peace with God through Christ's blood. With this message, they turned the world upside down. They valued truth more highly than safety. The threats of the opposition were not idle threats. Christians were in constant danger. Therefore, all of them needed to pray for boldness to speak God's Word.

To this day, we Christians face opposition from the world in which we live. Often, we must face ridicule, compromise, public opinion, false teachings, which want to undermine our faith in Jesus as Savior from sin.

Today, we need to pray that we may have the courage to stand up and be counted and to speak out against indifference, error, loose morals, unbelief, racial strife. If Jesus is the only hope for this world of sin—and we believe that He is—then we must by word and action boldly confess Him. We must let people know that we belong to Him and love Him because He gave His life that we might be cleansed from sin and have peace with God.

Lord Jesus, remove from my heart all fear of men, and help me boldly confess Thee as my Savior. Amen.

—w—

July 23, 1962

July 24

—∞—

Read Ephesians 2:1–10
Psalm 51
Do not grieve the Holy Spirit of God, by whom you were sealed
for the day of redemption. *Ephesians 4:30*

BRIDGING THE GAP

It has been called the longest eighteen inches on earth. No person can bridge it.

It is the distance between our heads and our hearts. It represents our helplessness to believe in God by our own power. We lack the ability to trust in God and live by faith unless moved by God's Spirit to do so. We can fill our heads with much knowledge—even about Christ and His redemptive work on the cross—but without the Holy Spirit, our heart is unaffected, unchanged.

But God bridges the gap with His Word and the Sacraments of Baptism and Communion. Then God's Holy Spirit goes to work on our hearts. He spans earth's longest eighteen inches and creates the necessary saving faith in Christ.

In Baptism, we are sealed by the Spirit—marked as God's own—in preparation for the day when God will take us to heaven. Then there will be no gap between our minds and hearts, as we live in God's glorious presence in sincerity and truth.

Until that day, our text urges us, we must not grieve the Spirit by resisting God's will or neglecting His Word and Sacraments, so that the Spirit may continue to bridge the gap in our lives.

Grant us Your Holy Spirit, O God, that our minds and hearts may be one in faith and love for our Lord Jesus Christ. Amen.

—∞—

July 24, 1992

July 25

—ᴙ—

Read Mark 10:35–45
Diotrephes, who likes to put himself first, does not acknowledge
our authority. *3 John 9*

LOVING THE PREEMINENCE

St. John complains about Diotrephes, who was causing trouble in the Church because he "likes to put himself first." The conduct of this would-be great toward the apostle revealed how very little he really was.

The work of many a congregation has been adversely affected because some members love to play to the grandstand. If they cannot head the committee, they decline to serve at all; if they cannot sing the solos, they resign from the choir; if a suggestion they make is not adopted, they are insulted. They must have the preeminence, or else.

Such conduct in the work of the Church often causes ugly divisions and offenses, and the most important work in the world, building the kingdom of God, may be seriously hampered.

It really matters little whether or not we occupy a position of preeminence in the Church. What matters is that we serve to the best of our ability with the talents God has given us. Nor is it important whether or not we are honored by men for the service we have rendered. God knows, and Jesus assures us: "If anyone serves Me, the Father will honor him" (John 12:26).

What more could anyone desire?

Heavenly Father, forgive us for Jesus' sake the sins of a proud and haughty spirit, of which we sometimes are guilty. Amen.

—ᴙ—

July 25, 1963

July 26

—⚏—

Read Hebrews 12:1–3
Psalm 125

Therefore, since we are surrounded by so great a cloud of witnesses, let us also lay aside every weight, and sin which clings so closely, and let us run with endurance the race that is set before us. *Hebrews 12:1*

SURROUNDED!

We're surrounded!" Those are not encouraging words if you're in battle. However, these words give great encouragement if you're running a race with the stands full of cheering fans!

"We're surrounded!" That's the cry as we Christians run the race set before us.

Imagine the cheering crowds as we run. There's Noah. "God helped me endure ridicule. Keep running." Abraham is cheering. "Don't give up. The Lord got me through great testing." Listen to Moses. "Nothing is impossible with God." The chant is deafening, over and over again. "God helped us. He'll help you!" (For a fuller listing of our fans of faith, see Hebrews 11.)

Surrounded by the faithful, we run in faith. Surrounded by the faithful, we repent and lay aside our faithless deeds. Surrounded by the faithful, we fix our eyes on the source of our faith, Jesus. Surrounded by the faithful, we run in awe that Jesus would find joy fixing His eyes on us as He endured the shame of our sin on the cross.

"We're surrounded!" Thank God!

Thank You, Jesus, for Your faithfulness and for our faithful fans, those who have gone before us in the faith. Amen.

—⚏—

July 26, 2009

JULY 27

—⁓—

Read 2 Corinthians 1:3–11
I can do all things through Him who strengthens me.
Philippians 4:13

A DYNAMO OF POWER

Paul is not making an idle boast. He was conscious of his own weakness. But he was confident of Christ's strength. Jesus was *his* Savior and Lord. He had yielded his life and will to the service of his King. Christ was his life and the will of Christ the determining influence of his actions and desires. To the Galatians, he had written: "It is no longer I who live, but Christ who lives in me. And the life I now live in the flesh I live by faith in the Son of God, who loved me and gave Himself for me" (2:20). The power of Christ had been infused into his soul so that without reservation, he had placed himself into the service of his Lord and Master, Savior and Friend. His accomplishments he then ascribes not to himself, but to the power of Christ.

Trust in self does not give us the right to say: "I can do all things." But trust in Christ's power in us makes us confident workers in the Kingdom, bold confessors for Jesus, patient sufferers in affliction, mighty victors in the battle against sin and temptation.

The influx of this power comes to us through the Gospel. Christians therefore must remain in touch with the source of heavenly energy by diligent use of the Word.

"Now to Him who is able to do far more abundantly than all that we ask or think, according to the power at work within us, to Him be glory in the church and in Christ Jesus throughout all generations, forever and ever." Amen. (Ephesians 3:20–21)

—⁓—

July 27, 1953
On this date in 1953, armistice ends Korean War

JULY 28

—w—

Read 1 Timothy 2:1–6
Psalm 47
[God] desires all people to be saved and to come to the knowledge
of the truth. *1 Timothy 2:4*

GOD'S DESIRE FOR THE LOST

Have you ever sat in a packed athletic stadium and wondered how many of those screaming fans knew Jesus as their Savior? Have you ever walked down a busy street or tried to drive on a busy freeway in rush hour and silently prayed that somehow all of the people around you would know and trust in Jesus as their Savior? It is easy to become numb to the mass of humanity around us. They become just so many nameless faces, a sea of people we never know or touch.

It is important that we remind ourselves that God's perspective is very different. He created, knows, loves, and yearns for each person on this planet. His Son is the way, the truth, and the life for everyone. Jesus' death on the cross and rising to life is the hope of salvation for everyone.

God's desire for the lost sends us into this world each day with the joy of loving people and sharing His love with them. As we share that joy in our daily lives, as we join with others in our congregation to share it in our communities, and as our congregation joins with other congregations to share that joy with the world, we are living out God's desire for all to be saved and to come to a knowledge of the truth.

**Lord of all, send Your whole Church forth to share the joy
of our salvation in Jesus Christ. Amen.**

—w—

July 28, 1999

JULY 29

—∿—

Read Matthew 5:1–13

Blessed is the man who walks not in the counsel of the wicked, nor stands in the way of sinners, not sits in the seat of scoffers; but his delight is in the law of the LORD, and on His law he meditates day and night.

Psalm 1:1–2

THE GREATER BLESSEDNESS

Most people desire to be popular. Many think that the favors and smiles of the world bring with them advantages and advancement. The wise of the world seem to forge ahead as they travel the broad way of life. They are surrounded by many companions and have fun wherever they turn. With withering contempt, they look down on those who walk with the Lord and serve Him in the beauty of His tabernacle. They try to make us Christians feel that we are missing the best things in life.

But the way of the transgressor still is hard. In the end, he has no peace of mind. He is afraid of God. He cannot face the eternal courts of the Most High, while he rejects the gracious invitation to come to the cross and be healed. In the end, the wicked shall be cut off.

Upon those, however, who walk in the paths of righteousness by faith, God pronounces His benedictions of peace. The believer finds the greater joy in the grace of God through Christ Jesus. He is unafraid because he is cleansed altogether from sin through the redeeming sacrifice of Calvary.

Gracious Lord, with joyful heart we praise Thee, who hast washed and cleansed us from all our sins and hast taken us by the hand today to lead us in the paths of righteousness, where we can serve Thee with a happy heart through Jesus Christ, our Lord and Savior. Amen.

—∿—

July 29, 1950

Read John 6:16–21

DO NOT BE AFRAID!

Man is haunted by fear. How often the word *fear* meets us in the Bible and the fact of fear in the lives of men! When the angel of the Lord appeared to the shepherds on the fields of Bethlehem, we read that they were sore afraid. When the disciples saw Jesus walking on the sea, they were afraid. Fear dogs the footsteps of men. Fears are as evil spirits dancing round a campfire. Fear is the characteristic of all pagan religions.

The most prolific source of fear is an evil conscience. The sense of guilt makes us afraid of God and fearful of His punishments. Fear makes us believe that nature has conspired to destroy us.

Because the heart of man has been swamped with fear and his countenance is wrinkled with anxiety, the Bible is filled with encouragement that asks us not to be afraid. The message of Jesus in the Gospel to fear-burdened men is "Do not be afraid"! Not afraid of God, of sorrow, of death when we see and know Jesus. Our Savior has atoned for our sins by His holy life and His innocent suffering and death and has earned for us the love and pardon of His heavenly Father. The assurance of the Fatherhood of God in Christ drives fear out of our hearts and gives unto our soul the calmness of peace.

When contrary winds blow and the waves of affliction roll and our heart is troubled by the thought that God has turned against us, we hear the voice of Jesus saying: "It is I; do not be afraid" (John 6:20). Christ is with us, and the contrary winds must blow us no ill. Faith in Christ is the antidote against fear.

—⟋⟍—

July 30, 1937

July 31

—⟋⟍—

Read Psalm 1
For this is the will of God, your sanctification. *I Thessalonians 4:3*

GOD WRITES THE SCORE

God established the purpose of life for all the children of men when He created Adam and Eve. He made them with a definite design for living. He gave them specific instruction for a God-pleasing life, having created them with a perfect righteousness and holiness. Man is to do God's will.

The score for godly living has not changed, even after Adam and Eve failed to play their part correctly. God kept the world intact and permitted man to remain, that His plan of life may be followed by His foremost creatures. To that end, He promised them a Savior and, in the fullness of time, sent Jesus, His only-begotten Son, to redeem the world. He empowers people with His Spirit to live the Christian life. To this day, we, together with all living mankind, are to take heed of God's plan of life. He has determined the purpose of living for all of us.

By nature, we do not follow God's direction but follow the leading of Satan. The devil leads men to play solo parts, to serve selfish desires, and to ignore God's score. This wrong reading of the score makes life a jangle of harsh discords to our heavenly Father as He beholds the sons of men. He alone knows how many discordant notes and how many wrong themes sound forth from the face of this earth. Yet it remains God's will that we lead sanctified lives.

Jesus, our Savior, has not only redeemed us, but has set the pattern for living according to the score written by God. Let us follow Him!

Dear Lord, "Let us ever walk with Jesus,
Follow His example pure." Amen. (LSB 685:1)

—⟋⟍—

July 31, 1955

August

Heavenly Father, let the same mind be in us that was also in Christ Jesus. Amen.

August 1

—ɷ—

Read 1 Corinthians 15:12–20
Set your minds on things that are above, not on things that are on earth.
Colossians 3:2

THE THINGS ABOVE

Without the hope of heaven in our hearts, life would be an empty and futile thing. It is good for us to remember that much of our weariness with life, much of our boredom and bitterness, arises from the fact that we do not think enough about heaven. There are some people who believe that religion should concern itself only with earthly affairs, and they like to say that if we talk too much and think too much about heaven, religion will cease to be a vital force in our daily life. We know this is not true. On the contrary, it is when we forget our heavenly destiny and begin to live only for this life that our lives become small and meaningless and fruitless.

When our affection is set on the things that are above, "where Christ is, seated at the right hand of God" (Colossians 3:1), then our hearts are filled with love for our Savior, who died to save us, and filled with a deep longing to be with Him where He is.

Such a faith will brighten every corner of life and influence every thought, every word, every deed.

These people who say that heavenly-mindedness makes life drab and confining are completely wrong. It is the wonderful prospect of heaven that makes our human life a glorious pilgrimage full of adventure, full of meaning, full of hope.

Blessed Lord Jesus, Thou hast died that we might live forever; help us to live in this life as heirs of the life to come. Amen.

—ɷ—

August 1, 1953

August 2

—⟋ꝏ⟍—

Read James 4:13–17
Psalm 118
You ought to say, "If the Lord wills, we will live and do this or that."
James 4:15

PLANNING FOR THE TRIP

When beginning a trip, you could just get in your car and start to drive wherever the roads might take you. Usually, however, it is better to do some advance planning—studying maps to know how to get where you want to go, gathering clothes and equipment for whatever you plan to do once you get there.

God's written Word is our map for the trail of life. Here, He shows us the way; it isn't by our goodness that we will get there. The only way is through Jesus, God's holy Son, who took our place and was punished for all our sins and all the sins of everyone. This is the message we need every day on our trail so that we don't lose the way.

God's Word also is the equipment we need along our daily way. He gives us guidance to meet the challenges and opportunities that will come. He also gives us the spiritual strength we need to face these and to remain faithful to Him.

Here, God comforts us that we are in His keeping also when the trail takes turns we don't expect or particularly enjoy.

So just as one does not look at a map only at the beginning but also throughout a trip, we keep using His Word daily on life's trail.

Thank You, Lord, for Your guiding Word. Amen.

—⟋ꝏ⟍—

August 2, 1990
On this date in 1990,
First Gulf War begins

AUGUST 3

—֊ຕ——

Read James 2:21–26
[Wisdom says,] "Blessed is the one who listens to me, watching daily
at my gates, waiting beside my doors." *Proverbs 8:34*

ATTENTIVENESS

Happy is everyone who hears, watches, waits on the Lord. As we gather for our family devotion or when we worship God in privacy, we speak to Him by means of our prayers. He, in turn, speaks to us in His Holy Word. When we read the Bible or when it is read to us at home or in church, let us pay the closest attention. Remember, God is speaking. It is our privilege, as God's children, to hear.

How often have we heard that what certain people hear goes in one ear and out the other? Such people sit through the family devotion and have their minds so fixed on something else that they scarcely hear one word that is read to them. They listen to the sermon on Sunday, but they do not concentrate on what is said; by Monday, yes, before Monday, they have forgotten all about it.

The great and important lesson for every Christian to learn is to pay attention to what he hears, to try to understand what it means, and to carry out in his daily life what has been taught him by the Word. Being attentive is not enough. Not they are blessed who merely hear the Word, but they who hear and keep it.

*Jesus, grant us both to will and to do according to Thy
good pleasure! Amen.*

—֊ຕ——

August 3, 1943

August 4

—∿—

Read Genesis 22:1–10
Abraham believed God, and it was counted to him as righteousness.
Romans 4:3

MOUNT MORIAH AND FAITH TESTED

These were strange orders that God gave Abraham to carry out: "Take your son, your only son Isaac, whom you love, and go to the land of Moriah, and offer him there as a burnt offering" (Genesis 22:2). For many years, God had been promising Abraham that he was to be the father of many nations, that his prosperity would be countless as the stars. Abraham and his wife found it difficult to believe these promises since they were without a single child of their own.

Then God gave them a son in their old age. This son was growing up to manhood as their only link between themselves and the countless descendants. But now, God commanded that this son should die.

This story tugs hard at a parent's heart. Just suppose this command were given today? How unbelievable it would be for the parent given such a command; how frightening for the son who is to be offered up! It was that difficult for Abraham and Isaac too. But Abraham had a strong faith grounded in mercy of God who would somehow be faithful to all He had promised. He believed that God was right when Abraham could not understand. Abraham believed God.

Do we believe implicitly in our God who is faithful, even when perplexing questions and pressing demands confront us?

Open our eyes to see Thy will and ways, O all-wise God. Amen.

—∿—

August 4, 1959

August 5

—⁂—

Read Ephesians 4:11–16
So we, though many, are one body in Christ. *Romans 12:5*

ONE BODY IN CHRIST

On any given Sunday millions upon millions of Christians gather with their fellow members of the Body of Christ to worship their Lord and Savior. Our churches have as the focal point in the chancel a cross or crucifix, a constant reminder that our worship is to be "in Christ."

This expression, "in Christ," pretty well sums up our faith and life. We stand acquitted before the Father because He looks at us "in Christ." One Bible student discovered 164 places in St. Paul's letter in which the apostle describes believers as being "in Christ."

When we remember that we "are all one in Christ Jesus" (Galatians 3:28), when we bear in mind the biblical picture of Christ as the Head and the believers as members of His Body, then we shall see the vital relationship we must maintain to be "in Him."

This one Body is the Holy Christian Church. This unity is invisible. Thus, an organized denomination dare never become an end to itself. Christians must guard against the danger of being fonder of their church body than of their Savior.

We would shake our heads at someone who would say he was for education but had no use for schools. Yet we hear some say they are for Christianity but not for the organized church. We are to build the kingdom of God through united effort. We need the organized visible church groups, but their church work must always be in Christ and for Christ.

Gracious Father, grant that we who are one Body in Christ may in thought, word, and deed glorify Him who is the Head of the Body, even Jesus Christ, our Lord and God. Amen.

—⁂—

August 5, 1956

Be watchful, stand firm in the faith, act like men, be strong.
1 Corinthians 16:13

Watchfulness

Watchfulness, alertness, vigilance is important in any warfare, as in this fight of faith. Rightly, we sing: "Rise, my soul, to watch and pray; From your sleep awaken! Be not by the evil day Unawares o'ertaken; For the foe, Well we know, Is a harvest reaping While the saints are sleeping" (*LSB* 663:1).

A good soldier is watchful. We have not forgotten the admonition—or have we?—"Be sober-minded; be watchful. Your adversary the devil prowls around like a roaring lion, seeing someone to devour" (1 Peter 5:8).

This vacation season, let us remember the devil takes no vacation. Nor can the Christian away from home afford to be less watchful. Yea, he ought to be doubly watchful. Putting on the armor of God, praying always, strong in grace, adding thereto watchfulness, we are more than conquerors through Christ. What can slumbering disciples be thinking? This "soul, take thine ease" attitude spells eternal ruin. Eternal vigilance is the price of any victory.

> *My soul, be on thy guard;*
> *Ten thousand foes arise,*
> *And hosts of sin are pressing hard*
> *To draw thee from the skies....*
> *Ne'er think the victory won*
> *Nor lay thine armor down;*
> *Thine arduous work will not be done*
> *Till thou obtain thy crown. Amen. (TLH 449:1, 3)*

—ɷ—

August 6, 1945
On this date in 1945,
atomic bombing of Hiroshima

August 7

—ᴍ—

Read 1 John 4
By this we know that we abide in Him and He in us,
because He has given us of His Spirit. 1 John 4:13

In

The little word *in* is the preposition of sanctification. We are *in* Christ, and He is *in* us. The Christian life consists in the fact that we dwell in Christ. This is a relationship so close, so intimate, that we cannot find words adequate to convey its full and sacred meaning.

Christ has made us partakers of His own nature and life. St. Paul says: "I have been crucified with Christ. It is no longer I who live, but Christ who lives in me" (Galatians 2:20). Luther described Christ and the believer as being "baked into one cake."

Since Christ dwells in us, our body is the temple of God and the abode of His Spirit. That makes life entirely different. We cannot ask our Lord to share His place in our heart with the false gods that want to crowd in—the cheap, tinny idols of pride, envy, greed, lust, hatred, sloth. If we let those intruders in, we say, in effect, to Christ: "Begone!"

But if we are true to the indwelling Christ and enshrine Him in our hearts, He will enrich and bless us with His presence. If we are thus joined with Him, we must strive to be like Him. "If anyone is in Christ, he is a new creation. The old has passed away; behold, the new has come" (2 Corinthians 5:17).

O enter with Thy grace divine;
Thy face of mercy on me shine. Amen. (LSB 340:5)

—ᴍ—

August 7, 1952

August 8

—⚊—

Read Revelation 3:14–22
Fire shall be kept burning on the altar continually; it shall not go out.
Leviticus 6:13

ON FIRE

Throughout the history of God's people in the Old Testament, there was to be a continuous fire on the altar of the tabernacle and of the temple. This was not to be a destructive fire, but it was to serve a twofold function. First, it was always to be ready to receive any burnt offering that anyone wished to bring. Then it was to symbolize the presence of Yahweh, who promised to be with His people in a cloud visible during the daytime and by a pillar of fire during the night.

Symbolically, there should always be a fire burning on the altar of our hearts; it should never go out. This is the fire of faith, faith in Christ as the Savior from sin. It is also the fire of a confident trust, never to go out, even though it might become "a smoldering wick" (Matthew 12:20). There is also the fire of love, love to God and love to man. It is to be burning brightly, so bright that men may see our good works and glorify our Father in heaven. There is also the fire of loyalty, loyalty to our vows to remain faithful to Christ unto death. Finally, there is the fire of enthusiasm about our faith, our Church, our religion. Unless there is this fire, there is little hope of God's blessing upon us. He is displeased and disgusted with the lukewarm, who are neither cold nor on fire. He threatens to spew them out.

Fire Thou me, O Christ, with heavenly zeal, that all my life, my time, my treasures, and my talents be dedicated to Thy service. Amen.

—⚊—

August 8, 1960

Read Romans 8:1–9
Those who live according to the Spirit set their minds on the things
of the Spirit. *Romans 8:5*

THINKING OF SALVATION

Thoughts are most important in the realms of the spiritual. Solomon said, concerning man, "For he is like one who is inwardly calculating. 'Eat and drink!' he says to you, but his heart is not with you" (Proverbs 23:7). And the Bible often reminds us, "Whatever is true, whatever is honorable, whatever is just, whatever is pure, whatever is lovely, whatever is commendable . . . *think about these things*" (Philippians 4:8, emphasis added). We know that transgressions are thoughts, words, and deeds contrary to God's will. Let us remember that thoughts come first. Before we speak a kind word or perform an act of charity, there must be a thought that moves the lips to speak and the hands to give.

In our devotions to God, participation of the mind is most important. The Bible is not only to be heard and read, but its precepts and promises should also be meditated upon. The finest commendation the Bible extends to a human being is this: "Mary treasured up all these things, pondering them in her heart" (Luke 2:19).

There is a reason why thoughts are so important: "For to set the mind on the flesh is death, but to set the mind on the Spirit is life and peace" (Romans 8:6). A mind constantly filled with evil thoughts must finally go to the place where those thoughts originate, and that's hell. But with Christ's Word and Spirit in our mind, always rejoicing that Jesus saved us from sin, we shall be guided on the path of life and peace and heaven.

Heavenly Father, let the same mind be in us that was also in Christ Jesus. Amen.

—⟋⟍—

August 9, 1944

—∿—

Read Psalm 17:6–15

HEAR MY PRAYER

Among the problems that have always disturbed the Christian heart, one of the greatest is the problem of unanswered prayer. Does God answer all prayers? Will He answer mine? If not, why not? For answers to some of our questions, we must wait until the gates of eternity open before us. Here on earth, we see as through a glass, darkly. But the question about unanswered prayer can be answered here: There never has been, and there never will be, anything like an unanswered prayer. Every true prayer, spoken in faith in the redeeming work of the Savior, whether it be the words of our lips or the sigh of our heart, is heard by God and answered. If we think of prayer as a great correspondence between earth and heaven, no letter is ever laid aside or left unanswered. God always hears our prayers.

This, however, is also true: Some of our prayers have been, and will be, *ungranted*. But there is always an answer. Sometimes, the answer may be "yes"; sometimes it may be "no"; most often in the Christian life, it is "Wait a little while! You do not see very clearly now. Your vision is dimmed by your sin and your tears. My ways are not your ways, and My thoughts are not your thoughts."

This we must remember when we plead with God to hear our prayers. He hears them, but the answer is His and not ours. He may want to take us a strange way, a way we do not want to go, through the fire and smoke of trials and temptations, to come out at last all steel and light. Our plea should be "Hear my prayer, O Lord; but Thy will, not mine, be done!"

Lord Jesus, who didst pray to Thy heavenly Father from the bitter altar of the cross, grant us grace ever to pray "Thy will be done." Give us a childlike faith and trust in the leading of our Father in heaven. Amen.

—∿—

August 10, 1938

August 11

—⟋∿⟍—

Read Romans 8:31–39
Psalm 133

If we live, we live to the Lord, and if we die, we die to the Lord. So then, whether we live or whether we die, we are the Lord's. *Romans 14:8*

MAKER AND PRESERVER

The smells, the sights, the sounds, even the movement of my own muscles speak to me of my Father in heaven, who created me and the world about me, who has created within me a clean heart through the forgiveness of Christ my Savior, who now gives me the privilege of serving Him this day.

Every moment of this day, I am determined to remember that my real Master is God the Father Almighty, my Maker and Preserver. I shall think, speak, and act in all things as though I were doing it for Him—for in fact, I really am! I would not want someone to say of me, "What a great person he is!" but rather, "What a great God he has!"

I do not know what will happen to me this day or tomorrow or the next day. But I do know that I begin each day with a clean slate, for all my sins are washed away by His forgiving love. I do know that each day must be a day of thankful service to my God. I do know that I live each day in His care and protection, so that whether I live or die, I am on my way to Him who created me for life everlasting.

Living or dying, Lord,
I ask but to be Thine;
My life in Thee, Thy life in me,
Make heav'n forever mine. Amen. (TLH 591:4)

—⟋∿⟍—

August 11, 1967

AUGUST 12

—॥॥—

Read Acts 16:6–10
They attempted to go into Bithynia, but the Spirit of Jesus did not
allow them. *Acts 16:7*

BAFFLED FOR GREATER USEFULNESS

The decisions of God leave us sometimes perplexed, especially when we try to serve Him and fail; a door closes mysteriously, and we have to abandon our purpose.

Thus the apostle Paul must have been perplexed. He had attempted to enter the province of Bithynia, intending to do God's work there. Yet the Holy Spirit Himself, whose very work is that of bringing sinners to Christ, barred the way in a manner to us unknown. The apostle must have wondered—for a while.

Then he learned why this had been. All unknown to him, a great door was now open into the whole continent of Europe. There he was needed most. God conserved his strength and his remaining years for the greater task by closing the way to the lesser.

The same reason lightens our bafflements too. We are poor judges of our own best abilities and opportunities. Sometimes, we try to undertake tasks for which we are unsuited. Or we are unaware of other tasks for which we are better suited. We sometimes mistake the less important for the more important. So God conserves our strength and time by making some things impossible for us. He guides our usefulness into more fruitful fields, often closing other doors.

We are to try to serve God as we think best. If we are wrong, we may trust Him to correct us and guide us. He will put us where He wants us, if necessary by closing doors. But He baffles us in the present only to guide us to greater usefulness in the future.

Heavenly Father, do Thou guide my days and service while giving me humility and trust to follow Thy leading. Amen.

—॥॥—

August 12, 1940

August 13

—᚜—

Read Matthew 20:17–28
He humbled Himself by becoming obedient to the point of death,
even death on a cross. *Philippians 2:8*

Success Story

From rags to riches, from office boy to president of the firm, from log cabin to White House—these are the great American success stories. Sometimes when I think of this, I say to myself, "When will you make your mark? Will you ever be a success?"

And then I think of my Lord's success story: from heaven to earth; from the right hand of God, the Father Almighty, to a peasant mother and a manger in Bethlehem; from popularity to indifference to hatred to crucifixion to death! And through it all, I see my Lord Jesus busy in serving everyone around Him. Guests at a wedding drank the wine He prepared for them; five thousand sat down on the grass and ate the bread and fish He served; scores of the sick received His healing; twelve chosen men sat around a table arguing about success, while their Master and Lord quietly washed their feet! Then came the highest service of all: ignorant soldiers jeered at Him, spiteful priests quoted the Scriptures at Him, cowardly disciples fled from Him—as He hung by nails to a cross, bearing the sins of all, even of His enemies!

This was our Savior's success story. True—He also arose from the dead and returned to His throne in heaven. But the success of His redemptive mission was assured on the cross of shame and agony when He cried out, "It is finished!"

Lord Jesus, let the story of Thy success move me to saving faith and humble service. Amen.

—᚜—

August 13, 1961
On this date in 1961,
construction of Berlin Wall begins

Read John 14:23–27
Psalm 119:73–80

Have this mind among yourselves, which is yours in Christ Jesus.
Philippians 2:5

THE MIND OF CHRIST

That man should possess the mind of Christ, that he should think like Christ, is without doubt the most challenging assignment God has ever given to a human being. The same Scripture that records this assignment reminds us that no one really knows the mind of God, that God's thoughts are higher than our thoughts. Are we to possess the infinite?

Many of our fellowmen are not too complex, and yet, when we think we understand them, they do or say something that is completely out of character. If we cannot even fathom a fellowman, how can we fathom God or His Son, Jesus Christ?

But the mind is tricky and sometimes arrogant. Man believes that he can understand God, that he can think like Christ. This was probably the essence of Adam's fall. "You will be like God, knowing good and evil," said Satan (Genesis 3:5).

To grow toward the mind of Christ and to possess His thoughts in increasing measure are challenges that can be achieved only if we make full use of Scripture, relive incidents of Christ's life, search out the full meaning of His words, and hear the interpretations of His life from those who were with Him. The challenge to think like Christ is a stunning admonition to immerse ourselves in His life and thought.

Lord Jesus, lead me to understand Thee. Amen.

—∿—

August 14, 1966

Read Jeremiah 23:1–6
This is the name by which He will be called: "The LORD is our
righteousness." Jeremiah 23:6

OUR RIGHTEOUSNESS

In these God-inspired words, Jeremiah says much more than that our Lord Jesus is righteous in His person and in all His works. Jesus, the Messiah from the house of David, he says, shall be made righteousness, the righteousness that avails before God, to those who believe in Him. The pastors and teachers in Israel in the days of this prophet had all but wasted the kingdom of God among men by their sinful neglect of the Word of God and their rejection of their redemption through Him who had been promised as the Redeemer. Therefore, the Lord Himself, the prophet says, would arise and gather what was left of His people from all the countries to which His chastisements had driven them and give them pastors to lead them to the green pastures of His Word and to make them unafraid. In those days, the days of the New Testament, the Messiah would rule and prosper, and the Church would be holy and dwell safely. And all who would be the Lord's in truth would call the Savior "The LORD is our righteousness."

By the redemption of the world through the blood of Christ, all sinners are not only forgiven all their trespasses, but they also have in Christ Incarnate Righteousness, Himself. O mystery of redemption: God made Jesus Christ to be very sin for all men "so that in Him we might become the righteousness of God" (2 Corinthians 5:21). This purpose of God is realized in us through faith. We behold Jesus Christ in the Gospel and in the Sacraments; by enlightenment of the Holy Spirit, we call Him "The LORD is our righteousness." *So* we are saved. *So* we enter the heavenly mansions.

Thou art, O Christ, "The LORD is our righteousness."

—⁓—

August 15, 1945
On this date in 1945, Japan surrenders

August 16

—⟵∭⟶—

Read 1 John 2:1–14
Comfort My people, says your God. . . . Cry to her . . . that her iniquity
is pardoned. *Isaiah 40:1–2*

WORDS OF COMFORT

We could use some comfort. God looks down on our poor, derelict world and sees man's cruelty to man, broken homes with which the sea of modern life is littered: crime, anger, contempt, and disdain. A note of comfort in the midst of all the anguish? Yes, we could use that.

There is one comfort we need more than any other, more than just the soothing of our sorrows and the calming of our cares. We need the comfort of sins forgiven. There is no comfort until the conscience is at peace. "Comfort My people. . . . Cry to her . . . that her iniquity is pardoned." Not just "speak tenderly" (v. 2). Proclaim, give it everything you've got. The world won't believe it at first. It sounds too good to be true. You have to make the news urgent. Proclaim that sin has been paid for!

On those battlefields where men and women struggle, you and I sometimes meet defeat. If things have happened in your life that ought never to have been, if the walls of sinful habit and indulgence have closed in around you, listen to your Father in heaven say, "The past is over and gone. Because of Jesus' sacrifice for you, you can start all over again."

Lord, how precious is Your assurance that I am forgiven
through Jesus' merit. Amen.

—⟵∭⟶—

August 16, 1999

August 17

—⚭—

Read Genesis 32
Psalm 30
Weeping may tarry for the night, but joy comes with the morning.
Psalm 30:5

JOY IN THE MORNING

We all have our nights of doubt and sorrow. How long the nights are when we water the couch with tears! Sleep does not come though we are weary, but the tears come easily. We try to block our doubts that haunt us, but the harder we try, the more real they become. Doubt, often the cause of sorrow, is as dark as the night.

The psalmist says that "joy comes with the morning." He celebrates God's goodness that had delivered him from great illness. He had experienced the depths of despair, but God lifted him up. He had walked in the vale, but God guided him. He counts this healing as a sign that God will always attend him and permit him to enjoy the morning after the night of weeping.

God has given us an even greater assurance of His love. God gave us the joy of Easter morning. When Christ greeted the dawn with His resurrection, victory broke the night of weeping over our sin and death. By the rosy dawn of Easter morning, God gave us the promise that He will dry all the tears of our nights of weeping. Joy will again fill our hearts no matter how long and how dark the night has been.

Father, help us to dry the tears of nightly weeping by assuring us of the joy of morning in Christ, our Lord. Amen.

—⚭—

August 17, 1977

August 18

—⚍—

Read Daniel 2:14–35
One's life does not consist in the abundance of his possessions.
Luke 12:15

PROGRESS

When we evaluate the progress that modern man has made and the greatness of his genius in bending the forces of nature to his purposes, we still have to face the bitter truth that all this progress, as stupendous as it is, has not saved us from insecurity and unhappiness. Our progress has not eliminated the radical wrong in the human heart. It has not done away with selfishness, pride, hatred, and all the other vices that tear down human relationships and threaten our peace. The way of modern progress is not the way along which we can find a reason for living or a hope against our dying. Our progress and the abundance of things that it places at our disposal cannot make life full and free and happy. The modern world has one great discovery still to make. It must discover the forgotten truth of God that life does not consist in the abundance of things that a man possesses. Life must have God in it and have Him there first and above all things.

The progress of the twentieth century cannot save us. We know that now, for we are afraid of the power we have discovered. We need desperately to know the Christ and the saving might of His boundless love. There is a green hill far away and of long ago where modern man can find life and immortality in the faith of the Son of God, who loved him and there gave Himself for him. This way lies the kingdom of God and eternal life.

—⚍—

August 18, 1949

AUGUST 19

—∿—

Read Exodus 20:8–11
Psalm 63
[Jesus said,] "Come away by yourselves to a desolate place
and rest a while." *Mark 6:31*

RETREAT!

S oldiers march, but soldiers also sometimes retreat. When you hear that your army is retreating, it sounds like you're losing. But history teaches that sometimes the wisest and bravest generals order a retreat. A retreat can lead to a better position, a replenishment of supplies, and an ultimate victory.

Christians also must wisely choose time to "retreat." Weekly worship is a retreat that replenishes us for a week back out in the world. Daily time with the Lord in His Word and through prayer is a retreat to our ultimate source of strength. Another time to retreat is when we find ourselves in a situation that would lead us to sin. When we find ourselves in locations or with people that pull us away from God, we may feel it is our responsibility to stay and witness. At times, it is. But at other times, the wisest course is to retreat, to pull back, to return to locations with people who support and encourage our faith rather than seek to corrupt it.

Jesus never backed away from battle, but He regularly took time in communion with His Father to replenish His strength for completing His mission of salvation for all humankind.

Jesus, lead me to gather new strength in Your Word and Holy Supper.
Amen.

—∿—

August 19, 2000

August 20

—⚬—

Read Mark 9:14–29
Psalm 130
Jesus said to him, "'If You can'! All things are possible for one
who believes." *Mark 9:23*

THE POWER OF FAITH

S ometimes, we get discouraged and think that our problems can't be resolved. Jesus had come back from the transfiguration, where Peter, James, and John were given a glimpse of His glory. Meanwhile, more people who had learned of Jesus' healing powers were bringing the demon-possessed and sick to Him to be healed.

A man brought his demon-possessed son to Jesus after bringing him to the disciples, who couldn't do anything. Though the man went to Jesus, he wasn't sure Jesus could help him. He said, "If You can . . . help us." And Jesus said, "'If You can'! All things are possible for one who believes" (Mark 9:22–23). The father replied that he believed, and Jesus healed his son.

Why couldn't the disciples help the man's son? The disciples caused their failure—they had lost confidence in God and forgot to pray to Him for help (v. 29).

Sometimes, we also forget that we have an all-powerful God who loves us and sent Jesus to die for our sins, including the sins of doubt and unbelief. We should not approach our problems in a spirit of hopelessness, but of faith, knowing God has the power and desire to help us.

Dear Lord, thank You that when I face tough problems, I can turn to You for help. Amen.

—⚬—

August 20, 2008

August 21

—ɷ—

Read Psalm 32
Pride in possessions—is not from the Father. 1 John 2:16

IN THE DARKNESS: PRIDE

In dim moonlight, even the plainest person may imagine himself good-looking, for in the darkness one can delude even oneself. In the darkness, we often delude ourselves spiritually as well. Our pride will not permit us to see ourselves as we really are. We spend our lives amassing wealth and possessions, but hide it behind the label of "security." We show a sickening lack of love to those of other colors and religions, but mask it behind "religious devotion." We live for ourselves, lazily neglecting others, but convince ourselves that it is "modern easy living."

We cherish a false image of ourselves. Criticism hurts because it threatens us so deeply. We want others to see us as we see ourselves. St. John includes all of this in his expression of "pride in possessions." He warns us that it does not come from the Father but from the world.

The solution appears simple: Let us stop pretending. But we won't do it. And why? We are basically afraid that there is nothing beneath the surface.

Only God can deal with this condition. Like the ancient psalmist, we discover that life turns bitter when we hide our sins. We must break through as David did, saying, "'I will confess my transgressions to the LORD,' and You forgave the iniquity of my sin" (32:5).

O Lord, hear our cry as we confess our many sins;
forgive us for Jesus' sake. Amen.

—ɷ—

August 21, 1959
On this date in 1959,
Hawaii is admitted as fiftieth U.S. state

August 22

—⟶—

Read Joshua 4:1–9
Psalm 98
Give thanks to the Lord of lords, for His steadfast love endures forever.
Psalm 136:3

UNFAILING LOVE

We may think the skyscrapers we have constructed will stand forever, but nothing made by human hands is permanent. Towering mountains appear immovable, but God's Word assures us that one day, when the Lord of lords returns, they will all crumble.

In the middle of change and decay, we come face-to-face with God's love and find it to be unchanging, uncrumbling, un-dimmed—yes, altogether unfailing. God's saving love in Jesus Christ is enduring and persevering. The unfailing love of God is demonstrated in that while we were still lost and dead in sin, Jesus Christ died for our salvation.

This is love that no wall can hold back. The devil cannot hold it in check. Our obstinate plunge into self-indulgent sin cannot destroy it. God's love sent Jesus. He came and walked the dusty, rocky paths of Israel and accomplished to perfection the will of the heavenly Father. Jesus gave Himself up to be nailed to the cross, to die in our place, then to rise again, promising to be with us forever. Yes, give thanks to Him—the Lord of lords! His love truly does endure forever!

Lord Jesus Christ, help us always remember that Your love never fails.
Amen.

—⟶—

August 22, 1993

August 23

—⟶—

Read Galatians 5:16–25
Psalm 25:14–20
If we live by the Spirit, let us also walk by the Spirit. *Galatians 5:25*

THE POWER FOR WORK

What magnificent graces the Holy Spirit gives the Christian! Hopeless is the life of thought and emotion, word and deed, of the man without God and Christ. But joyous, able, strong, is the life of the man filled with the Spirit of God.

Somehow, it often comes with the force of a surprise that every Christian has this Spirit and therefore this power. We are apt to look for the gifts of the Spirit in other men. Let us find them there and be glad. But let us see them also in ourselves. Let us not imagine ourselves weaklings. In us is the power that made Abraham the father of the faithful; that sent Samson forth to scourge God's enemies; that helped Isaiah say, "Here I am; send me"; that held Jeremiah to the consolations of God; that led the Magi to the Bethlehem crib; that flung Paul on through every woe to the victory of the cross—the power of the Spirit of God. What are we waiting for? Where else should the Spirit be? He is in us, the Spirit of counsel and might.

But let us remember also this: all the things we do as tasks for God must be done in the Spirit's power. Often, we are tempted in the work of the Church to use human means alone. That will not work. Freight trains are to be drawn not by dog teams but by locomotives. For divine tasks, we need God's own power, imparted by Word and Sacrament. Things done for God without the Spirit are nothing. God Himself must help us to see the power that He has given us and, seeing it, to work with it.

—⟶—

August 23, 1937

August 24

—∿—

Read 1 Peter 1:13–25
Psalm 89
Forever, O LORD, Your word is firmly fixed in the heavens. *Psalm 119:89*

GOD'S WORD STANDS

In the days of the French Revolution, enemies of Christianity said to a peasant, "We will pull down your church steeples. Then you'll no longer have anything to remind you of God and your religious superstitions." The peasant replied calmly, "But you will leave us the stars."

No one can tear down the stars. Neither can anyone destroy the Bible. Century follows century—there it stands. Empires rise and fall and are forgotten—there it stands. Storms of hate swirl about it—there it stands. Atheists rail against it—there it stands. Profane punsters poke fun at it—there it stands. Unbelief abandons it— there it stands. Thunderbolts of wrath smite it—there it stands. Flames are kindled about it—there it stands.

The Bible is as eternal as its author. God's Word will not pass away. We can lean our weight on it without risk. It will never crumble. In the Word, we come into the presence of greatness. The Word sweetens life. It is an armor plate against evil. It feeds the soul. It brightens the path. It sets the spirit ablaze. It is God speaking to us, cleansing us, holding us, leading us into life eternal.

Lord, the Scriptures testify on You. Therefore, help me to be a Word-lover and Word-keeper all my life. Let Your powerful Word grow in me and bring forth much fruit. Amen.

—∿—

August 24, 1975

Read Colossians 2:6–9
Psalm 92
Christ who is God over all, blessed forever. *Romans 9:5*

CHRIST IS GOD

W hen St. Paul calls Christ "God over all, blessed forever," he expresses the central truth of Christianity. If Christ is not God, Christianity has no foundation on which to stand.

To save us and the millions of our fellowmen from the awful consequences of sin, we need the promise of a divine redemption. No merely human leader can guide us to heaven. No man, no matter how self-sacrificing, can take our place before the bar of eternal justice and remove the penalty of our sins. Not even an angel can cleanse our hearts, forgive our sins, and open the gates to heaven.

What we with a life of endless penance could not do; what all the good works of all the ages could not earn; what all the angels in their dazzling brilliance could not grant—forgiveness, salvation, heaven—all this is offered to us by Christ. He is our true and gracious God. In the richness of His mercy, He became poor for our sakes. On the cross, He, as the substitute for sinners, gave up His blood. This eternal power of the cross and of His cleansing blood is grounded in the truth that Jesus Christ is true God.

Lord Jesus, we confess Thee as our God. Thou hast redeemed us by the shedding of Thy holy, precious blood. Amen.

—ᴍ—

August 25, 1969

August 26

—ᴍ—

Read 1 Peter 5:6–11
Psalm 37
Casting all your anxieties on Him, because He cares for you. *1 Peter 5:7*

He Cares about Me

There are many things that cause people to be anxious or to worry. Perhaps they do not feel well, or they are having some kind of trouble. Perhaps they cannot afford some things that they really need, or they don't know what to do in a certain situation. Often, people are troubled because of their sins; they are afraid that God will not forgive them. All these things we call anxieties or cares because they make people worry whether God still cares about them and whether He will continue to take care of them.

Christians often make the mistake of imagining that they must bear their burdens alone. They forget the Lord's invitation, "Casting all your anxieties on Him, because He cares for you."

Our heavenly Father dearly loves His children and wants to help them with their anxieties, burdens, and cares. That is why He sent Jesus into this world to take away our sins by becoming our substitute. He is also willing and able to take care of all our other needs and problems if we will only bring them to Him as children to their father and trust and obey Him.

Dear heavenly Father, I accept Your gracious invitation to cast my anxieties upon You, confident that You will help me again as in the past. Amen.

—ᴍ—

August 26, 1978

August 27

—∿—

Read Matthew 13:1–9, 18–23
He told them many things in parables, saying: "A sower went out to sow."
Matthew 13:3

THE DIFFERENCE IS IN THE SOIL

In our world, we see the same patterns as detailed in Christ's parable of the sower. The context of our text is a portrayal of the different ways people react to the preaching and teaching of the Gospel. Some are like soil on a pathway, so hard that the Gospel never penetrates. Some are like rocky places, where the Gospel produces faith, but the faith lives only for a short time and then withers and dies for lack of nourishment or care.

Some are soil in which weeds, the weeds being the distractions of life, crowd out and choke off the Gospel and the faith it produces. And finally, some are like good soil. In them, the Gospel—the Gospel that the Son of God took flesh, lived, died, and rose for the forgiveness of sin—takes root and thrives.

The Church finds it frustrating when people reject the message of salvation. It is a disappointment when someone does little to nourish and sustain his or her faith. Some reject outright the message of the Gospel. Yet our task is to sow the seed of the Gospel so that it can work. Then we are like St. Paul, who said, "I planted, Apollos watered, but God gave the growth" (1 Corinthians 3:6).

Lord, give me strength as I sow Your seed and patience to await Your harvest. Amen.

—∿—

August 27, 1996

AUGUST 28

—⁌—

Read Revelation 3:14–22
Psalm 40:1–8
Behold, I stand at the door and knock. *Revelation 3:20*

CHRIST AT THE DOOR

This spiritual gem from the inspired pen of St. John has served as an inspiration to both poets and artists. Here, our Lord Jesus is pictured as earnestly calling the sinner to repentance. The congregation that originally received this letter is one that had fallen into spiritual indifference. Its faith is described as neither hot nor cold, but only lukewarm. If it had been either hot or cold, the congregation would have more easily recognized its condition. But the members were only too happy to remain in their "wretched, pitiable, poor, blind, and naked" condition (v. 17). The earnest invitation goes out to them. "Behold, I stand at the door and knock."

This earnest invitation is one that goes out not only to congregations today but also to individual Christians. Indifference about our spiritual life is a constant danger. A minister once put it most aptly, "There is nothing more difficult to work with than the half-baked Christian." Such persons are content to function in spiritual indifference and cannot see the danger.

In this earnest call from God's Holy Word, Jesus stands at our heart's door with His earnest invitation, desiring to give us the fullness of His blessings.

Lord Jesus, keep me from spiritual indifference, and may my heart and life be Your dwelling place. Amen.

—⁌—

August 28, 2002

—ᴍ—

Read Judges 6:25–27
Psalm 66
The LORD said, ..."Pull down the altar of Baal." *Judges 6:25*

SKETCH OF A WRECKER

All who would lead people to Christ must be willing to remove obstacles. Gideon first had to lead his people to the knowledge of their sins before he could save them from their enemies. The purge of false religion had to come first.

Baal worship was a cancer in Gideon's community. To ensure spiritual healing, this cancer had to be cut out—the altars of Baal had to be pulled down in spite of reaction or resistance from either his father or the community. The spiritual health of Israel was an absolute necessity for its victory over oppressive pagan nations.

To be winners today, to participate in Christendom's victories, we, too, must pull down modern altars that obstruct vision and impede the progress of Christ's Gospel.

The undue attention we give to the altar of wealth and power must go. We cannot be slaves to mammon and servants to Christ at the same time. The dollar signs in our eyes blur our vision of Christ, who alone is our one and all. The altar of self-advancement—in business, profession, or social position—to the neglect of all else must also be pulled down. We must let God be God in our lives.

Gracious Father, help us remove from our lives all that keeps us from honoring Christ as our Savior and highest good. Amen.

—ᴍ—

August 29, 1982

August 30

—∿—

Read Ephesians 5:22–33
Psalm 138
This mystery is profound, and I am saying that it refers to Christ
and the church. *Ephesians 5:32*

True Fidelity

In Ephesians 5, St. Paul gives a beautiful, Christological description of holy marriage. Husbands are to love their wives as Jesus, who was willing even to die for His Bride, loved the Church. Wives are to submit to their husbands as the Church submits to Christ, that is, as the Church relies, trusts, and depends on Christ, the Bridegroom.

But suddenly, in the midst of this wonderful picture of marriage, St. Paul says these cryptic words: "This mystery is profound, and I am saying that it refers to Christ and the church." All of the talk about holy marriage is first a talk about Christ and the Church!

Christ is our Bridegroom, and we—as part of the Holy Christian Church—are His Holy Bride. He is utterly faithful in all things, even willing to go to a brutal death for us. Jesus will never leave us. He will never forsake us. He will always love us. And one day, we will most certainly live together with Him forever.

Faithful Bridegroom, Jesus Christ, I give You thanks for calling me to faith in You and making me a member of Your Holy Christian Church. Keep me ever as part of Your Holy Bride; when my last hour comes, do not forsake me, but love me forever. This I humbly beg You for the sake of Your holy name. Amen.

—∿—

August 26, 2009

August 31

—∞—

Read Matthew 6:19–21
Psalm 33:18–22
Blessed are those who keep His testimonies, who seek Him
with their whole heart. *Psalm 119:2*

Seeking Hearts

A strong cultural current urges young and old alike to adopt the advice to "follow your heart" as a litmus test when deciding which course for life is best to travel. The motto is attractive for its romantic whimsy, but cloaked within is real danger. Following our hearts can be sound advice only if our hearts are pure, blameless, and reliable. But because of sin, which taints everyone, our hearts are corrupted, guilt-ridden, and fickle. Little wonder that following our hearts has often landed us in many kinds of trouble.

Our hearts must be transformed if they are to be useful compasses, pointing us toward life with God that is good and meaningful. In our fallen condition, we are turned inward, so that following our hearts leads to endless self-centeredness and futility. That pointless cycle is broken only when we are fixed on a more trustworthy reference point.

God's testimonies found throughout Scriptures comprise the reference point that gives us true hope and direction for our lives; they are the core of His promises that lock our hearts onto our Lord Jesus Christ, whose undying love on a cross causes us to seek Him until we see Him when we rise from our graves. Hearts linked to Christ lead directly to God's eternal blessings.

Lord, turn our hearts and lives toward You. Amen.

—∞—

August 31, 2010
On this date in 2010, Operation Iraqi
Freedom ends by executive order

September

Dear God, uphold me at all times with Your righteous hand, and always strengthen me in faith and forgiveness through Your Son, Jesus. Amen.

Read Revelation 7:9–17
A great multitude ... standing before the throne and before the Lamb.
Revelation 7:9

A GREAT MULTITUDE

Here, we have a thrilling glimpse of heaven. It is a vision, seen of St. John when he was banished to Patmos. We read this passage, and our hearts are full to overflowing. Such is the end of faith for those who by God's grace steadfastly look unto Jesus. "For the joy that was set before Him [He] endured the cross, despising the shame, and is seated at the right hand of the throne of God" (Hebrews 12:2). Here is set before us the joy that awaits us. Surely we can endure our little crosses and despise shame with such a dazzling prospect to hearten us.

Before the throne and before the Lamb we shall stand, free from sin and from every curse of sin. The blood of the Lamb has made us clean, fit for heavenly honors. Troubles and tribulations, toils and conflicts are left behind. In our hands are the palms of victory. To serve Him who so graciously has redeemed us shall be our eternal delight. He shall meet and satisfy our every need.

A vast company shall share this blessed lot. All the holy angels shall with the great multitude of the redeemed join in an unending service of praise. From the corners of the earth, God has gathered His saints. On earth, they knew not each other; they spoke various languages, they were of different nationalities, they lived in every age of history. In eternity, they shall be one heavenly body, worshiping Him to whom all once looked to cleanse them through His blood and whom they all shall forever behold.

May God grant us grace to be one of that great multitude!

Jesus, in mercy bring me soon to that land of rest. Amen.

September 1, 1939
On this date in 1939,
Nazi Germany invades Poland

—w—

Read Matthew 2:1–13
Blessed is the one who finds wisdom, and the one who
gets understanding. *Proverbs 3:13*

THE LONG, HARD ROAD

When our Lord was born in Bethlehem, Wise Men from the East tried to find Him. They found Him because they were truly wise. They were wise enough to follow God's directions, wise enough not to be offended at where they found Him, and wise enough to come for the distinct purpose of worshiping Him.

There is something sudden, startling, and satisfying about the discovery of wisdom. It brings a sense of thrill and relief. To get understanding is equally satisfying, even though we must walk such a long, hard road to get it! Our God must teach us many lessons, and often we are such unwilling students!

To understand His love for us, He must teach us to understand our great need for His love. The more we understand how rebellious we are, the more we understand how reconciling He is. The more we understand our weakness, the more we understand His strength. So He leads us day by day in ways strange to us but clear to Him.

In hours of loneliness, we discover how close He can be. On sickbeds, we can take time to look up to see His face shine upon us. At the death of a Christian, we can learn better to know Him and the power of His resurrection. When He rebukes us for our sins, we realized that He is truly the friend of sinners.

*Lord, do not become impatient with us, but lead us on the way
to a better understanding of Thy great love in Christ for us. Amen.*

—w—

September 2, 1964

SEPTEMBER 3

—⚹—

Read Deuteronomy 31:1–8
Psalm 25
I have learned the secret of . . . abundance and need. I can do all things
through Him who strengthens me. *Philippians 4:12–13*

STRENGTH AND COURAGE FROM GOD

By AD 380, the emperors of Rome had become Christian, and so had many citizens of the empire. At this time, a great churchman, Ambrose, became the chief pastor in Milan, Italy. Emperor Theodosius was a member of his parish. On several occasions, Ambrose had to reproach the emperor for his sins—once publicly from the pulpit. A serious crisis arose when the emperor, in a fit of anger, ordered seven thousand people massacred in Thessalonica because someone had insulted the imperial authority. When Ambrose heard this news, he refused to permit the emperor to attend services or receive Communion until he had repented of this violent deed and had made such amends as he could. For a time, it seemed that more blood would be shed, but finally, the emperor repented and was forgiven by his pastor.

Ambrose had the courage of his convictions and was prepared to uphold justice and truth despite the cost to himself. In doing so, he took as his example Jesus Christ, who suffered and died even though He was innocent. From the risen Lord we, too, can take courage when we suffer because of our Christian convictions. "[God] will not leave you or forsake you. Do not fear or be dismayed" (Deuteronomy 31:8).

Lord Jesus, give us the courage to do what is right. Amen.

—⚹—

September 3, 1977

Nathan said to David, "You are the man!" *2 Samuel 12:7*

A PERSONAL BOOK

Martin Luther's wife studied his Small Catechism, and she was impressed especially with one feature: namely, that the contents of the Small Catechism seemed to be written just for and about her. That is the proper way to read a book, especially one that deals with our lives and our problems, our worries and cares.

God's Book is highly personal; it is written for and to the individual sinner and in no uncertain language. God did not reveal something to mankind that was so vague and indefinite that an individual should or could be in doubt as to whom the Lord might be talking or that a reader of the Bible might always think, Now, that means my neighbor. Anyone who reads the Book will find himself and his troubles and sins there on those pages; he is pictured so minutely that he can recognize himself even though his name does not appear.

David had sinned shamefully; God knew it, and David also knew it. God did not keep David in the dark very long as to his sin and the gravity of the offense but sent Nathan, a prophet of the Lord, to David to tell him point-blank: "You are the man!" This was just as personal as anything could have been, and there was no room for David to ignore the word or to think that probably someone else and not he was meant. He had to acknowledge his sin, and he received forgiveness too, through Nathan.

God speaks to us personally about our sins, about our Savior especially, about our troubles in this world, about the problems of our daily life and living, about our family, about our Church, about our government, about everything. All we need to do is to insert our names behind the verses and chapters as we read them.

—w—

September 4, 1942

Read Romans 8:18–25
Psalm 19
The heavens declare the glory of God, and the sky above proclaims
His handiwork. *Psalm 19:1*

THE SILENT SERMON

There is a sermon being preached, but you need special ears to hear it. There is a drama being acted out, but you need special eyes to see it. Nature, lying so silently around us, fairly shouts out God's glory. Martin Luther once commented, "Our Lord has written the promise of resurrection not in books alone but in every leaf in springtime." St. Paul noticed that nature preaches, for he wrote that the whole universe waits and waits for God's children to be revealed, groaning like a woman on the verge of giving birth.

Our Lord Jesus found heavenly illustrations in the birds of the air, the lilies of the field, a grain of mustard seed. But then, isn't it only fitting that all of creation should proclaim in countless ways Him through whom and for whom it was all created?

In the Gospel, God proclaims and imparts something greater. He tells us that He sent His Son to liberate us from sin, death, and hell. To give us everything else along with Christ is a small thing for God, and so He has given us all of nature too, that we might be filled with awe, thankfulness, and the knowledge of Christ.

Dear heavenly Father, open our spiritual eyes and ears so that we can understand nature's sermon today. Amen.

—⟋⟍—

September 5, 1982

SEPTEMBER 6

—m—

Read Romans 3:21–26
Psalm 35:1–10
For all have sinned and fall short of the glory of God, and are justified
by His grace as a gift, through the redemption that is in Christ Jesus.
Romans 3:23–24

OUR COMMON PROBLEM

There are some people who believe they do not sin. Apparently, they have not read, or do not believe, the words of the apostle John: "If we say we have no sin, we deceive ourselves, and the truth is not in us" (1 John 1:8).

If people have one thing in common, one problem that constantly eats away at them, it is sin. Paul reminds us of this when he preaches the Law to show us how we stand in relation to God. We stand condemned.

But then in the same breath, he relieves us of our shame and fear by telling us that we are saved despite our shortcoming. Because of Jesus' suffering and death on the cross, our heavenly Father has declared that we are forgiven and at one with Him. He declares us justified, made holy by His grace, because Jesus has redeemed us, that is, has purchased us at the price of His blood.

Christians should be the happiest people in the world. Once they were lost, but now are found; once dirty, but now clean; once sick, but now healthy. Because our sins are forgiven by Christ, we are heaven bound.

Thank You, Lord, for dying for me on the cross.
Increase my joy in Your great gift. Amen.

—m—

September 6, 2002

Read John 10:7–18
I am the good shepherd. I know My own and My own know Me.
John 10:14

THE PROMISE OF RECOGNITION

I f the Scriptures did not picture our Lord as our Shepherd and Christ as the Good Shepherd, we would undoubtedly carry with us a much different picture of the life of sheep. We certainly would not wish to be referred to as sheep; we resent even now being known as "sheepish," and many characteristics of the flock are unappealing to us.

Yet the picture of the Christian as a sheep and Christ as Shepherd has survived more bad poetry, second-rate music, and third-rate art than any other image of this relationship. Pastors know that Psalm 23 and the parable of the lost sheep are among the most requested portions of Scripture by those who walk in the valley of the shadow of death.

We like the picture because we like to see the Lord as the Shepherd. It is a figure He Himself chose. He wanted to assure us of His concern; unlike the hired man, He would not run away in time of danger. He cared. As a matter of fact, He laid down His life for the sheep when that was necessary.

How happy we are to hear again and again that He knows His own! He promises to recognize us and to give us the power to respond to Him. Earthly recognition may be a wrong quest; it may involve pride and self-seeking. Heavenly recognition by Christ is our hope, our assurance, our security already for this life. We are known of God today and forever.

Lead us, O Lord, our Shepherd, and never forsake us,
for Thy mercy's sake. Amen.

—ᴍ—

September 7, 1957

September 8

—⟋⟍—

Read Matthew 6:25–34
Psalm 62
Anxiety in a man's heart weighs him down, but a good word
makes him glad. *Proverbs 12:25*

THE ANSWER TO ANXIETY

Many people are beset by anxiety. The cares and concerns of life weigh them down. Jesus addressed Himself to the problem when He said: "Do not be anxious about your life, what you will eat or what you will drink, nor about your body, what you will put on" (Matthew 6:25). He repeatedly says "your heavenly Father." It is our heavenly Father who feeds us. If He takes care of the birds, He will take care of us also.

If that is not sufficient to calm our anxiety, we consider who is telling us this in the Sermon on the Mount. It is the Son of God, yes, God Himself, who is speaking to us. What He says is not simply a matter of words. He who speaks these words is the Word of God made flesh. That Word expressed Himself in direct action. The Son of God, Himself the Word, came to earth to prove His concern, not only for food and clothes but also for our eternal salvation. He Himself is the bread of life. Clothed in the robe of His righteousness, we can stand before God. St. Paul writes: "If God is for us, who can be against us? He who did not spare His own Son but gave Him up for us all, how will He not also with Him graciously give us all things?" (Romans 8:31–32). That should control our anxiety!

Lord, You know how weak I am. Give me strength in time of anxiety.
Amen.

—⟋⟍—

September 8, 1971

SEPTEMBER 9

—ɯ—

Read Psalm 26
Guard your steps when you go to the house of God. *Ecclesiastes 5:1*

REVERENT CHRISTIANS

S olomon asks for reverence by using a figure of speech in which a part—the foot—stands for the whole—the body. We are reverent when we use our feet to take us to church and never guide them upon paths of unrighteousness. We are reverent when, in God's house, we use our minds to concentrate devoutly upon the message. Our reverent attitude will not permit us to disturb, nor be distracted, lest we "offer the sacrifice of fools" (v. 1), an outward display of devotion without serious, prayerful, heart-deep mediation.

We are reverent when at home we seek to improve our souls and minds by reading the Bible and wholesome secular literature.

We are reverent when in the sanctuary of the Savior we use our eyes to see the beauty of God in sacred art and, above all, the loveliness of Jesus in sacred story. Outside the church, we will use our eyes to see the wonders of God in the grandeur of nature and turn them away from all that is shoddy, ugly, unclean, and evil.

We are reverent when we fold our hands in fervent prayer in public and private and open them to the needy, when we use our knees to kneel in adoration and supplication and never bend them before an idol of any kind.

We are reverent when we use our lips to sing with sincerity the praises of Him "who was delivered up for our trespasses and raised for our justification" (Romans 4:25) and to testify to Jesus, but never defile them, stain our souls, dishonor God by using them to take His name in vain.

Our reverent lives, refraining from all that is displeasing to God, will be, then, influential, exemplary, upright, noble, and sincere.

—ɯ—

September 9, 1954

September 10

—⁓—

Read 2 Samuel 15:1–6
Psalm 49
If your brother sins against you, go and tell him his fault,
between you and him alone. *Matthew 18:15*

SETTLING OUR DIFFERENCES

Absalom, a son of king David, desired to wrest the kingdom of Israel away from his father. One of the methods he used was to defame the king. He attempted to ruin his father's good name and thereby turn the hearts of the people toward himself. Such devious, evil actions are not uncommon today as well.

When disagreements occur, our human tendency is to make ourselves look good while making our adversary appear evil. Truth goes out the window and is forgotten. We may circulate evil reports for the purpose of injuring a reputation.

God outlines His strategy for us to follow when others sin against us. We should go directly to them with our concern. We are to tell them, not others. We are to resolve the dispute by going one-on-one.

God's Word urges every sinner to repent and trust in His forgiveness on account of Christ's sacrifice. The first to repent should be you and me; if we do not confess our sin and apologize, what right have we to expect others to do so? What a comfort it is to know that we have a merciful Savior who is eager to forgive our every trespass and grant us another chance!

O Lord Jesus Christ, You are so quick to forgive me. Grant that I may be so quick to forgive others. Amen.

—⁓—

September 10, 1992

SEPTEMBER 11

—⁂—

Read John 1:1–18
Psalm 29

That which was from the beginning, which we have heard, which we have seen with our eyes, which we looked upon and have touched with our hands, concerning the word of life. *1 John 1:1*

WE WONDER!

C an you imagine John writing these beginning words of his first letter? He is an old man, and by the Holy Spirit's inspiration, he desires to share the Jesus that he knew. John thought back to the many times he and the other disciples had sat with Jesus. Picture it? They sat with Jesus, directly across from Him. They could look Him in the eyes. They could tug on His sleeve and ask for an explanation of His teaching. They could hear every word—the pitch, the emphasis, the quality of His voice. John had heard and seen and touched the living Son of God, the world's Redeemer!

Wouldn't that be a wonder—to see and hear and touch Jesus and to do that at any time and in any place! Yet the fact that his readers had never experienced this did not stop John from writing about the Word of life. He knew that you and I would hear Jesus by the power of the Holy Spirit in His Word, the Bible. He knew that we would see and touch Jesus in the wonder of Holy Communion.

What a wonder!

Lord, open now my heart to hear,
And through Your Word to me draw near. Amen. (LSB 908:1)

—⁂—

September 11, 2001
On this date in 2001, series of coordinated
suicide attacks on U.S.

SEPTEMBER 12

—ɯ—

Read Ecclesiastes 5:1–7
Psalm 52
The LORD is faithful in all His words and kind in all His works.
Psalm 145:13

VANITY OF LIP SERVICE

Sometimes, we find ourselves in a jam and cry out to God for help. In our desperation, we even make rash promises or try to bargain with God: "If You will only do this, then I will do that." But after the crisis passes, these often become empty vows, promises we do not and cannot keep.

Again, we dishonor God when we mouth the words of the liturgy while our minds are on dinner or the afternoon's game. Perhaps we rush through our prayer time because we think we don't have time for God.

The preacher warns us to beware of every form of rash words, worthless vows, and empty utterances.

When we find ourselves guilty of giving lip service to God, we are called to repentance. "If we confess our sins, He is faithful and just to forgive us our sins and to cleanse us from all unrighteousness" (1 John 1:9).

How blessed we are that Jesus took our sins upon His shoulders to win forgiveness for us! Forgiven, we no longer carry the guilt of our thoughtless words and neglected promises. Unlike our broken promises, God's promises are certain and sure. God is faithful in all His words. We can count on Him.

Lord, forgive me for giving You lip service only. May I always remember that You are faithful and Your promises are everlasting. Amen.

—ɯ—

September 12, 2007

Read 1 Peter 3:13–15
Psalm 119:121–128
My ways are higher than your ways and My thoughts than your thoughts.
Isaiah 55:9

GOD BEYOND REASON

D o we have to leave our minds outside the church door? Is it intellectually defensible to believe in the God who has revealed Himself in the Bible? Some people doubt that faith and reason can be harmonized. They do not bother to check what the Bible actually says. Others find too many "contradictions." For them, there can be no unanswered questions, though they do not flinch when doctors cannot diagnose their illness or when scientists find conflicting sets of data.

This kind of thinking has influenced us more than it should. Although we may regard what the Bible teaches and what science teaches as true, we tend to think that science is more "true" than the Bible. We trust our reason more than God's revelation. At that point, God would remind us that He created us with the very power to reason. He expects us to use it but also to recognize its limitations. At times, our powers of perception and reasoning fail us. Sometimes, our God is above and beyond our powers of comprehension even if we could reason perfectly.

We cannot fully comprehend God's salvation in Christ, but we can believe it. Thank God that His thoughts are higher than ours!

O Lord, our Creator, Your thoughts and Your ways
are far beyond our comprehension. Amen.

—〰—

September 13, 1976

September 14

—⚬⚬—

Read Luke 6:12–16
Psalm 6:9
Always keep on praying. *Ephesians 6:18 (NIV)*

A Time to Pray

Have you taken time to pray today? Prayer is an important part of the life of every Christian. In His Word, God has a lot to say about prayer. The Bible tells us that the almighty God takes time and has the interest to hear our prayers, that He does so because by the death and resurrection of His Son we have been adopted as God's children. It tells us that God desires that we pray for those who do not know Christ and for workers of His kingdom and for all in need. It encourages us to be persistent in prayer.

Jesus took time to pray, sometimes all night long. He prayed before He selected His disciples. He prayed before He was arrested in Gethsemane. He prayed as He committed His soul to His Father when He was about to die for our sins.

Prayer ought to be an important part of our daily life too. Ask God for wisdom and direction for your life. Confess your sins every day in prayer and receive forgiveness, which is ours through faith in Christ Jesus. Thank God for giving you life and for giving you new life in Christ. Take time to pray. God is always ready and glad to listen.

Lord, hear our prayers for Jesus' sake. Amen.

—⚬⚬—

September 14, 1997

Read Romans 5:6–11
Psalm 113
My kingdom is not of this world.... For this purpose I was born and
for this purpose I have come into the world—to bear witness
to the truth. *John 18:36–37*

CULTURE SHOCK

Have you ever traveled to another country? The language is different. The money is different. The food is often a shock to our bodies. Behaviors acceptable in one place are often viewed as rude in another.

Jesus must have experienced a culture shock as well when He left His heavenly home to be born a man on this earth. He was perfect and holy. He left a perfect and holy place to come into a world full of sin and troubles—a world hostile to Him!

Would we choose to visit a country hostile to us? Would we want to help people who treat us as enemies? We might be willing to rough it a little bit, but not to the point of death. Jesus, however, wasn't at all like us! He is God's Son. He chose to come to the earth, knowing that He would innocently sacrifice His life for the very people who mistreated Him, doubted Him, and put Him to death. So great is God's love!

Whoever believes in Jesus will be received into His kingdom. The beauty of heaven will be "out of this world." And we'll fit right in because by God's forgiveness we have been made children of the King!

*Dear Father, thank You for caring for us. We look forward to living
in heaven with You! Amen.*

—ɯ—

September 15, 1999

Read Genesis 2:4–9
Psalm 63
The earth is the LORD's and the fullness thereof, the world and those
who dwell therein. *Psalm 24:1*

STEWARDSHIP AND THE FATHER

C hristian stewardship is built on a Father-child relationship, because what God gives us to care for as stewards
comes to us from His fatherly goodness. God the Father
created all things and placed us over His creation. That signifies
this relationship: the Creator-Father places us, His children, over
our Father's house here on earth. All of us stand in a direct and
personal relation to God by virtue of our existence, for we were
created to be stewards, or managers, for God. Therefore, all we
possess is ours as a gift from the hands of our Creator. And whatever we do in all of life is our response to God's dealings with us.

After explaining what we have received from God the Father,
Luther, in the Small Catechism (in the explanation of the First Article of the Creed), states: "For all this it is my duty to thank and
praise, serve and obey Him." That's stewardship! It's responding
to the goodness and mercy of the Father in creation. And it's more.
The stewardship life also has to do with responding to the goodness and mercy of God in Jesus Christ. He shed His blood for us on
the cross. That makes us spiritual children of God. Once again, we
are in a Father-child relationship—children serving our heavenly
Father.

Creator-Father, thank You for creating and redeeming us. Amen.

—ᘑ—

September 16, 1986

—ᴁ—

Read Colossians 3:12–17
Psalm 107
Oh give thanks to the LORD, for He is good. *Psalm 107:1*

GRATITUDE ATTITUDE

God provides everything. As self-evident as this truth is, we have to be reminded of it. Too often, we take things for granted. We go, for example, to the faucet; we turn it on; cool and refreshing water gushes out; our thirst is satisfied. We do this daily in a routine manner and forget that God is the giver of water.

Is common water such a precious gift? What answer would the rich man in hell give to this question? When he lived in this world, water was so common that he didn't appreciate it. Only expensive wines could satisfy his thirst. But when he was in torment, he begged for water, just plain water—and not too much of it, just one drop!

The sin of ingratitude is a besetting one, especially in days of affluence. So we must keep this truth in mind always: no matter how good the days may be, we are still dependent upon God for everything—dependent upon His mercy to forgive our sins through the merits of His Son, Jesus Christ our Lord, dependent upon Him for all our temporal goods. True are the words of the psalmist: "The eyes of all look to You, and You give them their food in due season" (Psalm 145:15). Yes, God is the giver of every good and perfect gift.

Lord, we give thanks to You for all Your benefits. Amen.

—ᴁ—

September 17, 1979

Read Luke 15:11–32
Psalm 51
Now the tax collectors and sinners were all drawing near to hear Him.
Luke 15:1

JESUS TAUGHT IN PARABLES

A tough audience gathers around Jesus as He teaches. These people are not accustomed to talking about religion. Rather, they are outcasts, judged by peers to be transgressors of God's Law and outside God's kingdom. Tax collectors and "sinners" are the least likely of listeners for Jesus, the traveling Rabbi.

Nevertheless, they are coming in droves to hear Him. What a Teacher, this Jesus! Jesus knew the hearts of His listeners. He tells them stories that describe perfectly their situation before God. The stories are not about criminals getting what they deserve, but about family members being forgiven.

Jesus' lesson plan includes bringing down the self-righteous and lifting up the penitent. His objectives lead His hearers to the Father, who loves all His children and wants them to rejoice within His household.

Jesus continues to touch the hearts of "least likely listeners." Wherever there are people whose hearts ache to go home but who fear their reception, Jesus says, "Come home; your heavenly Father wants you and forgives you for My sake. Come home."

Lord Jesus, lead those who have strayed from You to return, and prompt us to receive them with love. Amen.

September 18, 1995

September 19

—ɷ—

Read 2 Corinthians 11:7–12
Psalm 66
Did I commit a sin in humbling myself so that you might be exalted?
2 Corinthians 11:7

HUMBLED TO EXALT OTHERS

How far are we willing to go so that others may share in God's Gospel of free grace in Jesus Christ? The apostle Paul was willing to humble himself. He proclaimed the Gospel free of charge. He was accused of bringing a message worth nothing, of lowering himself, and sinning. He had the right to payment for his services, but he humbled himself, working with his hands to supply his own needs and the needs of those with him.

Paul did these things to "exalt" the Corinthians. They now had a new relationship with God: they had forgiveness of sin and the hope of eternal life. That cost God His Son. It cost them nothing. Even the one who brought the Gospel would not be a burden to them. What Paul could not supply himself was supplied by other Christians so that the Church at Corinth would know that salvation was a gift.

Our desire is that those who have not yet come to faith in Jesus Christ be exalted by our gracious God to be His sons and daughters. Our approach is one of humility. It is to hold before them God's forgiving grace in Christ, without condition, without price. Freely we have received, freely we give (Matthew 10:8).

Lord, help us to humble ourselves that others may be exalted.
In Jesus' name. Amen.

—ɷ—

September 19, 1998

SEPTEMBER 20

—ɯ—

Read John 13:3–17
For what is our hope or joy or crown of boasting before our Lord Jesus
at His coming? Is it not you? For you are our glory and joy.
I Thessalonians 2:19–20

FOOT WASHERS

Evangelism involves more than just witness. The responsibilities of the evangelist go beyond exposing men and women to the Good News of salvation in Jesus. Jesus said: "Go therefore and make disciples of all nations, baptizing them in the name of the Father and of the Son and of the Holy Spirit," and then He added: "teaching them to observe all that I have commanded you" (Matthew 28:19–20). There is a nurturing aspect to evangelism too. There is follow-up.

As Jesus sat at the table for His Last Supper with His disciples, He demonstrated the full measure of His commitment to them. He got up, bent before them and gently washed their feet. He had not only called them into His kingdom but, once there, also He loved, nurtured, and comforted them as they grew in faith. He taught them God's will and showed them God's will in action.

St. Paul taught the Thessalonians the Good News of salvation and stayed involved in their lives. He concerned himself with their growth in the faith. He protected them against false teaching and gave them constant hope and comfort through the Word.

Like St. Paul, like Jesus Himself, shepherd and cherish those whom you have brought to Christ.

Dear Jesus, help me to love and serve those who have come to You by my witness. Amen.

—ɯ—

September 20, 1996

—⟋ᗰᐯ⟍—

Read Matthew 13:24–30
Psalm 126
Let both grow together until the harvest. *Matthew 13:30*

SEEDS AND WEEDS

Each year, it happens. Our lawn begins to grow as it is thoroughly watered with spring rains. We eagerly await the lush green growth. Then the dandelions and crabgrass appear. They have taken root and compete for space with the grass.

In this particular parable, Jesus speaks of a farmer's field in which weeds grow along with the good seed. The reference is to the outward appearance of the Church, in which disguised unbelievers are mingled with believers. Rather than pulling out the weeds immediately, the Lord lets both grow together. At the harvest on the Last Day, God will separate the crop from the weeds.

Christians live in a world filled with the growing weeds of those who are outside God's kingdom of grace. They are mixed in with Christians, and we may not be able to distinguish them from those who are growing in their faith.

As God's people, we may wish to eradicate the "weeds" from the visible Church. But the same mercy that God extended to us in His Son, He extends to all, including unbelievers. He wants them to hear the Word and be saved. We still have time to witness to them about Christ through our words and life before the harvest of judgment.

Holy Spirit, help us grow in faith through Your Word, and may faith also grow in the hearts of others. Amen.

—⟋ᗰᐯ⟍—

September 21, 1994

Read Isaiah 41:1–10
Psalm 105:1–11
Fear not, for I am with you; be not dismayed, for I am your God;
I will strengthen you, I will help you, I will uphold you
with My righteous right hand. *Isaiah 41:10*

UPHELD BY GOD'S RIGHT HAND

A friend once told me that faith is not most valuable when you are at the end of your rope; rather, faith is most valuable when there is no rope. In pastoral ministry, I have often found this adage to be true, not only for myself, but also for those I serve. It is easy to think we can take care of ourselves as long as life is comfortable or just manageable. But when things go all wrong, we become fearful, dismayed, and weak.

When we are weak, God is strong. When we are confused, God speaks with clarity. When we fall down, God picks us up. My friend's favorite hymn, "How Firm a Foundation," is based on today's Bible passage from Isaiah. The lyricist, John Rippon, included these words in the hymn: "Fear not! I am with you, O be not dismayed, For I am your God and will still give you aid; I'll strengthen you, help you, and cause you to stand, Upheld by My righteous, omnipotent hand" (*LSB* 728:2).

The foundation of our faith is sure in Jesus Christ, our Lord. And that is sure! He gave His life that we might be His for time and for eternity!

Dear God, uphold me at all times with Your righteous hand, and always strengthen me in faith and forgiveness through Your Son, Jesus. Amen.

—⚹—

September 22, 2004

—ᴍᴍ—

Read Acts 14:8–18
Psalm 19
And God saw everything that He had made, and behold,
it was very good. *Genesis 1:31*

ALIVE—TO THE PHYSICAL WORLD

To see the physical world through the eyes of faith is to see the Creator behind the creation and to stand in awe at the magnificence and mystery of it all. The psalmist saw the glory of God in His creation. The poetically inclined person sees God painting the sunset in radiant colors. The observant Christian sees the beautiful world around him as a reflection of the love and concern of his Maker.

But often, we walk as though blind and deaf to the message of God's love in creation. Much beauty escapes us as our insensitivity shuts out the messages God is sending through the sun, the moon, the stars, the clouds, the wind, the rain, the flowers, the birds, the grain, the vegetables, the shrubs, the grass, the animals, and every living thing that proclaims—if we are alive to hear—the greatness of our Creator. God made us, they all say. When we hear this, we rejoice, for God's work is very good.

The more we learn about the wonderful physical world around us, the greater must be our faith in God, Father Almighty, Maker of heaven and earth, our Creator, and our Redeemer in Christ.

For the beauty of the earth, for the wonder of each hour, Lord, we thank You. Amen.

—ᴍᴍ—

September 23, 1972

September 24

—✖—

Read Psalm 91
And the Lord said to Paul one night in a vision, "Do not be afraid, but go on speaking and do not be silent, for I am with you, and no one will attack you to harm you, for I have many in this city who are My people."
Acts 18:9–10

ENCOURAGEMENT FROM ABOVE

Ventures in the kingdom of God call for courage. Obstacles and difficulties dampen ardor and enthusiasm. Often, we meet with determined opposition, and fear of failure begins to paralyze our efforts.

Let us never forget that the cause is the Lord's. Success or failure rests in His hands. He uses us as His tools. Whatever we achieve, we achieve with His help and by His benediction.

He encouraged Paul by telling him that He had many people in the notoriously wicked city of Corinth. Paul was to be unafraid in spite of all resistance his labors might encounter.

We preach a divine Savior to a perishing world. "In Christ God was reconciling the world to Himself, not counting their trespasses against them" (2 Corinthians 5:19).

People may not rush to hear and accept our message. They may even threaten violence and persecution, but we should be undismayed. "I am with you," the Lord said to Paul. His promise bolsters our courage and imbues us with new zeal and devotion.

Lord, Thou ruler of the hearts and the affairs of men, Thou hast committed to us the building of Thy kingdom on earth. Trusting in Thy gracious presence, we continue in our labors even though others may plot to thwart our work. Thou art our shield and very great reward, through Jesus Christ. Amen.

—✖—

September 24, 1951

September 25

—⟋⟍—

Read Acts 8:26–40
Open my eyes, that I may behold wondrous things out of Your law.
Psalm 119:18

OPEN EYES

The Holy Scriptures are full of marvelous things. The Bible is a wonderland. God has laid up great treasures in His Word. It not only tells of miracles, but also the Bible itself is a miracle. Even the best-read student of the Scriptures has not found all the treasures that God has laid up in His Book. The wonders of God's love are so many that there is no end to them.

No one knew this better than David, the sweet singer of Israel. He knew that there were glories in the Word that he had not yet fully seen, marvels that he had not yet beheld.

The psalmist asks for no new wonders. He does not call for a simplified, much less a shortened, edition of the Scriptures. David prays for the opening, the unveiling, of his eyes that he might understand better and better the wondrous things out of God's Law.

The Scriptures need opening and unveiling. But the veil does not hang over the inspired Book. The veil lies on our hearts. The darkness is in our eyes and understanding. David had read the Bible of his day from end to end, and yet he felt the need of more light. He felt that he needed to see deeper and deeper into the wellsprings of revelation. His understanding needed to be sharpened and its range lengthened.

Only God can unveil and open the eyes of our understanding. The Holy Spirit is the unveiler. He illumines the heart and the mind. He gives insight and faith. God's Holy Spirit opens, expounds, and applies God's life-giving Word.

"Open my eyes, that I may behold wondrous things out of Your law."
Amen.

—⟋⟍—

September 25, 1954

—ɷ—

Read Psalm 23
For you know that the testing of your faith produces steadfastness.
James 1:3

A RESULT OF FAITH

Who has patience these days? What some people call patience is more fitly called lack of interest, apathy, or just plain indolence, laziness.

The believer in Jesus Christ has patience. Faith gives patience. We all have probably learned patience in the manner in which God's children generally learn it, through trial.

God puts His people's faith to the test. They are in some trouble. God seems to pay no attention to their prayers. Exasperating! Why does God not *do* something about my trouble? Why must *I* suffer? Why do other people get *everything*, while I must do without?

As long as we think like that, we are not getting practical value out of our faith.

However, if we have a problem, a loss, a disappointment, a bereavement, a misfortune in any form, we should tell God about it and then let the matter rest in God's hand. Trusting in faith that God will do what needs doing on His part, we shall discover that our faith is stronger, and, besides, we shall have become quiet in our mind, fretting will have been overcome, and we will be patient, for we *know* God will take care of us.

Dear Jesus, we pray that the trials of life may strengthen our faith and bear such fruit as You will be pleased to give. Amen.

—ɷ—

September 26, 1956

—ᴍ—

Read Matthew 28:16–20
Psalm 119:137–144

Whoever speaks, as one who speaks oracles of God; whoever serves, as one who serves by the strength that God supplies—in order that in everything God may be glorified through Jesus Christ. *1 Peter 4:11*

SAY SOMETHING!

There is no doubt about it: Christians are to speak. This was true also of the believers of old, as the psalmist said, "Let the redeemed of the LORD say so" (107:2). Peter's statement answers the question: *How* should a Christian speak? He should speak as the spokesman of God. Surely this is binding on those called to preach and teach publicly. But what is expected of ministers in public is expected of all Christians in their daily contacts with other people.

What is there for Christians to say? As God's spokesmen, let them repeat and apply what God Himself has said to people in their several conditions and needs. To the *godless*: "The fool says in his heart, 'There is no God'" (Psalm 14:1). To the *penitent:* "Though your sins are like scarlet, they shall be as white as snow" (Isaiah 1:18). To the *weak*: "As your days, so shall your strength be" (Deuteronomy 33:25). To the *lonely*: "I will never leave you nor forsake you" (Hebrews 13:5). To the *troubled:* "All things work together for good, for those who are called according to His purpose" (Romans 8:28). To the *fearful:* "Fear not, for I am with you; be not dismayed, for I am your God; I will strengthen you, I will help you, I will uphold you with My righteous right hand" (Isaiah 41:10). The fact that these are God's words gives force to what we say.

Dear God, let me speak of Thy justice and Thy love. Amen.

—ᴍ—

September 27, 1970

SEPTEMBER 28

—⚹—

Read 1 Corinthians 10:11–13
Psalm 73
God is faithful, and He will not let you be tempted beyond your ability.
1 Corinthians 10:13

HE CARES FOR YOU

A t times, the weary Christian feels that God is asking too much. Illness, loss of job, and deep sorrow fall upon us. We may even complain that God is not fair. We see no point in suffering, hardship, and trials. They tempt us to despair of God's goodness and mercy.

Just as athletes know that muscles and endurance are strengthened by the stress of weights, Christians confess that suffering and trials are among God's tools to strengthen and refine faith (1 Peter 1:6–7). We have this confidence because Christ has entered into our trials, carried their weight, and given us His victory.

But God also knows that sorrow, grief, trials, and temptation can crush us. He knows our breaking point and promises never to exceed it. Because Christ put on our created flesh to suffer and die for us, we may be confident that His promises are faithful and true.

God also provides a way for us to escape every temptation that we may be able to bear it. That way is Jesus Christ, who bore the real brunt of our sins. He endured the real suffering and pain, even death. He removed the real burden of our sins and promises us that beyond the cross is the crown of everlasting life. Even in our deepest depression, we know that He is faithful and that He cares for us.

Grant us, Lord, the heavenly vision that lies beyond this troublesome life, for Jesus' sake. Amen.

—⚹—

September 22, 2005

SEPTEMBER 29

—∿∿—

Read Genesis 32:22–32
Psalm 28
The people of Israel do not eat the sinew of the thigh that is on the hip
socket, because he touched the socket of Jacob's hip on the sinew
of the thigh. *Genesis 32:32*

SACRED SCARS

He walked with a limp. It could have been a reminder of a tragic injury. Instead, it was a reminder of God's mercy. God met Jacob in the middle of a desperate, fearsome night. God injured Jacob's hip, but blessed him as well. That hampered hip would remind Jacob of the blessing and the new name God had given him. He would no longer be "heel grabber" Jacob, but Israel—"he who struggles with God." Israel's descendants counted as sacred, as a remembrance of God's grace, the joint that was touched.

We all carry scars. Some scars appear on our bodies, others in our thoughts and feelings. Scars remind us of injuries we have survived—by God's grace.

God Himself has scars. Even Jesus' glorified body in heaven still carries the scars of His crucifixion. These sacred scars are reminders of what He suffered for us and that the price for sin has been paid. They are also the pledge that whatever God may allow in our life, the purpose is not to damage, but to build up and heal. Strengthened by His promise, we cling to Him in faith.

Lord Jesus, remind me by Your scars that Your gracious power is always at work, accomplishing Your purpose of love in my life. Amen.

—∿∿—

September 29, 2006

SEPTEMBER 30

—⟶⟵—

Read Zechariah 4:1–6
Psalm 143
When the Spirit of truth comes, He will guide you into all the truth.
John 16:13

ON BEING FILLED WITH THE SPIRIT

Someone asked Martin Luther, "Sir, do you *feel* you are saved?" He answered, "No, I don't *feel* I am saved; I *know* on the ground of God's Word that I am saved."

His certainty and that of other Christians came not from feelings, but from God's Word. Feelings are not the way to certainty; certainty is the way to feelings. When we rest on feelings, our certainty vanishes when we don't feel well.

The work of the Holy Spirit centers in functions, not feelings. Feelings do not cause us to be filled with the Spirit, nor are they the sign that we are so filled. What is important is the actual presence of the Holy Spirit, not the sensation of His presence.

In possessing and expressing the fruit of the Spirit—"love, joy, peace, patience, kindness, goodness, faithfulness, gentleness, self-control"—we show that we are filled with the Spirit (see Galatians 5:22–23).

Like every other gift of God, the filling or anointing of the Holy Spirit is received by faith. Believing that we are filled with the Spirit is taking God at His Word. To continue in the Holy Spirit is to continue in Christ's Word. Then we are truly His disciples.

O Holy Spirit, You brought us to Christ; now keep us in Jesus Christ, and make us like Him in all things. Amen.

—⟶⟵—

September 27, 1980

October

Give us grace, dear Lord, that we may receive with gladness the salvation offered us through Jesus Christ. Amen.

OCTOBER 1

—⚋—

Read Exodus 20:1–21
Psalm 14
The fool says in his heart, "There is no God." *Psalm 14:1*

THERE ARE NO REAL ATHEISTS

The Bible has little interest in proving the existence of God. That God exists is assumed. Only a fool would believe otherwise. The Bible is much more concerned with idolatry, that is, dedication and devotion to the substitute gods that the human mind makes for itself. These idols are anything that a person fears, loves, and trusts more than the living God. They are as endless as the human imagination.

Mark Twain once quipped that in the beginning, God created man in His own image, and ever since, man has been returning the compliment. Homemade gods are most often reflections of the self. If we forsake the Word of the Lord, it is not that we become godless but that we fashion something in creation, such as wealth or health, an ideology, or maybe even our own reputation, as the object of our trust. Whatever your heart trusts is, in fact, your god.

Self-made gods will always fail. They promise life but give death. They entice with pleasure but deliver pain. The true God, the God and Father of our Lord Jesus Christ, is trustworthy and true. He stands behind His name and His Word. He keeps His promise to be your God and Lord in life and in death. Where He is Lord, there is room for no rivals.

Lord Jesus, keep my heart and mind anchored in You alone. Amen.

—⚋—

October 2, 2007

OCTOBER 2

—⁂—

Read Genesis 18:1–14
Psalm 103
Sarah conceived and bore Abraham a son in his old age at the time
of which God had spoken to him. *Genesis 21:2*

IS ANYTHING TOO HARD FOR THE LORD?

Abraham and Sarah had waited for God to keep His promise of an heir. Eventually, it seemed—at least by all human standards—that it was no longer possible. They were both simply too old for children. Then, when God visited them and reminded them of His promise, Sarah laughed. She was sure that she knew better.

To her laugh, God asked this rhetorical question: "Is anything too hard for the LORD?" (Genesis 18:14). God then used His limitless power to set in motion His plan of salvation in spite of her disbelief. Sarah, in bearing Isaac, became an ancestor of Jesus.

That promise of salvation exists for each of us. How can we, so full of sin, be saved? Even while we laugh like Sarah at what seems to be an impossible task, God chides our unbelief, saying, "Nothing is too hard. Your salvation has already been accomplished. I have sent My only Son. He died for you. You are Mine."

Now we laugh with the joy of a beloved child secure in her father's arms. We are forgiven. Through the power of the Spirit, faith lives and grows within us, and nothing can pluck us from the hand of God.

Father all-powerful, I would believe; help my unbelief. Amen.

—⁂—

October 2, 2010

OCTOBER 3

—m—

Read Exodus 15:1–21
Psalm 88
Singing and making melody to the Lord with your heart, giving thanks
always and for everything to God the Father in the name of our Lord
Jesus Christ. *Ephesians 5:19–20*

THE URGE TO SING

Isn't it strange how the urge to sing may come to us? Driving on an interstate highway, we may flick on the CB and suddenly hear some happy fellow driver joyfully singing along with a tune on the radio. We may have just heard some good news in the doctor's office, and we have an urge to sing out of joy and gratitude.

Our heavenly Father calls on us to have the urge regularly to sing. He gives us ample reason for breaking out in song. His design for our singing is that it grows out of music in our hearts to the Lord. Moment to moment, we are filled with the memory of God's goodness and mercy. Our hearts have reason for bubbling over with music as we eagerly thank God the Father for everything. That is a rather challenging word, isn't it? *Thank* God for everything! *Thank* God for some of the troubles and burdens we have? Can we ever forget the prisoner Paul and his companion Silas as they sang praise to God at midnight? Thinking of what Jesus means to us—He is our Savior from sin—gives us reason for having the urge to sing.

*Gracious God, help us to have music in our hearts as we experience
Your goodness in Christ. Amen.*

—m—

October 3, 1990
On this date in 1990, reunification of Germany

OCTOBER 4

—∿—

Read Matthew 10:7–13
Psalm 142

Acquire no gold nor silver nor copper for your belts, no bag for your journey, nor two tunics nor sandals nor a staff. *Matthew 10: 9–10*

YOU CAN TAKE HIM WITH YOU

Today is the feast day of Francis of Assisi, to commemorate the date Jesus summoned Francis from the Church Militant on earth to the Church Triumphant. St. Francis's battle against sin, death, and the devil is a fascinating story. As he listened to the Scripture reading of Jesus sending out the Twelve, Francis personally heard the commission of Christ. The once wealthy cloth merchant dropped his cloak, sandals, and staff at the church door. With nothing but a peasant's tunic, he set out to preach the Gospel and serve God's people. Francis's journeys for the cause of Christ took him as far as Egypt. His care for the poor inspired thousands. At age 44, Francis lay blind and ill in a little hut near his hometown. Singing Psalm 142 with his friends, he died. Throughout his adult life, nothing could distract him from his call to serve his Lord.

Jesus gave His all to save us. Nothing could distract Him from that mission. Should we not turn aside from every distraction to serve Him? With all who have followed Jesus before us, we rejoice that He gave up everything for us. Because Christ has given all for us, let us give our all to serve Him, to give Him honor and praise.

Heavenly Father, let us gladly listen to Your call and serve You with faithfulness. In Christ's name. Amen.

—∿—

October 4, 1997
On this date in 1957, the Soviet
Union launches Sputnik 1

OCTOBER 5

—∿—

Read Colossians 3:16–25
God settles the solitary in a home. *Psalm 68:6*

ARE YOU LONESOME?

In His wise and kind providence, God permits us to grow up in families and through life supplies us with relatives and friends. But you are alone? You are living all alone? Do not cultivate loneliness. Beware of indulging in self-pity and becoming self-centered! Still it is true what God said in creation: "It is not good that the man should be alone" (Genesis 2:18). There may be circumstances beyond your control that compel you to *live* by yourself; but you need not *keep* to yourself. Relatives and old friends may have departed; but you need not *remain* alone. Still, it is true: "God settles the solitary in a home."

Your congregation is the spiritual family into which God has placed you. There, you will find brethren and sisters in the faith. There are those who for Christ's sake will take an interest in you, be kind, sympathetic, and helpful. If your health permits, go forth from your lonesome quarters; bring helpful companionship to another who may be in greater need than you. Forget yourself in ministering to others.

In any case, Jesus, your heavenly friend, is ever with you. He assures you: "I will never leave you nor forsake you" (Hebrews 13:5). The covenant He made with you in Holy Baptism stands.

Jesus, my heavenly friend, teach me to value Thy presence;
by Thy love, move me to help others. Amen.

—∿—

October 5, 1949

OCTOBER 6

—⚡—

Read Matthew 3:13–17
Psalm 29
This is My beloved Son, with whom I am well pleased; listen to Him.
Matthew 17:5

VOICES FROM HEAVEN

L istening is a lost art. As more and more stimuli are presented to us through an ever-growing variety of media,
our ability to focus our attention decreases. If a wife has
trouble getting through to her husband because of the newspaper
or football game on TV, or if a parent has difficulty being understood by the teenager because of headphones, how likely is it that
distractions prevent us from hearing God's Word?

For all those present at the Baptism of Jesus by John in the
Jordan River, or for Peter, James, and John at the transfiguration of
Jesus, attention was no problem. A voice was heard that affirmed
what they were seeing, a voice cutting through every distraction
and announcing that Jesus is the beloved Son of God, who is worthy of all our attention: "Listen to Him"!

That same voice comes to us through the Holy Scriptures. By
the work of the Holy Spirit, that Word gains our complete attention as it exposes our sin and leads us to our Savior, who died on
the cross for our sins. God has the power to restore in us the art
of listening to Him. Though the clamor of competing faiths and
philosophies is deafening in our world, His voice speaks the truth
that leads us to eternal life.

Dear heavenly Father, open my ears that I might always eagerly hear
Your truth in Jesus Christ. Amen.

—⚡—

October 6, 1998

October 7

—ᴍᴍ—

Read Proverbs 6:16–22
Psalm 25
There are six things that the LORD hates, seven that are an abomination
to Him: haughty eyes, a lying tongue, and hands that shed innocent blood,
a heart that devises wicked plans, feet that make haste to run to evil, a
false witness who breathes out lies, and one who sows discord among
brothers. *Proverbs 6:16–19*

WATCHING FOR THINGS GOD HATES

In the face of the things God hates, who can plead innocence? See further delineation of these in Matthew 15:19-20: "Out of the heart come evil thoughts, murder, adultery, sexual immorality, theft, false witness, slander. These are what defile a person."

These are the specific behaviors of people that produce uncleanness in themselves and suffering for others—things that are detested by God. On the Lord's Day, as on every day, it is time to take stock of our lives. We have opportunity to receive forgiveness and Christ's strong nourishment in the Lord's Supper for the strength and power to amend our ways.

We come to the foot of the cross, and there we lay our sins of rebellion against God's holy will. We leave God's house of worship clean of the stains of our sin, for God has bestowed on us the forgiveness won for us by the death of His Son on the cross.

*O God, when I do the things You despise, remind me that I am
nevertheless the object of Your love, for whom You gave Your Son
that I might be with You forever. In His name. Amen.*

—ᴍᴍ—

October 7, 2001
On this date in 2001,
war in Afghanistan begins

OCTOBER 8

—〰—

Read Genesis 29:31–35
Psalm 42
[Leah] conceived again and bore a son, and said, "This time I will praise the LORD." *Genesis 29:35*

SECOND BANANA

L eah felt like what modern slang would call a "second banana." Jacob was in love with her sister Rachel, who was very beautiful. Leah had "weak eyes." Leah's conniving father, Laban, had exchanged Leah for Rachel on Jacob's wedding night. Jacob was married to Leah, and her whole life was filled with Jacob's overt favoritism for her sister. Leah tried to win Jacob's love by providing sons for him.

Leah's strategy did not work; her life was torture. Favoritism hurts. Leah was desperate. She gave hopeful names to her first three sons: Reuben (I'm seen), Simeon (I'm heard), and Levi (I'm attached). But with son number four, Leah's attitude changes: "This time I will praise the LORD" (Judah).

Look in the mirror. Do you sometimes see a Leah? Do you ever feel like a "second banana"? There are no "second bananas" in God's family! What God sees when He looks at you is His beautiful child, for whom His Son gave His life on the cross. That's you!

Leah turned to the source of love and praised the Lord. God heard her anxious cries. Leah's fourth son, Judah, became an ancestor of God's own Son, Jesus. What a beautiful blessing God placed on her! And beautiful are His daily blessings of love to us.

Jesus, thank You for blessing me with Your holy love. Fill me with the joy of Your salvation! Amen.

—〰—

October 8, 2002

Read James 1:22–25
Psalm 96
The one who looks into the perfect law, the law of liberty,
and perseveres ... he will be blessed in his doing. *James 1:25*

TRUE CHRISTIAN FREEDOM

Jesus says in the story of the publican and the Pharisee that the Pharisee wanted to justify himself. Self-justification is one of the great human drives. Nearly all people will admit to their personal imperfection in some way, but all want to be regarded as acceptable to God and others. They do not understand that God demands perfection.

Part of Christian life is daily looking into the mirror of God's Law. Through self-examination, we see ourselves as sinners who constantly offend God. God's Law as a mirror gives us a chance to see our faults and correct them. If we look into a mirror to check our appearance and don't correct what is amiss, that mirror serves no purpose. Unless we do something with our sinful lives, the Law has no purpose.

Because the Law has been fulfilled by Christ, it no longer accuses the Christian. We can live victoriously because Christ has borne the Law's curses and accusations. Christians are righteous not because of their own righteousness but because of Christ's. This gives true Christian freedom to live according to God's Law. We do it not because we have to, but because we want to.

Lord Jesus, I have found freedom through the Gospel. May Your righteousness be seen in my life. Amen.

—⚏—

October 9, 1979

Read Matthew 5:33–37
Let what you say be simply 'Yes' or 'No'; anything more than this
comes from evil. *Matthew 5:37*

SAY WHAT YOU MEAN; MEAN WHAT YOU SAY!

Several popular television programs present guests before a panel of experts who try to guess their occupation or some event in their life. Rules of the program call for questions that can be answered with yes or no.

When a person is on trial in court, witnesses are instructed to answer questions with yes and no. Responses modified by reservations like "maybe" or "I think so" are not acceptable.

Many people have not learned the art of plain and simple language. They flavor their speech with too many needlessly emphatic words. Some people feel we do not trust them unless they enforce their words with an oath.

Jesus tells us, "In your talk, all you need is a simple 'yes' and 'no'." That is sufficient. True words need no oaths. Oaths may be spoken when required. Jesus Himself used one in court. Everyday speech with our friends and neighbors should be plain. God does not permit every kind of oath. The person whose heart is true to God utters every statement as made in His presence and finds no reason to add anything to "yes" and "no."

O God, keep my speech free from words that are not pleasing to Thee.
Amen.

—ᵐᵐ—

October 10, 1957

OCTOBER 11

—ᴍ—

Read Matthew 8:23–27
What sort of man is this, that even winds and sea obey Him?
Matthew 8:27

WHAT SORT OF MAN?

The disciples marveled time and again at the evidences of Jesus' supernatural power. He gave sight to the blind; He healed the lepers; He made water into wine. And now, crossing the storm-tossed Sea of Galilee with His disciples in a frail boat, He speaks a word to the elements. At once, the wind dies away, and the waters become smooth as glass. Small wonder that the astonished disciples cried: "What sort of man is this, that even winds and sea obey Him?"

The cry "What sort of man?" has echoed down the ages as men have beheld the miracle-working power of the Son of God. What sort of man is this, whose coming changed the course of history? What sort of man is this, who has power on earth to forgive sins? What sort of man is this, who calls Himself the way, the truth, and the life? What sort of man is this, whom even the bonds of death could not hold?

What sort of man? He is the God-man. He is the Lord of glory. He is our Savior, our dearest Friend.

Unheard, because our ears are dull,
Unseen, because our eyes are dim,
He walks our earth, The Wonderful,
And all good deeds are done to Him. (John Greenleaf Whittier,
    "Saint Gregory's Guest," 1886)

*O Thou, whose voice can still the restless waves, speak words
of peace to our troubled hearts. Amen.*

—ᴍ—

October 11, 1959

OCTOBER 12

—ɷ—

Read Hebrews 11:1–6
Now faith is the assurance of things hoped for. *Hebrews 11:1*

BY FAITH

People in the Western Hemisphere celebrate the discovery of America today. By coming upon this new land, Columbus touched off a series of changes in world history. Columbus believed he was sailing to a rich land. But the problems aboard ship nearly disrupted his plans. Discouraged sailors were at the point of mutiny.

Faith was restored before they sighted land. Green leaves and branches of trees floated toward them. Reassured, Columbus sailed on in confidence to the Bahamas.

This is an illustration of Christian faith. "Now faith is the assurance of things hoped for, the conviction of things not seen."

We hope for the glory of heaven. We are certain of redeeming love through Christ. We are confident that in some way, all things work together for our good. We know God forgives our guilt through the completed work of Jesus.

Yet our faith weakens when we fail to "see" His helping hand. Troubles discourage. Burdens load our thoughts. Our lack of trust wants to lead to a rebellious mutiny against God.

Here, God reassures us. As leaves floating on the sea strengthened Columbus, so evidence of God's love comes to us. He answers a need through His Word. He provides an unexpected solution to a problem.

These blessings move us to say, "Why was I ever uncertain of His love?"

Lord, make me certain of Thee and Thy love. Amen.

—ɷ—

October 12, 1955

OCTOBER 13

—᙮ᙡ᙮—

Read 2 Corinthians 2:14–17
Psalm 40
For we are the aroma of Christ to God among those who are being
saved and among those who are perishing. *2 Corinthians 2:15*

THE AROMA OF CHRIST

We all know that the same aroma may cause two different responses. To me, the aroma of liver and onions frying in a pan is fragrant. To my wife, it repels! Have you ever thought of Christ as an aroma that gets different reactions? Have you ever thought of yourself as being that aroma? That's what Paul would have us do in today's verse.

When we share the truth about Christ, we are His aroma. To those clinging to their own truth, the aroma of Christ repels. They reject Christ's truth. They do not want to hear it because it contradicts their chosen lifestyle or way of thinking. Tragically, to them, the aroma of Christ is the smell of death.

To those who realize that relying on themselves only leads to heartache and destruction, the aroma of Christ is fragrant! The truth about Christ on the cross becomes the fragrance of forgiveness. The truth about being reconciled to God becomes the fragrance of peace. The truth about Christ's resurrection becomes the fragrance of hope. Wonderfully, to those who believe, the aroma of Christ is the fragrance of life!

Lord God, help us to be the aroma of Christ so that those trapped in the cycle of sin and death may come to know the fragrance of life. In His name. Amen.

—᙮ᙡ᙮—

October 13, 2003

OCTOBER 14

—∿—

Read I John 3:7–10
Little children, let us not love in word or talk but in deed and in truth.
I John 3:18

CREED AND DEED

Have you ever wondered if you are really a Christian? Apply this test. Does love for my fellow man well up in my heart? If Christ is in me, it will.

But what about my many failures to love? God knows what is in our hearts. He knows our love. But He also knows that this love is at times dim and feeble. And He knows how sorry we are when we fail in love.

Two things, says John, every Christian must do. One is to believe that Jesus Christ is God's Son and his Savior. The other is to love his fellow man. Christian life depends on right belief and right conduct. Pure doctrine and pure life go together. Satan chuckles when a man of impure life insists on pure doctrine.

We begin the Christian life when we receive Jesus Christ as our Savior and Lord. Thereafter, our attitude is the same as His, an attitude of love. Because He lives in us, we will want to go His way. Whenever we fail, we are sorry, we repent of our failures and bring them under His victory. In His strength we strive to do better, to reflect His presence.

Thou great lover of all mankind, praise be to Thee for leading us to the fountain of divine love. Fill our hearts with love for all mankind, especially for those who, with us, are the children of God. Amen.

—∿—

October 14, 1962
On this date in 1962, Cuban Missile Crisis begins;
ends on October 28 with the announcment
that Soviet missiles will be withdrawn from Cuba

October 15

Read 2 Timothy 3:14–17
Psalm 119:97–104
From childhood you have been acquainted with the sacred writings,
which are able to make you wise for salvation through faith
in Christ Jesus. *2 Timothy 3:15*

WISE FOR SALVATION THROUGH FAITH

L uther found one principal cure for his depression at the Wartburg, and it worked. He wrote. He also translated the New Testament into his native German.

Luther wanted the people to be able to read the Scriptures in their language. Paul insisted that the Scriptures are "God-breathed." He is speaking here of the Old Testament; the New Testament was not yet established. Paul's description is just as true of the New Testament, which shows Christ fulfilling the Old.

The Scriptures are useful in teaching. Only in the Scriptures do we get a firsthand look at Jesus, His life, teaching, work, and gifts. The Scriptures are valuable for rebuking. They convince us of the error of our ways and point us to Christ Jesus, our Savior. The Scriptures give correction. Everything is to be tested by the Bible. And this use of Scripture is always to be done under Luther's rule that "Scripture interprets Scripture" with Christ as its heart and center.

Paul's final point is also important. Salvation is ours through the Scriptures, yet they bring us to Christ not for ourselves alone, but to equip us also to faithfully confess the Lord, who freely gave Himself to save the world.

Holy Spirit, through the Scriptures, fill me, mold me, and send me
in the name of Christ, who loves me. Amen.

October 15, 2005

OCTOBER 16

—⟋⟍—

Read 2 Kings 5:15–27
Psalm 32

Gehazi, the servant of Elisha the man of God, said ... "I will run after him and get something from him." *2 Kings 5:20*

GOD'S GRACE IS NOT FOR SALE

Would you recognize a good deal if you saw one? Gehazi thought he did. And so did Naaman. Naaman had been healed of leprosy. Elisha, the prophet of God, has instructed Naaman to bathe seven times in the Jordan River. Healed, Naaman was ready to reward the prophet generously. Elisha said, "No, thanks; it was the gift of God." Gehazi thought of all those "goodies" and went after Naaman. "My master has changed his mind. He could use some clothes and money for students." Gladly, Naaman gave them to Gehazi.

Maybe Gehazi felt that what Elisha didn't know wouldn't hurt him. But God's prophet knew. Gehazi was punished by receiving Naaman's leprosy.

In the day of the apostles, a man named Simon came to Peter, asking to buy the gift of God's grace. He wanted it so he could heal and sell his service to others. To this day, the selling of God's free gifts is named after him: simony. God intended that His grace in Christ be a free gift. It is not to be bought with either money or works. God said simply: "By grace you have been saved through faith. . . . It is the gift of God, not a result of works, so that no one may boast" (Ephesians 2:8–9).

Give us the grace to accept Your gifts of forgiveness and life, dear Lord. In Jesus' name we pray. Amen.

—⟋⟍—

October 16, 1989

OCTOBER 17

—ɷ—

Read Psalm 84

WHY DOES A CHRISTIAN GO TO CHURCH?

A Christian attends church *because of its blessings.* Which are these? What is man's greatest blessing? Well, what is man's greatest need? Man's greatest need is to have a reconciled God, to obtain the forgiveness of sin. This is the essence of religion. And now, what means yonder altar? the baptismal font? What does the pulpit stand for? Nowhere does God so richly dispense His grace and pardon as there. For all that this earth can offer, a Christian would not forego the quickened conscience, the hallowed thought, the sacred delights of devotion and strengthened hearth, the assurance of sins forgiven, the noble sentiments and emotions experienced in the house of God.

A Christian goes to church *for inspiration and Christian growth.* The body needs the Sunday to regain the energy lost during the week, and the soul needs worship to replenish it after the decline through the week. What we need is new strength, reinforcement. Where shall we find it? There is many a one who, when he has missed the services on the Lord's Day, feels that he has been robbed of "the weekly tonic."

The Christian goes to church *for comfort.* To wipe the tears of sorrow from the eyes, to drop balm into hearts that are desolate and rent, to aid men to bear courageously and submissively the burdens of life, to lift up, cheer, and invigorate the drooping spirit and fainting heart, there is nothing like a visit to the house of God.

Should we not, then, welcome entrance to it? Should it not claim our loyalty, our zeal, our regular attendance of the services?

—ɷ—

October 17, 1937

October 18

—∿—

Read 2 Timothy 3:1–9
Psalm 119:137–144
I will arise and go to my father, and I will say to him, "Father, I have sinned
against heaven and before you." *Luke 15:18*

A Plan for Action

The plan for action announced here is daring and bold, particularly since the young man's self-evaluation is a rationally accurate one. He is really saying to himself here: "I am a grievous sinner before both God and man, especially before my own father. Him I have despised and insulted; him I have shamed and dishonored. Of him I demanded my share of the inheritance and have squandered it. I am no more a son, nor am I really worthy of his consideration even as a hired hand."

So, having said all this, what conclusion does he reach? The one we would least expect: "I will arise and go to my father." There is no right or reason for this plan for action, except that the son still feels that, despite all, the father who gave him his inheritance will even now not turn away from his own sick, sad, sinful, but somewhat wiser son. He was correct on both counts: his estimate of himself and of his father.

How true of us, and how wonderfully true of our gracious Father! When we are in sin's distress, there is only one resolve: let us arise and go to our Father in Jesus' name. "If anyone does sin, we have an advocate with the Father, Jesus Christ. . . . He is the propitiation for our sins" (1 John 2:1–2).

Thanks be to Thee, O Father, for Thy forgiving arms that are ever open
to Thy unworthy children. In Jesus' name. Amen.

—∿—

October 18, 1969

Read John 5:39–47
And sent his servants to call those who were invited to the wedding
feast, but they would not come. *Matthew 22:3*

WHY SOME MEN REFUSE

Nowhere in secular history do we hear of a people so rude to their king as these people in the parable. Most men would call it a great honor to be invited to the palace and to sit at the royal table. It is only the Lord God Himself whom men treat so ill, for it is He who sent His servants to call men to the wedding feast, and the King's Son of whom the parable speaks is our Lord Jesus Christ.

They would not come. That has been the sad story down through the ages. God's own people in ancient times begged to be excused. This has always been the case wherever the invitation has been given. Men will not come.

Nothing difficult is asked of them. No large sum of money is needed to gain a place in the banquet hall, and no effort is required on man's part. It is not a weary task that is demanded of man but rather an invitation to a joyous festival, the marriage of the King's Son.

It is man's own unbelief that causes him to refuse God's wedding invitation. We cannot by our reason and strength *choose* to believe in the saving power of the Lord Jesus, but we have the awful power to *refuse*. It is man's own sin that causes him to turn aside and be lost.

Give us grace, dear Lord, that we may receive with gladness the salvation offered us through Jesus Christ. Amen.

—〜〜—

October 19, 1942

OCTOBER 20

—꩜—

Read Revelation 2:24–29
My teaching is not Mine, but His who sent Me. *John 7:16*

ON THIS ROCK

Too many people feel that what they believe is not really important. It is only important that they believe something.

This is the kind of thinking that allows many parents to raise their children as spiritual delinquents. When it comes to eating, no parent allows his child to grow up only on candy and pop, no matter how much the child begs. Neither does the wise parent leave his child adrift in the field of religion without encouragement and counsel.

No student would think of inventing his own formulas in the field of physics. He would not be allowed to set up his own multiplication table. But in religion, too many forget that *what* they believe is as important as belief itself.

The Bible simply does not allow us to invent our own faith. For those who questioned His teaching, Jesus had the ideal answer. "My teaching is not Mine," He said, "but His who sent Me" (John 7:16).

Our answer should be the same. God's truth does not change. Not only did Jesus proclaim it during His years on earth, but also through His apostles He left an inspired record for all to trust and to consult for all time.

This Word is a trustworthy guide, able to lead us through the hills and valleys of our earthly way.

Make Thy Word, O Lord, the lamp to our feet and the light to our path. Amen.

—꩜—

October 20, 1960

OCTOBER 21

—w—

Read Acts 26:24–32
Psalm 29
Agrippa said to Paul, "In a short time would you persuade me
to be a Christian?" Acts 26:28

THE PERIL OF POSTPONEMENT

St. Augustine, in the early days of his spiritual struggle, prayed, "Lord, save me from my sins, but not just yet." That made him even more miserable than he was before. Later, he came to a point where he prayed, "Lord, save me from all my sins except one." That made him feel like the greatest sinner on earth. Finally, he learned to pray, "Lord, save me from all my sins, and save me now." When he was finally led to quit postponing his complete surrender to the grace of God, he found his Savior, and that was the end of his struggle.

Many people try to postpone their relationship with Jesus Christ. It may be natural to postpone the more disagreeable things in life, but why does a person postpone the salvation of his or her precious soul and say with King Agrippa, "In a short time would you persuade me to be a Christian?" It doesn't make sense. These people rob themselves of living their lives with Christ, and if they persist, they will live forever without Him.

Let us remember that God sent His Son into the world not to suit our convenience as sinners but to save our souls.

Lord, save me from all my sins, and save me now. Amen.

—w—

October 21, 1986

OCTOBER 22

—ɷ—

Read Luke 22:39–46
Being in an agony He prayed more earnestly. *Luke 22:44*

PRAYING EARNESTLY

We all pray. We would not be Christians if we did not pray. But the questions follow: How do we pray? How often? How much? In what spirit? And how earnestly?

We all know that to pray means more than to "say prayers" morning and night. The short prayers memorized in childhood days are certainly not without value, even in adult life. But our use of them may so easily become routine and mechanical. The Lord's Prayer is a priceless jewel; but, as Luther has remarked, it is "the greatest martyr" because it is so much abused. As adult Christians, we should learn to use the Lord's Prayer as a guide, a line of thought, a framework about which to build our own prayers. From our beloved Master, we are to learn how to pray first for the glory of God and then for our own and our neighbor's spiritual and physical wants.

Then there will be critical hours in our lives when we must learn from our Savior to pray "more earnestly." In Gethsemane, crushed under the burden of the world's sin, Jesus gave Himself more earnestly to prayer and thus found strength and peace. When we are in agony of mind and heart, wrestling with some perplexing problem or burdened with a great sorrow, we also shall find relief by praying more earnestly.

Lord, teach us to pray in faith and in submission: to pray
sincerely, earnestly, perseveringly.

—ɷ—

October 22, 1948

OCTOBER 23

—𝔪—

Read Psalm 46
Come away by yourselves to a desolate place and rest a while. *Mark 6:31*

TAKE A BREAK

Tradition has it that when the apostle John was overseer in Ephesus, his hobby was raising pigeons. One day, another elder, returning from hunting, saw John playing with one of the birds. The man rebuked him for spending his time so unproductively. John looked at the hunter's bow and commented that its string was loose. "Yes," the elder said, "I loosen the string in my bow when I am not using it. If I kept it tightly strung, it would damage the bow and fail me when I need it." John then said, "And I am now relaxing the bow of my mind so that I may be better able to shoot the arrows of divine truth."

We cannot do our best work when we are under constant pressure. We need, sometimes, to take a break. In the midst of all the activity recorded in Mark 6—casting out demons, healing the sick, the death of a dear friend—Jesus takes His friends aside for some rest.

You needn't feel guilty when you take a break. Whether it is with a hobby, a good book, a vacation, take a break with Jesus. Go off to a quiet place to spend some time with Him. Taking a break with Him is important for a productive walk with Him through life.

Dear Lord, let me find a quiet place where I can rest with You. Amen.

—𝔪—

October 23, 1996

OCTOBER 24

—∿—

Read 2 Timothy 4:16–18
Psalm 34
Many are the afflictions of the righteous, but the LORD delivers him
out of them all. *Psalm 34:19*

DELIVERANCE

We all have troubles and worries that plague us. In our wishful thinking, peace of mind often begins with the words, "If only . . . " Psalm 34 says, "Many are the afflictions of the righteous, but the LORD delivers him out of them all." Our response to that may be, "*If only* He would deliver me . . . *and right now!*"

Consider the troubles Jesus had when He lived among us. He was harassed and accused by His enemies, betrayed and denied by His closest friends, condemned in an unjust trial, and tortured to death on a cross. Yet through Jesus' suffering, God was carrying out His plan to deliver us from the troubles of sin, guilt, and eternal death.

Peace of mind doesn't begin with "if only." Peace comes in knowing that through Jesus' grief and suffering, God was steadily at work to deliver us. And as surely as God was at work in Jesus to save us, He is now at work in our lives as well. "He who did not spare His own Son but gave Him up for us all, how will He not also . . . graciously give us all things?" (Romans 8:32). The promise still stands: "Many are the afflictions of the righteous, but the LORD delivers him out of them all."

Christ, our Lord, deliver us according to Your promises! Amen.

—∿—

October 24, 1999

OCTOBER 25

—ɷ—

Read James 2:14–26
Psalm 119:153–160
They who wait for the LORD shall renew their strength; they shall
mount up with wings like eagles. *Isaiah 40:31*

UP AND AT THEM!

Time and time again, we hear the remark, "I've had it! I just can't do any more." From a human point of view, that is probably true. The demands of our daily routine, the demands placed upon us by the family, the requests for help that come from the congregation—all seemingly come at us at the same time and seem to swamp us! Probably the first reaction is not one of "up and at them." On the contrary, it may be the desire to drop everything for the time being and take care of oneself. After all, the adage says, "If you don't take care of yourself, nobody else will."

However, as we arrange our priorities and put them in order, beginning with our responsibilities to the Lord, everything will fall into place. The prophet Isaiah learned this well in his time. He spelled it out very clearly: "He gives power to the faint, and to him who has no might He increases strength" (40:29).

What a great God He is, providing us with all that we need for body and soul! He invites us to draw upon His strength and His power—His sufficient grace in Christ, our Savior. To Him shall be all glory and honor forevermore.

Father in heaven, grant us the courage and strength to fulfill
all our responsibilities; in Jesus' name. Amen.

—ɷ—

October 25, 1982

Read Revelation 11:15–19
Psalm 128
The kingdom of the world has become the kingdom of our Lord and
of His Christ, and He shall reign forever and ever. *Revelation 11:15*

KING FOREVER

When the eighty-six-year-old Polycarp, an early Christian Church Father, had been burned at the stake, the congregation at Smyrna wrote an account of it, dating the martyrdom of their pastor with the triumphant words: "Statius Quadratus being proconsul, but Jesus Christ being King forever." Where today is Statius Quadratus? and Herod? and Nero? and the dictators of the World War II era? and all who set themselves against the Lord and His Anointed?

Truly, Jesus Christ is King forever. And His kingdom, the Church, remains forever. "For not like kingdoms of the world, Thy holy Church, O God, Though earthquake shocks are threatening her And tempests are abroad" ("O Where Are Kings and Empires Now," st. 3; Arthur C. Coxe, 1839). The eternal Christ—the same yesterday, today, and forever! What a King we have! And it is His pleasure to give us the Kingdom and in it make us kings and priests, as John declares: "To Him who loves us and has freed us from our sins by His blood and made us a kingdom, priests to His God and Father, to Him be glory and dominion forever and ever" (Revelation 1:5–6). Human rulers are puppets for a day, but Christ is King forever.

Jesus, my eternal King, You have made me Yours, that I may live under You in Your kingdom and serve You. Amen.

—⟡—

October 26, 1981

Read Revelation 2:8–11
Psalm 73
Then I discerned their end. *Psalm 73:17*

THE BOTTOM LINE

In the business world, people do not judge a project by its ups and downs. The bottom line, showing final profit or loss, determines the success or failure of a venture.

The psalmist Asaph, chief musician at the Lord's tabernacle in the days of King David, learned that also life has a bottom line. For a time, he could not understand why he, a faithful servant of the Lord, was obliged to endure much trouble and hardship while wicked and arrogant people, who mocked God, seemed to be carefree and to have no problems or ills. Their prosperity made him envious. Almost, he confesses, he was persuaded to follow the example of the ungodly to see if things would go better for him.

The problem was too difficult to grasp until he entered the sanctuary of God. Then he understood the end of the wicked. The bottom line was not how well things might be going at a given time, but where a person stands at the end.

The end of the ungodly is destruction and eternal damnation, but for the godly, who by faith have the righteousness of Jesus Christ, who remain faithful to the Lord and let Him lead them, it is everlasting life with God in glory.

Help us, Lord, to understand that what really counts is a blessed end.
Assist us to remain faithful and obtain the crown of everlasting life.
Amen.

—᙮᙮—

October 27, 1984

October 28

—ᴍ—

Read 1 Corinthians 15:9–11
Psalm 119:89–96
But by the grace of God I am what I am. *1 Corinthians 15:10*

By Grace I Am What I Am

Paul's past haunted him. The wrong he had done kept accusing him. But every time it did, he could say, "God forgives me, for Jesus' sake. Because of Jesus' death and resurrection, my sin is not counted against me. I am actually one of God's saints. By grace I am what I am."

Paul most likely would have continued his opposition to the Gospel if Christ had not stopped him on the way to Damascus. But God's grace brought this straying sinner to believe in the very Savior whom he had been opposing.

Where would we be if it were not for the grace of God? We, too, by our very nature, are straying sinners. We want to do our own thing. The Gospel of Christ seems foolishness to human reason.

But by the grace of God, our sin is not counted against us. We've been rescued. By the power of His Word and Sacraments, God moves us to trust in His mercy. By His grace, He will keep us in that saving faith.

Whatever we may face in life—a task in school, a choice of vocation, a challenging job, a project in our congregation—we need to remember that we succeed only by the grace of God. That grace keeps us going, gives us a goal, and guides us as we move through life.

Gracious Lord, preserve us in the true saving faith and help us safely move through life to eternity in heaven with You. Amen.

—ᴍ—

October 28, 1994

—m—

Read 1 Peter 3:18–22
Psalm 69:1–18
Baptism … saves you … as an appeal to God for a good conscience.
1 Peter 3:21

YOUR WORKING BAPTISM

An adult man was baptized. A few minutes after leaving the church, he came running back inside. "Pastor," he said, "I just had a horrible thought. So why didn't my Baptism work?" The pastor asked if he wanted that thought to be washed away and for pure, honorable thoughts to arise. The man answered, "Yes!" The pastor said, "Your Baptism is working just fine."

Holy Baptism is not a one-time shot or a merely symbolic act. It continues to save us. Yes, this holy washing defines and affects the whole of our lives in Christ Jesus while we are on this earth.

We live in a world drenched in the thoughts and works of sin. Baptism daily drowns in us every sin and evil desire so that we cry to God, yearning and pleading, "Let all that is hostile toward You be washed away. May Your loving child arise to delight in You!" Baptism daily raises us up clean and holy in God's sight through Christ Jesus (Titus 3:5).

Our sinful minds and hearts may rage, entice, and dream up horrible things. In Baptism, God gives us hearts that long to be free of every sinful thought, word, and deed (Galatians 2:20) and gives us good consciences and hearts that want to please Him.

Father and Son and Holy Spirit, thank You for the gift of my never-failing, ever-working Baptism. Amen.

—m—

October 29, 2008

Read 2 Corinthians 6:1–10
Psalm 20
Go to the ant, O sluggard; consider her ways, and be wise.
Proverbs 6:6

THE ANT'S EXAMPLE

The author of the Book of Proverbs has no use for the lazy man, nor patience with the loafer who lacks the initiative to develop his talents. He urges us to go to the ant and learn a lesson from it. He writes: "Consider her ways, and be wise. Without having any chief, officer, or ruler, she prepares her bread in summer and gathers her food in harvest. How long will you lie there, O sluggard? When will you arise from your sleep? A little sleep, a little slumber, a little folding of the hands to rest, and poverty will come upon you like a robber" (Proverbs 6:6–11).

There is no time like the present. This applies especially to our salvation, as St. Paul says: "Behold, now is the day of salvation" (2 Corinthians 6:2). Here in time, we must come to Christ's cross to be cleansed and healed. Then both now and in the life to come, we shall have a full supply of the bread of life.

O Lord, in Your goodness You have given us not only our daily bread but also Your grace in Christ crucified. Amen.

—w—

October 30, 1975

OCTOBER 31

—∽—

Read John 8:31–36
Psalm 46
The LORD is a refuge to His people, a stronghold to the people of Israel.
Joel 3:16

A MIGHTY FORTRESS IS OUR GOD

Some of the most impressive structures in Europe are the ancient castles that have stood for centuries. Virtually impenetrable, these miniature cities were a safe haven and ultimate source of security for those who lived within their walls. The fact that they still stand is a testament to their great strength.

Martin Luther's metaphor of God as a "mighty fortress" is especially fitting. Luther lived among castles, even in them at times. He saw them as silent reminders of awesome strength and security. He chose his words well. No longer fearing God as a wrathful judge, Luther now saw Him as a tower of strength.

On this Reformation Day, we give thanks for the sweet simplicity and awesome power of the Gospel message of redemption by grace through faith in Christ Jesus. By faith, we are able to see, as did Luther, that God is our refuge and strength. As God's beloved children, we turn to Him in every situation, knowing that we can totally entrust our lives to Him, be still, and know that He is God.

Let Satan try his best. Our God, our "fortress," is stronger. Eventually, all the ancient castles will crumble and fall, but the Word of the Lord will endure forever. "The kingdom ours remaineth."

**O almighty God, be our mighty fortress throughout our lives.
In Jesus' name we pray. Amen.**

—∽—

October 31, 1995

November

O God, we thank
Thee that Thou has
assured us that there
is forgiveness with
Thee, for Thou art
gracious and plenteous
in mercy. Amen.

November 1

—ᴧᴧ—

Read Revelation 7:9–17
Psalm 33

After this I looked, and behold, a great multitude that no one could number, from every nation, from all tribes and peoples and languages, standing before the throne and before the Lamb, clothed in white robes, with palm branches in their hands. *Revelation 7:9*

A Glorious Company

Today is All Saints' Day, dedicated to the memory of all whom God has welcomed into eternal joy. Gathered about God's throne, John saw a glorious company, drawn from every nation and race, dressed in white robes and singing praises to God and to the Lamb. They have been cleansed from sin by the blood of Jesus. They have been delivered from all troubles, trials, and sorrows. Now they enjoy the endless bliss of heaven and delight in serving God. These are God's saints, redeemed by the precious blood of Jesus.

Here is a blessed hope for all who "have washed their robes and made them white in the blood of the Lamb" (Revelation 7:14). Here on earth, we have our troubles and sorrows. But the Christian can face the future with hope and good cheer. For him the best is yet to be. One day, God will deliver him from all the evils of this life and welcome him into the glorious company of the saints in heaven.

For all the saints who from their labors rest,
Who Thee by faith before the world confessed,
Thy name, O Jesus, be forever blest. (*LSB* 677:1)

Grant, O God, that by Your grace we may be numbered among Your saints in glory. Amen.

—ᴧᴧ—

November 1, 1977

November 2

—⟪⟫—

Read Romans 12:9–21
Love one another with brotherly affection. Outdo one another
in showing honor. *Romans 12:10*

When Light Is Darkness

How is your disposition? Are you letting the Holy Spirit make you beautiful and attractive for Christ? Few things hinder the cause of Christ more than the bad attitude of some church members. A bad disposition has been called the "vice of the virtuous." A woman who would not think of gambling or drinking or attending places of worldly amusement may yet show a churlish temper, which puts her Christian confession under a shadow. A man may fight for the faith once delivered to the saints, yet be so hard to live with that he constantly keeps his family in hot water.

These are the coffin nails that have hurt many a church: irritability, fault-finding, peevishness, a hasty temper, resentfulness, lack of charity. These are attitudes far more like Satan than like Christ. The effect of Sunday services can be cut to splinters by choice bits of gossip on the front steps. Many a soul has been turned away from the Church by the ugly disposition of those who profess to be Christians.

The Holy Spirit offers us power to live lives of purity and love. He gives us power to repent when we have failed to reflect Christ accurately. Without this divine power, we will be church breakers. True Christians, however, are kingdom builders and display Christlikeness.

O Savior, help us in the Spirit to become sweet-tempered, true, sincere, good, as is proper for those who profess Thy holy name. Amen.

—⟪⟫—

November 2, 1958

NOVEMBER 3

—∿—

Read Genesis 3:8–15
Psalm 69
The LORD God called to the man and said to him, "Where are you?"
Genesis 3:9

A QUESTION OF HIDING FROM GOD

It is a tragic scene when people flee from our good and gracious God. He knew full well where Adam was and why Adam was trying to hide. Sin had brought shame on the first man.

Adam learned—and we know too—that trying to hide from an all-knowing and all-seeing God is not the solution to our problem of sin. Nor does it help to try to minimize the problem, or to pretend that our sin does not place us under the curse of God's Law, or that there is no eternal death or hell.

The solution begins when God searches for us. Adam soon learned that the God who asked "Where are you?" was not just condemning his guilt, but also planning his salvation. After Adam and Eve were both convicted of their sin, God immediately spoke His first messianic promise: The woman's seed or offspring, Jesus Christ, would crush Satan's head for them. Their sin forgiven through Jesus, they would have no more need to hide from God.

God comes looking for us. We cannot—we need not—hide. He comes offering forgiveness and new life in Christ. He comes to enrich us with every spiritual blessing, to make us fruitful in every good work to His glory.

Teach us, Lord, never to run or hide from Your loving presence,
for Christ has reconciled us to You. Amen.

—∿—

November 3, 1992

NOVEMBER 4

—w—

Read Luke 17:11–19
Psalm 121
One of them, when he saw that he was healed, turned back, praising God
with a loud voice. *Luke 17:15*

BE THE ONE

Jesus was on His way to Jerusalem. From a distance, a group of men, all afflicted with leprosy, called to Him, "Jesus, Master, have mercy on us" (v. 13). To have leprosy in Jesus' day was to live as an outcast, separated from loved ones and neighbors and all. Jesus directed them, "Go and show yourselves to the priests" (v. 14). Priests served as health officers in those days. As the men went, they were cleansed. They were cured of their leprosy, even though leprosy was not considered to be curable in Jesus' day. But these lepers were cured.

What separates us from one another? What separates us from God? Sin. How grateful we can be that we have a Savior who chose to enter this world to cure us of the sin that separates us. Jesus faced it and defeated it and did the impossible. He cured us of our sin and won the victory for us through His life, death, and resurrection.

From the group of ten lepers in our text, only one returned to give Christ thanks. Only one paused to rejoice and give credit to the Redeemer. Join the one who was thankful for Christ's love. Be one who turns to God daily with gratitude for the gift of Christ Jesus.

Lord, thank You for giving Your life for me. Help me every day
to be grateful for restored health and salvation. Amen.

—w—

November 4, 1997

November 5

—∿∿—

Read 1 Timothy 2:1–7
Psalm 103
Bless the LORD, O my soul, and all that is within me, bless His holy name!
Psalm 103:1

BLESS THE LORD!

I t is easy for people to forget favors. As we look at the world about us, the sin we see most often is the sin of ingratitude. Children forget the loving care of parents, friends forget the days of friendship, young people forget the guiding hand of pastors and teachers. No one will ever be able to measure all the tears shed over the sin of ingratitude. It is the world's most common sin and most constant pain.

There is, however, a more terrible ingratitude: the forgetfulness of God's mercy and love. Everything we are and have we owe to Him: our lives, the salvation of our souls, every breath we take. Yet how often we forget to join David in his song: "Bless the LORD, O my soul, and all that is within me, bless His holy name!"

The life of a true Christian is a thankful life. Think for a moment of all the gifts of God to us, one by one. We count our blessings, and suddenly we know that God loves us and cares for us, down to the very smallest need of life. Our heart beats with thankfulness. For every gift, we praise His holy name. Our life becomes an unceasing song of praise and thanksgiving.

Almighty God, Father of all mercies, we give You most humble and hearty thanks for all Your blessings to us. Amen.

—∿∿—

November 5, 1975

NOVEMBER 6

—ƴ⁊—

Read Matthew 5:38–48
Psalm 119:25–32
Love your enemies and pray for those who persecute you.
Matthew 5:44

LOVE YOUR ENEMIES

There are some people in the world who are so caring that you can't help loving them. There are also a few people who make it difficult for us to love them, people who are negative or hateful, people concerned only with themselves. We tend to ignore them or treat them the way they treat us.

Then we encounter Jesus' words: "Love your enemies and pray for those who persecute you." It almost seems impossible. Impossible for us, maybe, but not for God, who does love His enemies. Left to ourselves in our sin, we are enemies of God, we are the people who are difficult to love, concerned only with ourselves. As the sun rises on the evil and the good, so God's Son sacrificed Himself for all people. God loves us. We are to love one another and also our enemies. Our daily failure to live up to God's commands drives us back to His love, grace, mercy, and forgiveness won for us on the cross by Christ. The storehouse is full of those good gifts. The sunshine of God's love rises over us each day to be reflected in our lives to others.

O God of love, lead us and our enemies from prejudice to truth; deliver us and them from hatred, cruelty, and revenge; and grant us all forgiveness of sin for the sake of Your Son, Jesus Christ, our Lord. Amen.

—ƴ⁊—

November 6, 1998

November 7

—⟋⟍—

Read Romans 8:31–39
Psalm 63
By sending His own Son in the likeness of sinful flesh and for sin....
He who raised Christ Jesus from the dead. *Romans 8:3, 11*

Two Great Miracles

Was Jesus, born of the Virgin Mary, God's only-begotten Son? Did He truly rise from the dead after His crucifixion and death? These two questions present bewildering mysteries to minds that are reluctant to accept the possibility of such miracles.

St. Paul states the answers in the affirmative as historic fact and established truth. The apostles, who were with Jesus before and after His resurrection, witnessed to the world that God became man in Jesus Christ, that He laid down His life for the sins of the world, and that He rose again from the dead. They were sure of it. On it, they staked their lives in this world and in the world to come. On the basis of these truths, they preached repentance and forgiveness of sins.

The witnesses of Christ assert that God wrought and brought salvation by being born of a woman, dying for sin, and rising again from the dead. This is a stumbling block to some and sheer nonsense to others. To us who have the Holy Spirit's gift of faith, it is the power and wisdom of God, our hope and comfort, and the cause for our joy and thanksgiving. He gives us power to become the sons of God and has promised us His Holy Spirit.

Lord, I believe. Increase my faith and help me to live it. Amen.

—⟋⟍—

November 7, 1966

November 8

—❧—

Read Matthew 8:5–13
Out of my distress I called on the Lord; the Lord answered me.
Psalm 118:5

Answered Prayer

When the Augsburg Confession was being presented to Emperor Charles V, Luther was at Coburg, praying for his associates. He wrote to them: "I am truly standing by you with groaning and prayers. I pray for you and have prayed and will pray. And I doubt not that I shall be heard. If what we wish does not come to pass, then it will be something better than this." Especially by the 118th Psalm, his favorite psalm, did he strengthen his assurance that God would hear his prayers. He wrote verse 17 on his wall with notes above the words to sing them: "I shall not die but live and declare the works of the Lord."

Spurgeon said in his Luther sermon: "Luther's faith abounded in prayer. What supplications they were! Those who heard them tell us of his tears, his wrestlings, his holy arguments. He would go into his closet heavy at heart and remain there an hour or two, then come forth singing, 'I have conquered, I have conquered.' 'Ah,' said he one day, 'I have so much to do today that I cannot get through it with less than three hours' prayer.' I thought he was going to say, 'I cannot afford to give even a quarter of an hour to prayer'; but he increased his prayer as he increased his labor. This is the faith that saves—a faith that lays hold on God and prevails with Him in private supplication."

"The prayer of a righteous person has great power as it is working" (James 5:16). God promises us, "Call upon Me in the day of trouble; I will deliver you, and you shall glorify Me" (Psalm 50:15).

Come, Lord Jesus, be our guest, and let these gifts to us be blest.
Amen, amen, amen. (LSB 776:1)

—❧—

November 8, 1940

November 9

—⟋⟍—

Read Romans 8:18–25
Psalm 139

I consider that the sufferings of this present time are not worth comparing with the glory that is to be revealed to us. *Romans 8:18*

No Comparison

There are times in the life of every one of us Christians when we think we cannot continue. Pain, agony, loss of a love one, loneliness, divorce, sickness, unexpected events—unpleasant experiences like these discourage us.

In the midst of pain, agony, and sorrow, we may readily think that God is causing us to suffer too much, that He has gone past our limit. This can never occur. God reminds us and comforts us through these words of St. Paul: "He will not let you be tempted beyond your ability" (1 Corinthians 10:13).

Even though it is true that "through many tribulations we must enter the kingdom of God" (Acts 14:22), the apostle reminds us that all our sufferings here on earth are not worth comparing to the great happiness that awaits us in heaven.

Because Jesus is our Savior, we know that God is not punishing us for our sins; He punished His Son on the cross. God now offers and gives us the power to cope with all our sufferings. Our goal is heaven. What a wonderful home awaits us!

This is great encouragement for all of us. The best is yet to come!

Lord God, heavenly Father, for me to live is Christ and to die is gain. Amen.

—⟋⟍—

November 9, 1989
On this date in 1989,
the Berlin Wall falls

—ɷ—

Read James 1:5–15
Psalm 146
Those whom I love, I reprove and discipline, so be zealous and repent.
Revelation 3:19

THOSE WHOM HE LOVES

No one whom God loves escapes chastening. It is in love that God chastens His sons and daughters. Human reason disagrees. It cannot understand God's love. The "I love" here by the Lord is best translated "I love dearly." God shows deep affection for His redeemed and restored children by bringing them under His heavy hand.

His motive? Is it because He enjoys seeing us squirm in distress? Surely not; He loves us dearly. He desires our spiritual well-being. He chastens us to remind us we are still under the cross and the influence of sin in the world. He must convict us of our sin and lead us to daily repentance. Both are essential in His care for us. Only as we feel helpless as sinners can we cherish the saving power of the Redeemer.

The Lord loved the Church at Laodicea (Revelation 3:14–22) with all its faults, its pride and self-satisfied security in which so little need of repentance was felt. In that love, He reproved and chastened. Nor has the unchanging Lord altered His approach. Nothing hits the saints by chance. It is not only the grace but also the glory of the believer to be reproved and chastened.

Lord Jesus, send me what You will if it will help me accept the fullness of Your redeeming love. Amen.

—ɷ—

November 10, 1980

—ᴧᴧ—

Read Colossians 3:12–17
Psalm 130
Jesus said, "Father, forgive them, for they know not what they do."
Luke 23:34

FORGIVE US . . . AS WE FORGIVE

When Jesus teaches us to pray about forgiving, He touches the very core of every human relationship, as well as our relationship with the Father, as the basis of it. Forgiving "those who trespass against us" is an essential ingredient in getting along with any other person. Each human life is marred by sin, and we are all in need of forgiveness, both God's and that of one another.

Our sin affects the way we interact with our boss or employee, our children, spouse, neighbor, brother, sister, or stranger. Likewise, the sin of other people affects us.

When we are abused or insulted by someone, how do we respond? If we take Jesus' Word seriously, we say, "Father, forgive them, for they know not what they do." We do this because, as Christians, we have received the greatest forgiveness in the world— the forgiveness Jesus earned for us on Calvary's cross.

When God's forgiveness fills our hearts, it drives out thoughts of revenge and fills us with the love He has for us in Jesus Christ. The power to forgive, then, is ours because of God's great forgiveness to us.

Father, fill us with thankfulness for Your forgiveness, that we may forgive as we have been forgiven in Jesus. Amen.

—ᴧᴧ—

November 11, 1982

—∽∾—

Read Revelation 21:1–7
Psalm 103
When the perishable puts on the imperishable, and the mortal
puts on immortality, then shall come to pass the saying that is written:
"Death is swallowed up in victory." *1 Corinthians 15:54*

LIFE EVERLASTING

C an you imagine a life without tears, hunger, sorrow, pain, or suffering? That is the promise we have in Christ, but it strains our imagination to conceive of what that might mean. Life seems all wrapped up in precisely those things that God says will pass away as former things (Revelation 21:4). Tears, sorrow, pain, and suffering just seem built into our existence.

Jesus, however, gave hints of that life when He healed the sick, fed the hungry, raised the dead, removed suffering, and made people whole again. Through these miracles, as through pinholes in the wall between us and the new heaven and new earth (v. 1), we glimpse what life should have been without sin and still can be by the grace of God.

Jesus' suffering, death, and resurrection are doors through which we enter the new life. Through Him, "death is swallowed up in victory." We see what happens when our perishable lives put on immortality and our mortal lives put on immortality. We see in Jesus what "new things" we can expect.

Lord, open my eyes to see in You all that I can hope for. Amen.

—∽∾—

November 12, 1986

—⁂—

Read 2 Corinthians 9:6–11
Psalm 103:1–19
Bless the LORD, O my soul, and forget not all His benefits, who forgives all
your iniquity, who heals all your diseases, . . . who satisfies you with good.
Psalm 103:2–3, 5

THE JOY OF GIVING

With the above words, the psalmist David calls to mind the manifold gifts of God to His human creatures. God "satisfies you with good," he declares. And chief among these, he lists first—the Lord "forgives all your iniquity." To David had been given the promise of a Savior, the Messiah, who was to come to bear our sin and destroy its consequence, eternal death.

We have seen the fulfillment of that promise. Through the coming to earth, life, death, and resurrection of God's own Son, we possess even now all the treasures and joys of the life that will never end.

God promises to grant us all that we need to live as His children with no end to His giving. In Jesus Christ, our Savior, we receive "more abundantly than all that we ask or think" (Ephesians 3:20).

"You received without paying; give without pay," our Lord admonished His disciples (Matthew 10:8). Recalling the treasures showered with abundance on us and His grace in Christ, we are to be moved to give generously and joyfully of our firstfruits to Him that His kingdom of grace may be extended to the ends of the earth.

*Dear Father, thank You for Your abundant giving. Move us to respond
in grateful praise of our Redeemer, Jesus, Your Son. Amen.*

—⁂—

November 13, 2003

NOVEMBER 14

—ɯ—

Read Hosea 13:1–3
Hebrews 11:13–16, 39–40

When Ephraim spoke, there was trembling; he was exalted in Israel,
but he incurred guilt through Baal and died. *Hosea 13:1*

GOD, THE WAITING ONE

Sometimes our words to God or about God can become too smooth and too glib. This can happen in church, where our memorized responses roll off our lips so easily. It can happen in our personal prayer lives, when we repeat familiar words and phrases without much thought about their meaning and power.

It was when Israel became too smooth in her worship life, says Hosea, that she offended the Lord. The people might as well have prayed to Baal, because they weren't taking God seriously in their empty rituals.

On the other hand, when the people spoke tremblingly and hesitantly, speaking spontaneously from the heart and from a sense of dependent faith in God, then they were lifted up and strengthened by their worship.

When we come to God quietly, humbly, and repentantly, He speaks to us words of promise that impart confidence and strength. "Whoever exalts himself will be humbled, and whoever humbles himself will be exalted" (Matthew 23:12). So said Jesus, who for our salvation humbled Himself and was then raised up to sit at God's right hand.

*We speak tremblingly to You, O Lord, so that You may speak to us
Your words of power and peace. Amen.*

—ɯ—

November 14, 1984

—⚒—

Read James 2
If you were of the world, the world would love you as its own; but
because you are not of the world, but I chose you out of the world,
therefore the world hates you. John 15:19

CHRISTIANS ARE DIFFERENT

Faith that produces no change in our lives is not saving faith in the Lord Jesus Christ. As the true faith is enshrined in our hearts, we will be different people than those who do not know our Lord.

When we belong to Christ, we must make up our minds that there is a certain amount of shame we shall have to bear. Our Savior has forewarned us of the enmity of the world. "If the world hates you, know that it has hated Me before it hated you" (John 15:18).

It is not easy to confess Christ before men in word and deed. When somebody uses the name of our Savior in a vile curse, it is not easy to say: "Please, do not insult my friend." When unbelievers invite us to join in sinful courses, it is not easy to say, "I can't go with you; I am a Christian." In taking your stand, you will experience the truth: "All who desire to live a godly life in Christ Jesus will be persecuted" (2 Timothy 3:12).

If unbelievers do not find any difference between Christians and themselves, they will never be led to Christ. The best testimony for Christ is still a life that is truly devoted to Him. Having invested so heavily in us, God has a right to expect the faith that links us to Him and produces in our lives the beautiful fruits of righteousness.

Give me courage, O Lord, that I may have no fear except the fear
of being untrue to Thee, my dearest friend. Amen.

—⚒—

November 15, 1944

—m—

Read Romans 5:1–11
God so loved. *John 3:16*

So Loved

Some people would take emotion out of the Christian religion. It cannot be done. You cannot keep the warm, pulsating, eternal, forgiving love of God out of the religion of Jesus Christ. We must remember that God is love.

"I have loved you with an everlasting love; therefore I have continued My faithfulness to you" (Jeremiah 31:3).

The Creator's heart yearned for His fallen, helpless creatures, who had disobeyed Him, but who could not save themselves, who would be lost eternally unless He did something about it.

When thinking about this fact that God *so loved*, we must not tarry at the manger, we must not only listen for the echo of those angel voices and picture the glory that shone round about, but we must also go to Calvary and linger at the cross, we must hear the earth quake and behold the darkness. We find there not a beautiful babe, but a man in great agony of body and of soul. God *so loved* that the slaying of His Son was His answer to man's need of forgiveness and salvation.

Behold the Savior of mankind
Nailed to the shameful tree!
How vast the love that Him inclined
To bleed and die for thee! (*TLH* 176:1)

And now we are to love. We are to love Him because He first loved us. We are to love Him with all our heart and all our soul and all our mind.

O Father in heaven, we thank Thee that Thy love was so great that even the agony of Calvary was not too much for Thee to endure. Amen.

—m—

November 16, 1941

—⟊—

Read Acts 13:49–52
Psalm 113
They shook off the dust from their feet against them and went
to Iconium. *Acts 13:51*

LET'S GO ON

Let's not expect everyone to receive us with open arms every time we tell them about Jesus. When we talk about Him, some people may give us no more than a tolerant smile or may even hint that we change the subject.

Paul and Barnabas had such an experience at a place called Antioch. Some of the people in that city were enemies of the Gospel. They stirred up the crowd to persecute the apostles. When Paul and Barnabas realized that there was no chance for them to get a fair hearing, they decided to go elsewhere. For the time being, they could do more good by going to another place.

There are times when sharing our faith with those around us shows no result. People of the congregation may stay away, or members of our family may become indifferent toward God. No amount of talking seems to do any good. At such times, it may be best to change the subject, to walk away, and even to stay away. Perhaps another time will be better.

God's Word is always powerful. It will bear fruit in His good time. Our task is to witness about Jesus, the Savior. God will produce the response.

Give us patience, Lord Jesus, to keep on witnessing. Permit us to see favorable results in accordance with Your will. Amen.

—⟊—

November 17, 1990

Read Romans 12:9–21
Psalm 20

They sat with him on the ground seven days and seven nights, and no one spoke a word to him, for they saw that his suffering was very great.
Job 2:13

THE MINISTRY OF PRESENCE

Job's friends didn't always provide him with the best advice, but soon after Job lost his family, property, and possessions, they gave him a great present. They came and sat with him for a week. Realizing his great suffering, no one said one word to him.

Job's friends ministered to him not with words, but with their loving presence. Have you ever avoided making visits to hospitals, nursing homes, or funeral homes because you didn't know what to say? While God certainly uses words to minister through people, just being there for someone in need is a powerful gift. Your presence might be the best present at times. A hug. A touch. A shared tear. A look. Each expression of empathy is important. Yet Gospel ministry does even more. It speaks of Jesus.

When Jesus reveals His presence, He goes beyond empathy. He actively takes upon Himself our sins and sorrows. He daily helps and heals us, giving us faith and hope in His Word. One Friday, Jesus took all our cares and troubles, nailing them to the cross. He broke their power to destroy us and made them His servants for our good. Because of His resurrection, even death no longer has power over Him—or over those who belong to Him. When Jesus reveals His presence, He gives us salvation.

Lord, thank You for ministering to me with Your presence, and teach me to do the same. Amen.

—〰—

November 12, 2004

—⚞—

Read Matthew 16:13–28
Psalm 106:1–12
For I do not do the good I want, but the evil I do not want is what
I keep on doing. *Romans 7:19*

REALISTIC CHRISTIANITY

Psychologists say that an addiction is a recurring behavior that cannot be altered or changed. Do you have such an addition: fits of anger, dishonesty, a tendency to gossip? Paul was honest enough to admit that some negative sinful behavior, some sinful addictions, were so much a part of his life that without help, he could not rid himself of them.

One reason we sin is because we enjoy it. We love the taste, the feel, the smell, the sound. There is no power in ourselves strong enough to pull us away from the lure of some sins. We repeat them again and again.

Paul was realistic about our inability to resist sin. He knew that people have no power to combat it except through Christ. Jesus has prevailed over evil. Our best chance for overcoming a pet sin is to run to Christ as fast as we can. He has already defeated sin's power through His death and resurrection. From Him comes the desire to do the good we would do and the energy and commitment needed to do it.

O dearest Christ Jesus, come quickly into our lives that we may be strong to do the good that we would do. Amen.

—⚞—

November 19, 1995

—ww—

Read Matthew 21:1–5
Psalm 24
To the King of ages, immortal, invisible, the only God, be honor and glory
forever and ever. Amen. *1 Timothy 1:17*

CHRIST THE KING

K ings rank above the ordinary citizenry. They live in palaces, eat rich foods, and are chauffeured in limousines. They wear the finest clothes and adorn themselves with jewelry, including a gem-studded crown. Servants care for the king's every desire while he builds his empire, amasses fortunes, and makes decisions. Some kings even demand to be worshiped.

The people of Israel awaited their King, the Messiah, but didn't understand that He would be different from any other king who ever lived. He rode a donkey. He was born in a stable. Rather than amassing riches, He died a humiliating death on a cross for His people. What kind of king is this?

This King does not demand to be served; He serves. The King of love, Jesus, took for Himself the punishment we deserve for our sins. And in exchange, He gave us His innocence. The sacrifice and benefit of His body and blood is distributed in Holy Communion. There, Jesus loves, forgives, and saves.

Because of His death and resurrection, we shall live with Him forever. In eternity, every knee will bow to Christ, the King of love and mercy. This King alone is worthy of our worship and praise.

Christ, You are the King of the universe and the King of my heart.
Thank You for Your merciful reign. Amen.

—ww—

November 20, 2005

—ᴍ—

Read Psalm 102:11–28
From everlasting to everlasting You are God. *Psalm 90:2*

THE EVERLASTING GOD

W hat is eternity? Only God really knows. He is eternal. With Him, there is no time, no hour, day, year, or century. With Him, yesterday and tomorrow are like the present, a thousand years are like one day, and Methuselah's 969 years are like a watch in the night.

Everything else comes and goes; only God is everlasting. The glory of this world passes away. The most precious things in this life slip through our fingers and are gone. In the middle of this change and decay, God gives us everlasting treasure.

We are not "from everlasting" because we are born. Without God, we are not blissfully "to everlasting," but are lost forever. But Christ brings us back to God. The eternal Son of God by an eternal redemption cleanses us from sin and rescues us from vanity and destruction. In the eternal Christ, the eternal God becomes our God. Living with the everlasting God, we are, like Him, everlasting. "Whoever believes has eternal life" (John 6:47).

Frail children of dust
And feeble as frail,
In Thee do we trust,
Nor find Thee to fail.
Thy mercies, how tender,
How firm to the end,
Our maker, defender,
redeemer and friend! Amen. (LSB 804:5)

—ᴍ—

November 21, 1958

NOVEMBER 22

—m—

Read Matthew 25:31–40
For whoever has despised the day of small things shall rejoice.
Zechariah 4:10

THE DAY OF SMALL THINGS

Life is made up of small things. The workman tightening a screw, the housewife baking a cake, the schoolboy doing his arithmetic—life is just one small thing after another. Great moments, exciting adventures—these are few and far between.

The danger, however, is that we may be inclined to despise the small things that make up our life. Just because they are routine and trivial, we tend to regard them as unimportant. We may even chafe at our humdrum, "ordinary" way of living.

Who has despised the day of small things? Certainly not the Lord. He blesses the cup of water given in His name. He sanctifies the hammer and nails that He uses in Joseph's carpenter shop. He multiplies the fishes in Peter's net. Small things, perhaps! But God regards them highly.

We must regard them highly too. We must realize that these things belong to our vocation, the calling into which God has placed us, the responsibilities that He has entrusted to us. The test of good stewardship will lie in the faithfulness and care which we apply to the "small things" of life. For these "small things" are God's things and He holds us to account for their proper use. And upon these small things God will bestow a blessing.

All that we have is Thine alone,
A trust, O Lord, from Thee. Amen. (LSB 781:1)

—m—

November 22, 1963
On this date in 1963, President John F. Kennedy
is assassinated in Dallas

NOVEMBER 23

—∞—

Read 2 Samuel 12:7–14
Psalm 130
Repent and be baptized every one of you in the name of Jesus Christ
for the forgiveness of your sins. Acts 2:38

REPENT AND BELIEVE

Adam and Eve hid themselves from God when their eyes were opened and they realized that they had sinned. Children hide physically or lie when they know they have disobeyed their parents. Workers try to hide errors and cover up the wrong things they have done. It is difficult for us to admit that we make mistakes, especially in matters of considerable importance.

King David had a similar problem. But God sent Nathan to show David that his sin could not be covered up. David confessed that his sin was not merely against Uriah but also against God. We must come to a similar realization about our sins.

True repentance is more than admission of guilt and sorrow for the mistake. Mere confession without faith results in despair, as it did with Judas. God's hand of love and mercy reaches out to us to save us from such despair. God's grace enables us to turn our backs on evil we have done and to turn toward His will. By His Spirit, He leads us to turn from sorrow to joy, from wrong to right, from evil to good. True repentance means a new life of forgiveness and service to others. It is the fruit of faith in Christ.

O God, turn us from evil. Enable us to change our lives and do those things that serve others and please You. Amen.

—∞—

November 23, 1987

November 24

—∿—

Read Revelation 7:9–17

You make known to me the path of life; in Your presence there is fullness of joy; at your right hand are pleasures forevermore. *Psalm 16:11*

FOREVER WITH THE LORD

With wondrous understanding of things to come, David foresees the glorification of Jesus. Through the mouth of David, Jesus speaks. Our Savior's path of life had a glorious destination, the salvation and eternal blessedness of sinful humanity. This path of life led through dark places: shame and persecution and death. But our Lord arose to everlasting glory and honor. To all eternity, men and angels will sing His praises.

By God's grace, the Savior's destiny has become ours. By faith in Him, we may confidently look ahead to a glorious resurrection of the body, to fullness of joy in God's presence, to pleasures at the right hand of God forevermore. While it is true that this is not as detailed a description of heaven as we would like to have, it is sufficient to create in us a longing to live in that heavenly home. It is enough to know that we shall be with God forevermore, that nothing will spoil our joy—no tears, no sickness, no pain, no sin, no death. This hope is ours as sure as Christ is risen from the dead, lives, and reigns to all eternity.

O Lord, show us the path of life, that we may live with Thee forever. Amen.

—∿—

November 24, 1957

November 25

—⁊⁊—

Read Revelation 21:1–4
Psalm 74
And He who was seated on the throne said, "Behold, I am making all things new." *Revelation 21:5*

ALL THINGS NEW

Everything in life grows old and wears out: rugs, furniture, cars, roads, buildings. We human beings are victims of the aging process too. Veins and arteries that have functioned as the lifeline of the body for a lifetime clog up or break down. Eyes grow dim. Memory fails us. We die.

Decay and death infect our lives as a curse that rests on us for our evil. We have cut ourselves off from God, the source of our life. Like a flower without rain and sun, our life shrivels and dies.

God knows and cares. He has acted to deliver us from decay and death. Through the death and resurrection of Jesus Christ, He triumphed over death and opened up the way to eternal life.

Now God holds out a blessed promise to us: "Behold, I am making all things new." This heaven and earth will pass away. God will bring a new heaven and earth into being. He will dwell with us there. In His new order of life, death will be no more. The old way of life will be at an end.

As we experience the aging, decaying, dying process of our present life, we can look to the future with hope. For God makes all things new.

Finish then Thy new creation,
Pure and spotless let us be;
Let us see Thy great salvation
Perfectly restored in Thee. Amen. (LSB 700:4)

—⁊⁊—

November 25, 1972

November 26

—⋙—

Read 1 John 2:15–25
Psalm 1
Do not be conformed to this world, but be transformed by the renewal
of your mind. *Romans 12:2*

A Transformed Life

One of the most difficult requirements for Christian living is to be a nonconformist in the world. Instinctively, we want to be accepted by the people around us. This tendency is obvious in the behavior of people generally. This becomes a problem for Christians when the world sets its own standards of ethics and morality and implies that we are hopelessly old-fashioned if we do not go along.

We constantly need to be reminded that by God's grace we are a separated people. Our high calling in Christ is to follow after Him in righteousness. This means not to conform to the world. This required of us self-denial, crucifixion of the flesh with its lusts, and forsaking the evil ways of the unbelieving world.

If we were left to our own resources, we would fail. As Christians, we are what we are by the grace of God in Christ Jesus. It is only in the renewing power of the Holy Spirit that we can be transformed and strive mightily to live in conformity with the perfect will of God. We have not achieved this perfectly. We need God's forgiveness daily. We also need the Holy Spirit's help to live holy lives to God's glory.

*Holy Spirit, mercifully guide us in the way of righteousness
through the renewal of our minds. Amen.*

—⋙—

November 26, 1978

Read Matthew 26:36–46
Psalm 121
My Father, if it be possible, let this cup pass from Me; nevertheless,
not as I will, but as You will. *Matthew 26:39*

CRUCIAL TESTS OF LIFE

We can face crucial tests of life in several ways. We can pray to be spared the anguish they may impose on us. And we can ask for the necessary courage and faith to accept the challenges they thrust before us.

When Jesus, in the Garden of Gethsemane, was confronted with the "cup"—His mission of dying for our salvation—He prayed earnestly, "If it be possible, let this cup pass from Me."

As disciples of Christ, also we can pray: O Father, let this cup—this suffering of body and mind, this critical surgery, this painful task, this demanding challenge, this heavy responsibility—let this cup pass from us!

But can we continue with the crucial test of our faith as expressed in the word "nevertheless"? If it is not possible for the nails and the cross to be removed, nevertheless not our will but Thy will be done, heavenly Father?

God's will was done by His Son. He did put the cup of our guilt to His lips, so that our "cup" might run over with His forgiving love and with the power He grants to trust in His gracious will, especially in the crucial tests of our life.

Heavenly Father, strengthen my faith, that I, too, may pray,
"Nevertheless, not as I will, but as You will." Amen.

—ᗰ—

November 27, 1981

November 28

—✠—

Read John 20:24–31
Psalm 104
[Thomas] said to them, "Unless I see in His hands the mark
of the nails . . . I will never believe." *John 20:25*

PORTRAIT OF A DOUBTER

Our name is Thomas, for we, too, have had our moments of doubt. We, too, have refused to believe the testimony of others, preferring sight to faith. We, too, have placed limits on God's ability to perform. We, too, have prescribed to God the exact conditions under which we'd accept His truths.

And because we have been where Thomas was, it is good to see Christ's sensitivity toward doubters. Jesus came to deal especially with the doubter. He did not reject him. Christ faced Thomas with love and forgiveness. He followed minutely the prescription Thomas had laid down as absolute: "Unless . . . I will never." Christ does not cast off even the most arrogant doubter with his unreasonable demands.

When tormenting and disquieting doubts besiege and assail us, we can with joy recall the understanding and completely forgiving attitude of our Lord in dealing with "doubting Thomas." We remember how He led him, step by step, to the glorious confession "My Lord and my God!" (v. 28) and then assured him that his doubts had been overcome and replaced by genuine faith. Oh, the blessed patience of Him who died for us and rose again!

*Gracious and patient Savior, we thank You for removing our doubts
and renewing us in our faith in You. Amen.*

—✠—

November 28, 1979

—⟋⟍—

Read Revelation 21:9–27
As I live, declares the Lord GOD, I have no pleasure in the death of the
wicked, but that the wicked turn from his way and live. *Ezekiel 33:11*

WHAT GIVES GOD PLEASURE?

One of the most subtle devices of Satan and unbelievers to prevent a sinner from turning to God and seeking forgiveness is to misrepresent Him as a hard and merciless Lord. And when some people once get this false idea of God, they often become hardened in heart and willfully go on in their sinful ways.

In the statement above, as if to end once and for all this ghastly belief that He finds delight in human misery and destruction, God affirms with a solemn oath that He has "no pleasure in the death of the wicked." Can anything be stronger than that? What God states under oath must be true. Let no man, no matter how clever in his argument, ever persuade us to entertain any doubt about it.

On the contrary, God affirms that He has pleasure in seeing a sinner turn from his wicked way and live. When we have sinned and now begin to cry in sincere repentance, "God be merciful to me, a sinner," we can be certain that He has pleasure; for the very purpose for which He gave His own Son is about to be accomplished: the salvation of a sinner. Jesus said, "There is joy before the angels of God over one sinner who repents" (Luke 15:10).

O God, we thank Thee that Thou hast assured us that there is forgiveness with Thee, for Thou art gracious and plenteous in mercy. Amen.

—⟋⟍—

November 29, 1949

November 30

—᙮᙮᙮—

Read Matthew 4:18–22
Psalm 127
And He said to them, "Follow Me, and I will make you fishers of men."
Matthew 4:19

FISHERS OF MEN

At first, Andrew was a disciple of John the Baptist, whose designation of Jesus as "the Lamb of God" prompted Andrew to follow Jesus. His first act after having found Jesus was to find his brother, Simon Peter, and tell him: "We have found the Messiah" (John 1:41). Andrew became the first personal missionary of the Lord.

The day came when Jesus called Andrew to become an apostle. This time, as he looked up from his nets, Andrew heard Jesus say: "Follow Me, and I will make you fishers of men" (Matthew 4:19). Like his companions, Andrew acted at once, out of deep conviction. It is said: "Immediately they left their nets and followed Him" (v. 20).

In the call of Jesus to Andrew, we find a precise formula for our lifelong mission. Fishers we are to be—fishers of men, proclaimers of the Gospel. When we, through Holy Baptism, entered into fellowship with Christ, we, too, were called to be His followers. Because the work is Christ's, He empowers us for our mission under Him.

Andrew followed implicitly, even to death. Only God knows the cost of our discipleship. But whatever the road, whatever the price, we have found the Messiah and cannot but follow Him.

Almighty God, grant us grace to follow Your Son. Amen.

—᙮᙮᙮—

November 30, 1971

December

O blessed and powerful
Holy Spirit, help me to
find the light of my life
in Jesus Christ, the light
of the world. Amen.

December 1

—✺—

Read Psalm 24

THE KING OF GLORY

G lory be to the Father and to the Son and to the Holy Ghost, as it was in the beginning, is now, and ever shall be, world without end. Amen."

The Son whom we glorify every Sunday in this ancient "Gloria" of the Christian Church is none other than our Lord and Savior Jesus Christ, whom we welcome today as the King of glory.

Glory! What is glory? Is it the honor and praise of men? Is it the power and fame that wealth or achievement will bring? Is it beauty, pomp, and splendor? Indeed not. This is but earthly glory. Like all earthly things, such glory will pass away. Our King's glory is eternal. It consists in the beauty and grace and love of our King's redemptive work, the mercy He has shown to sinners in suffering and dying for them, the compassion He shows today in seeking and saving them. No glory is like unto His glory. As Moses prayed, "Please show me Your glory" (Exodus 33:18), so we pray in these Advent days that we may behold His glory, "as of the only Son from the Father, full of grace and truth" (John 1:14).

But even as Moses was unable to look upon the full revelation of the glory of God, so we shall be able to perceive only a faint resplendence of His glory in His Savior's love. What we may see and appreciate of His glory is our salvation. But someday we shall see Him face-to-face in the glory of heaven. Then He shall remain forever our King of glory.

Dear heavenly Father, graciously enable us to behold the glory of our Savior King, and fill our hearts and lives with His glory. Amen.

—✺—

December 1, 1937

Read Acts 8:26–39
"What prevents me from being baptized?" *Acts 8:36*

THE ETHIOPIAN

On a highway, under the direction of God's Holy Spirit, the disciple Philip overtakes an Ethiopian reading out of the Book of Isaiah. He is a man of prominence, secretary of the treasury in a queen's court.

Philip asks this man a few questions and then begins to expound to him the Scriptures and tells him about Jesus.

The eyes of the Ethiopian are opened. He sees the light. As they ride together, they come to a place with water. The new convert wants to be baptized. Confessing his faith, "I believe that Jesus Christ is the Son of God," he is baptized by Philip.

Philip disappears, and a reborn man goes on his way rejoicing. What happiness comes into the life of those who find the Savior! What a simple and beautiful account of a great event! Another man's eternity is changed.

The Word of God is read in our day also and is being explained. Men find their Savior, and an unspeakable joy comes into their lives as they learn that Jesus has died on the cross for all their sins. We should distribute more Testaments and Gospel tracts; we should send out more missionaries; for faith comes only through the hearing and reading of the Gospel.

True Christianity is built on this truth that Jesus is the Son of God, that He shed His blood to pay for our transgressions, that believing this, we have forgiveness and peace.

We Christians must hold fast to the doctrine of the deity of Jesus Christ. That is the rock upon which the Church is built. The Godhood and the Saviorhood of Jesus Christ must be believed.

Lord, keep us in this saving faith. Amen.

—ᵐᵕ—

December 2, 1941

December 3

—៣–

Read Luke 1:5–17
Psalm 92
The angel said to him, "Do not be afraid, Zechariah, for your prayer
has been heard." *Luke 1:13*

Do Not Be Afraid!

One day, the angel of the Lord said to a priest named Zechariah, "Do not be afraid." You and I need a message like that for a time like ours, when many of us must live behind locked doors, protected by electronic alarms, guarded by watchdogs, afraid to go out at night.

Many were living in fear when the angel issued the announcement. God's message was that Zechariah and his wife, Elizabeth, would have a son—John the Baptizer. John would prepare the way for the Lord Himself; for this reason, his birth would be the occasion for great joy. Christ Jesus, the Messiah who was preceded by joy, came to earth to reconcile God with all people. He came as the Savior to bear the sin of the world, to sacrifice His life on the cross as the peace offering to the Father. He makes possible for us a peaceful relationship with God and with our fellow human beings.

The Gospel message is designed to bring great joy to all who hear it. God comes at Christmas in love and mercy—not to punish, but to set free; not to destroy, but to deliver us. In His mercy, He says, "Do not be afraid!"

Lord God, through the Spirit's power, may Your great mercy in Christ Jesus drive fear out of our hearts and provide us with comfort and joy. Amen.

—៣–

December 3, 1992

December 4

—๛—

Read Revelation 5:9–14
Your kingdom come. *Matthew 6:10*

Your Kingdom Come

The world of today and world of tomorrow lie before us uncertain and sad. Facing the future, we should feel, above all else, the need to pray for ourselves and for our world, "Your kingdom come." The disciples had often heard their Master pray. They seem to have felt that if they could only pray like that, what a power would come into their lives! The prayer that the Master taught them is the opening up of sources of world-conquering power. In no petition, perhaps, is this power seen more clearly than in the petition "Your kingdom come."

In the days of Advent, we remember the coming of the kingdom of God and its power. We know that it came when Christ was born in Bethlehem. We know that this kingdom of the eternal Christ comes today wherever His Word is preached to bring to men the mighty faith that conquers sin and the forces of hell. The kingdom of God will continue to come as long as there are todays and tomorrows. The reign of the babe of Bethlehem in our life and in the world cannot be broken by death or disaster.

"Your kingdom come" is our prayer for the deliverance of our world from the rule of Satan. It is also our prayer for the full opening of our heart to the coming Christ and to His kingdom within us. In its answer is the fulfillment of all of our hopes and all of the hopes of our world.

Help us, O King of kings, to pray "Your kingdom come" with an unshaken faith in its continuous coming to our hearts and to our world. Amen.

—๛—

December 4, 1943

DECEMBER 5

—ɷ—

Read Romans 8:31–39
Psalm 78
Come, you who are blessed by My Father. *Matthew 25:34*

BLESSED OF THE FATHER

Advent comes with the blessing of the Gospel of Christ. It lights up a person's whole existence. All the saints have proved it. Paul and Silas proved it lying broken and bleeding in a dungeon in Philippi. They remembered Christ, and they broke into song at midnight. Francis of Assisi proved it. Thoughts of Christ had him skipping his way around Italy in beggar's clothes.

What a difference Christ makes! We are our own best proof. The most burdened among us is happy that Christmas is coming. We welcome faces that smile for a change and music that lifts the spirit. The old worries make room for other interests. The common routine gives way a little because there is more to the day than the same old grind. There's a freshness, a newness, a difference now.

But Advent comes with the blessing of the Gospel. It is not just a general improvement. It is specific and distinctive. It is balm for our particular burdens and relief for our personal loneliness. The blessing of the Gospel of Advent is the reminder that Christ is coming so that we don't have to carry that load by ourselves anymore or walk the daily path in solitude. He is coming to be with us.

Give us Your blessing, heavenly Father. Amen.

—ɷ—

December 5, 1989

DECEMBER 6

—m—

Read Isaiah 35
Psalm 119:17–24
Say to those who have an anxious heart, "Be strong; fear not!"
Isaiah 35:4

ON BEING STRONG

During these Advent days, we prepare ourselves for the coming of the Christ Child at Christmas. We also prepare ourselves for the second coming of our Lord.

In Advent especially, our chief thought must always be, in the words of Isaiah, that God may give us a strong faith to remain firm. Our faith is strengthened through close communion with God in His Word. We read the Holy Scripture, we hear the Word proclaimed at home and in church, we commune at the altar, we remember our Baptism. The Holy Spirit works through these means to make us strong Christians.

Martin Luther, in one of his Advent sermons, said: "When a man with strong faith receives this King into his inmost heart, he is saved. Sin, death, hell, and all distress he dreads no longer; for he knows well, and does not doubt, that this King is the Master over his life and death, over sin and grace, over hell and heaven, and all things are in His hands."

In these days, we are especially mindful that our glorious King comes both as Savior and as Judge. May we, being made strong in faith, receive Him joyfully.

O Christ, our glorious King, make us subjects who will receive You in strong faith and without fear. Amen.

—m—

December 6, 1974

Read Matthew 15:1–9
In vain do they worship Me, teaching as doctrines
the commandments of men. *Matthew 15:9*

VAIN WORSHIP

Think of it: men substitute their ideas for God's truth. It is unbelievable, but it has been going on for a long time. Such human ideas are vain, useless. They accomplish nothing; they do not save; they destroy the souls of men.

A Christianity with the deity of Christ taken out of it, a Christianity with the atoning blood of Christ taken out of it, a Christianity with the virgin birth and the miracles of Christ explained away, is no Christianity. Christ crucified for our sin must be the center of our faith. Scripture warns: "Behold, I am against the prophets, declares the Lord, who use their tongues and declare, 'declares the Lord'" (Jeremiah 23:31). "Beware of false prophets, who come to you in sheep's clothing but inwardly are ravenous wolves" (Matthew 7:15).

Men in Christian churches are replacing God's teaching with their own. What flagrant misrepresentation of the religion of Jesus Christ! What an insult to God! It is ruining souls. It is bringing confusion into the Church. Rightly Christ has told us, "If you abide in My word, you are truly My disciples" (John 8:31).

It is like taking some expert's book on a given subject and having some ignorant person rewrite it. Let not man with his limited knowledge tamper with the truth of an all-wise God.

We all know what we think of imitations and substitutes in other things. How much worse when it comes to the things of God and the soul and eternity! No one has a right to add or take from this redeeming message found in the Scriptures.

Keep us steadfast in Thy Word, O Christ. Amen.

—✺—

December 7, 1941
On this date in 1941, Pearl Harbor is attacked

DECEMBER 8

—ᴍ—

Read Psalm 43

At that time separated from Christ, alienated from the commonwealth of Israel and strangers to the covenants of promise, having no hope and without God in the world. Ephesians 2:12

WITHOUT GOD

M en who have substituted their own ideas of Christ have not the true Christ and are without hope and without god in the world. Men may think they have God. Men may say they have hope, but it is all vain unless they believe that Jesus, by the shedding of His blood, has saved them from all sin.

No substitute will do. We need a genuine Christianity if men are to have real, abiding hope.

Bring a Christianity out of which the real Christ of the Bible has been taken into the midst of life's needs, and what have you? No real solution to any of life's problems. Bring a Christianity without the resurrected, living Lord alongside the grace, and what have you? A religion without hope, without comfort.

We have a sure prophetic Word
By inspiration of the Lord;
And tho' assailed on ev'ry hand,
Jehovah's Word shall ever stand.

By pow'rs of empire banned and burned,
By pagan pride rejected, spurned,
The Word still stands the Christian's trust
While haughty empires lie in dust. (*TLH* 290:1–2)

Through Thy Word, O God, we are citizens of Thy kingdom and are no longer foreigners. Keep us from the influences of man-made substitutes. Amen.

—ᴍ—

December 8, 1941
On this date in 1941, U.S. declares war on Japan

December 9

—⚍—

Read Isaiah 40:6–11
Psalm 73
I see Him, but not now; I behold Him, but not near: a star shall come out
of Jacob. *Numbers 24:17*

A Star of Jacob

As the children of Israel stood at the border of the Promised Land, their enemies, the Moabites, called on the prophet Balaam to curse the Israelites. Three times Balaam prophesied, and each time, his words proved a blessing instead of a curse. When asked to leave, Balaam spoke once more. Looking into the future, he cried: "I see Him, but not now; I behold Him, but not near: a star shall come out of Jacob."

The Messiah of God's promise had apparently become very real to Balaam. The Messiah would come from the descendants of Jacob and would be a star—someone to give light.

Stars bring cheer to the darkness of night. And the darker the night, the brighter the stars. A star provides guidance, just as it did years later for the Magi from the East. Christ would be like that too!

In many languages, an outstanding person is called a "star." Christ, the God-man, would indeed be a star! The loving rays of Christ, God's star, have been shining on people in all places and in all conditions for all time. Let us, then, love Him and worship Him.

*O blessed and powerful Holy Spirit, help me to find the light of my life
in Jesus Christ, the light of the world. Amen.*

—⚍—

December 9, 1980

DECEMBER 10

—ɷ—

Read 1 Thessalonians 5:1–11
Psalm 122

So then let us not sleep, as others do, but let us keep awake
and be sober. *1 Thessalonians 5:6*

KEEPING AWAKE

We all have heard comments about people who have a hard time staying awake in church. We may have been eyewitnesses to such incidents. Perhaps we saw a man's head bobbing up and down in a pew ahead of us. The next thing was a poke in the ribs from his wife's elbow.

The incident just related has overtones for our spiritual life as a whole. We are not to fall asleep in our faith. Our text for today encourages us to keep awake and be sober. Understood in its full context, it admonishes us to be ready for the second coming of Christ.

"The day of the Lord will come like a thief in the night," writes St. Paul (1 Thessalonians 5:2). Mankind will be caught unawares, for no one knows when Christ will come again. On that day, there will be no more uncertainty, for all—believers and unbelievers alike—will see Christ returning to earth in all His majesty and power.

The point should be obvious. The time to make spiritual preparations for our Lord's second coming is *now*. The Advent season calls us to repentance and to faith in the salvation that Jesus Christ has won.

Lord Jesus, awaken us from the sleep of sin. Strengthen our faith in Your promise of the forgiveness of our sins. Amen.

—ɷ—

December 10, 1976

December 11

—⁓—

Read 2 Corinthians 11:24–33
They gave themselves first to the Lord. *2 Corinthians 8:5*

Giving Oneself

We Christians of this generation should be more ready to give ourselves to the Lord. There must be actual denying of self and sincere following of Christ.

We withhold too much from Christ; do we not? Too often, time and strength, abilities and money, are used up in pleasure and recreation and too little is given to Christ and God's great enterprise. The right balance is all too frequently missing.

Our Lord speaks to us in the words of a human. As we read it, let us think ourselves at the foot of the cross, gazing upon the suffering Christ, and from His lips there come these words:

Oh, let thy life be given,

Thy years for Me be spent,

World's fetters all be riven,

And joy with suffering blent!

I gave Myself for thee:

Give thou thyself to Me. (*TLH* 405:6)

Can we do too much for Christ? Did Paul do too much? Did Barnabas give too much? The widow?

We should think more of what Christ has done for us, think more of the everlasting life that is ours, the eternal rescue, the greatness of God's cause, the crying need of others for the Gospel.

Did God do too much when He gave His Son?

O Christ of our salvation, we give ourselves anew to Thee. Amen.

—⁓—

December 11, 1941
On this date in 1941,
U.S. declares war on Germany and Italy

December 12

―ᴡ―

Read 1 John 5:11–13

And I will put enmity between you and the woman, and between your offspring and her offspring; He shall bruise your head, and you shall bruise His heel. *Genesis 3:15*

War and Peace

The story of mankind is one of constant struggle between good and evil. When everything seems to be quiet and orderly and progress is being made, suddenly conflicts arise to disturb the peace. Many a sensitive soul worries about this, wondering when peace might come to the world.

This struggle and how God planned to meet it was foretold in prophecy in the very beginning of time. It is the struggle between Satan and God, between the serpent and the Seed of the woman—between the devil and Jesus, our Savior. The devil and his whole evil force would fight against God and His chosen Redeemer—His Son, the Seed of the woman. This would be a fight to the finish.

The promised Savior would crush the power of the devil, but to do it, He had to receive the serpent's bruise: He had to die. Jesus came into this world as the babe of Bethlehem, born of the Virgin Mary. He completed the struggle when He died on the cross of Calvary and arose again from the dead. The war against eternal death has been won by Christ. He tells us now: "Peace I leave with you. . . . Let not your hearts be troubled, neither let them be afraid" (John 14:27).

Lord Jesus, our victor, fill us with true peace by believing in Thee. Amen.

―ᴡ―

December 12, 1959

December 13

—ꝏ—

Read I John 1:1–4
Psalm 119:97–104
In these last days [God] has spoken to us by His Son. *Hebrews 1:2*

God Spoke through His Son

God spoke to Moses face-to-face, to Samuel in an audible voice, and to many prophets in visions and dreams. They were His spokesmen and wrote down His words.

Prophets wrote history as God wanted it written. To them God revealed His plans, thoughts, desires, and the judgments to come. He gave promises to be fulfilled with announcements of a coming Savior and of His kingdoms of grace and glory.

But no matter how much revelation they gave us in the Bible, nothing could compare with the revelation through Christ. All that God is, Christ is. Christ is God's full and last Word.

St. John wrote, "In the beginning was the Word, and the Word was with God, and the Word was God" (1:1). This Word "became flesh and dwelt among us" (v. 14). He came in grace and truth to give His life for us. The kingdom of grace is His. He fulfilled all promises.

When we wonder what God is like or what He thinks of us, we turn to Jesus. God made all things through Him. He personifies all God's wisdom. He accomplished what no human wisdom and power could accomplish: forgiveness of our sins, resurrection of our body, and life everlasting.

Dear Jesus, the kingdom, the power, and the glory are all Yours.
What a joy it is to know You! Amen.

—ꝏ—

December 13, 1988

DECEMBER 14

—m—

Read Galatians 4:4–7
Psalm 96
When the fullness of time had come, God sent forth His Son.
Galatians 4:4

GOD'S TIMETABLE

Our God works according to plan and schedule. Nothing just happens with God; neither are there "accidents" with Him. The birth of Jesus was arranged from eternity. It had to occur exactly when it did, for it was part of God's plan of salvation. God sent His Son as our Savior when the fullness of time had come, and no sooner!

Jesus was born after Judah had been chastened through captivity and after Alexander the Great had made Greek the universal language in the known world. Thus the Gospels written in Greek could be spread far and wide. Jesus was born when Rome had built its famous military roads. Over these, Paul and other missionaries could speedily travel with the Word of life, carrying out the Great Commission: "Go therefore and make disciples of all nations" (Matthew 28:19). Yes, God's timing is always good, always right.

Because sin often beclouds our judgment, we become restless and impatient. We want to hurry God and urge Him to do certain things soon—now!

Let us remember that God is still "on schedule." No one frustrates Him in His plans. He still says, "Be still, and know that I am God" (Psalm 46:10). We can trust His timetable.

God, keep me patient, believing that Thou wilt help me at the right time and in the right way. Amen.

—m—

December 14, 1972

Read Luke 1:26–38
Psalm 15
Behold, you will conceive in your womb and bear a son, and you shall
call His name Jesus. He will be great and will be called the Son
of the Most High. *Luke 1:31–32*

MARY, THE MOTHER GOD CHOSE

Mary is the most honored of all women because God chose her to be the mother of His Son and of the world's Savior. How strange are God's ways! He passes by the palaces of kings and the mansions of the rich and reaches into a poor home in the unlikely village of Nazareth. There, He chooses a humble maiden to be the most blessed of women.

Mary was a person of humble faith. The angel's message that she was chosen for this great honor puzzled her. But when the angel told her that she, though a virgin, would conceive and bear this Child by the power of the Holy Spirit, she accepted it in simple faith and submitted to God's word and will. She was content to do His will and serve His purposes.

Mary was a woman with a great faith in a great God and in His mercy and power, willing to put herself into His hands, bow to His will, and accept His plan for her. She serves as an example for every believer and an ideal for every Christian girl and mother.

Let us honor Mary. But let us worship and praise not Mary, but God, who showed such grace to her, and God's Son, born of her to be the Savior of all.

Give us the grace, O God, to accept in simple faith, as Mary did, the mystery of Thy Son's birth. Amen.

—ɷ—

December 15, 1971

DECEMBER 16

—w—

Read Joel 2:28–32
Psalm 143
In the last days it shall be, God declares, that I will pour out My Spirit
on all flesh. Acts 2:17

THE SPIRIT'S POWER

Advent is a time to remember the work of the Holy Spirit. On Pentecost, the apostle Peter recalled Joel's prophecy concerning the "last days." God had said: "I will pour out My Spirit on all flesh" (Joel 2:28).

Peter was convinced that the New Testament era would be filled with the power of the Holy Spirit, the Holy Comforter. The Spirit was powerfully poured out on the disciples on Pentecost, the day when the Christian Church was given the power to carry out Christ's mission. The Pentecost event was accompanied by signs that point toward the fulfillment of God's promises about the end. His might and power were present on that day through the great outpouring of His Spirit.

During Advent, we can rejoice that we who belong to the fellowship of the Christian Church live by the power of the Spirit's presence. In the Gospel of Jesus Christ, we have the means through which the Spirit brings people to faith. By the power of the Spirit, hearts of stone are turned into God's living temples. Although we cannot see Jesus, the Holy Comforter assures us that He is our Immanuel: God with us.

Come, Holy Spirit, Lord divine, Your peace to us impart. Amen.

—w—

December 16, 1987

Read Acts 4:5–12
Psalm 72
Are You the one who is to come, or shall we look for another?
Matthew 11:3

THE RIGHT ONE

As Christmas Day comes closer, our thoughts focus more on the One whose birthday we will celebrate. We honor Jesus as the Savior, the Messiah. But there was a time during Jesus' ministry when He was asked if He indeed was the right one, the true Messiah.

This important question was the one that John the Baptist asked his followers to ask Jesus. Perhaps both John and his followers were discouraged. John was in prison, placed there by wicked King Herod. The king had become enraged because John had criticized him for living with his brother's wife. Perhaps John's followers wondered why God had allowed this to happen to John.

This Advent season, we can profit from what Jesus told John's disciples: "The blind receive their sight and the lame walk, lepers are cleansed and the deaf hear, and the dead are raised up, and the poor have good news preached to them" (Matthew 11:5). All this was proof positive that He was indeed the Messiah, true man and true God!

Yes, indeed! Jesus is the right one. Today, we still receive that answer as we read the Holy Scriptures. They bear witness to Jesus, the God made flesh, who is Christ, our Savior (John 1:14–18).

Lord Jesus, we believe that You are the one sent by the Father to be our blessed Savior. Amen.

—w—

December 17, 2008

—⚮—

Read Matthew 24:31
Psalm 1
The Son of Man is going to come with His angels in the glory
of His Father. *Matthew 16:27*

THE GLORY OF THE LORD'S RETURN

No man was present when at the beginning the glory of the Lord broke the silence of eternity to speak His mighty "Let there be!" Neither did any angels witness the majesty of the first creation. Both men and angels, however, saw the glory of the Lord in Christ Jesus in His first appearance upon earth, in the mighty acts of His ministry, and in the magnificent event of His ascension. And men and angels shall be there when on the Last Day of earth, He shall return in glory to judge the living and the dead and to lead His congregation of believers into the cathedrals of heaven.

God alone knows the day and the hour of Jesus' appearing. However, as His birth was foretold and the hearts of men were prepared to await His coming, so likewise is His return foretold in the sure word of prophecy, clearly announced to the world where once He lived, with the urgent call to all men to make ready to stand before Him on the Last Day.

We are still living in that period of preparation when, in repentance for our sin and in faith in the atoning work of the Savior, we may prepare our hearts to receive Him. To this opportunity of grace, we much respond! "Blessed are those servants whom the master finds awake when he comes" (Luke 12:37).

Teach us, O God, to make ready for the return of Thy Son, that at His appearing we may be found in the saving faith. Amen.

—⚮—

December 18, 1965

DECEMBER 19

—⟋⟍—

Read Luke 1:67–80
Psalm 81
The sunrise shall visit us from on high. *Luke 1:78*

THE BENEDICTUS

The priest Zechariah, father of John the Baptist, sang a beautiful hymn of praise to God on the day of his son's circumcision and confirmation of his name John, already given by the angel Gabriel long before the child was born.

It is significant, however, that the dominant theme of the song of Zechariah was the birth not of his own son but of a far greater Son, God's own, the Christ in whom all the world would be blest.

Zechariah gave this Child yet to be born a striking name: "the sunrise . . . from on high," or, as we may say, "the dawn of the morning from on high." With the dawn of every new day comes the sun with its light- and life-giving power to a world waiting through the darkness of night. So Christ, the sunrise from on high, comes to give spiritual light and life to people who sit in darkness and in the shadow of death. No one on earth is excluded from the light of the dawn of a new day. The all-embracing love of God in the sunrise from on high includes all people in all the world. The angel's message to the shepherds expressly proclaimed, "I bring you good news of great joy that will be for all the people" (Luke 2:10). Thank God for that! We, too, are included.

Lord Jesus, help us to reflect Thy light and love in our daily lives. Amen.

—⟋⟍—

December 19, 1967

Read Luke 18:9–14
God, be merciful to me, a sinner! *Luke 18:13*

SINNER YET SAINT

There are times when we feel, like the publican, that we have no right to enter our church. We recall how we have lived in the past week. We did not speak with a Christ-like tongue. We did not prove our faith by avoiding those things that we knew to be wrong. We simply went ahead and sinned. Now, it is so hard to lift up our heads because we are ashamed.

This tax collector was a sinner, and he knew it. That was his advantage. Not all are ready to admit that they are sinners. There was another man in the temple the day the publican was there. He was a Pharisee who could only think of thanking God that he was not a sinner like that publican. But in God's sight, the sinner was a saint, and the self-appointed saint was a great sinner!

We who love Jesus are saints, but not in our own right. It sounds strange to be called saints when we know we are sinners. We are saints because God has made us holy. He has declared us to be just and righteous through Jesus, our Savior. Jesus said that the publican who prayed "God, be merciful to me, a sinner" went down to his house justified.

Which, then, are we? Sinners who have become saints through Christ or self-appointed saints who in God's sight are impenitent sinners?

We sinners give Thee thanks, good Lord, that by Thy grace
we are numbered with the saints. Amen.

—〰—

December 20, 1958

—w—

Read John 14:1–7
Psalm 85
Thomas said to Him, "Lord, we do not know where You are going.
How can we know the way?" John 14:5

THOMAS FINDS HIS WAY

Advent hails the coming of Jesus, God's Son and our Savior. The Father had directed His Son to come and save us, to show us the way to His heavenly kingdom. His triumphant cry from the cross, "It is finished," signals His triumph over the power of sin. His resurrection celebrates our victory over death and the life we now have by grace through faith.

Apostle Thomas did not yet have the benefit of hindsight when he asked Jesus, "How can we know the way?" He was asking for direction from his Lord. The events that followed, culminating in the scene on Calvary and the open tomb, cleared it up for Thomas. "My Lord and my God!" he confessed (John 20:28). No longer any doubts there.

Passing through life, we ask for directions too. "Why, God? Why did You let this happen?" our imperfect faith may cry. "Why don't my children believe in You?" parents may ask. "My spouse has deserted me, God. Why did this happen to me?" moans a lonely voice.

Apostle Thomas points us to Jesus. And while quandaries still remain, we know that in Jesus, God is with us! For His name is Immanuel, God with us. We know where we are going and with whom!

Thank You, dear Father, for showing us, through Jesus, the way to Your side. Amen.

—w—

December 21, 2003

December 22

—∽—

Read Isaiah 9:2–7
In the beginning was the Word, and the Word was with God,
and the Word was God. *John 1:1*

THE ETERNAL WORD—OUR SAVIOR

Christmas is at hand. Faintly as from the distance of youth, we seem to hear the echoes of "Silent Night, Holy Night." "Christ, the Savior, is born" they seem to tell us. Worshipful, we fold our hands and bow our knees in adoration before the Christ of Bethlehem. It is right that we do so. The Christ of Bethlehem is the eternal Word of God, who was in the beginning, who was with God, who was God, as John tells us in the opening words of his Gospel.

John is speaking of Jesus as the Word of God. There can be no doubt that John is speaking of Jesus. A little later in his Gospel, he says that this Word was made flesh. Still later, he writes of Jesus Christ through whom grace and truth came.

Our Jesus is God. Wonder of wonders! God made flesh, born a child in Bethlehem. He who was in the beginning, who was God, has been made one of us. And so have been fulfilled the promises of old.

Even though the world is dark and dreary, yet our spirit rejoices in God, our Savior. So long as the world stands, the Christmas bells will ring on and on to cheer the hearts of men.

Blessed Redeemer, fill our hearts with the joy of faith as we make ready to receive Thee anew. Grant unto us and our beloved ones far and near a blessed Christmastide. Bring us Thy peace. Amen.

—∽—

December 22, 1944

—∿∿—

Read Matthew 2:1–9
[Herod] inquired of them where the Christ was to be born. They told
him, "In Bethlehem of Judea, for so it is written by the prophet."
Matthew 2:4–5

THE PLACE OF JESUS' BIRTH

Humanly speaking, Jesus might easily have been born at the wrong place. According to God's promise in Old Testament prophecy, He must be born in Bethlehem of Judea, the city of David. Yet Mary, who was to become His mother, lived sixty-five miles north of Bethlehem, in Nazareth of Galilee. As far as we know, Joseph and Mary had no intention to move from the northern part to the southern part of the Holy Land. Such moving causes much work and trouble and annoyance and expense. But Mary must be in Bethlehem when the days would be accomplished that she should be delivered. What will bring her there? What will make her move to Bethlehem?

The mighty Caesar Augustus, interested very much in the affairs of his great Roman Empire and not at all interested in the affairs of the kingdom of God, must at the appropriate time issue his taxing decree, according to which everyone went into his own city, that is, the city where the family had originated. Consequently, Joseph, out of the house and lineage of David, went with Mary to the city of David, which is called Bethlehem. There Jesus was born.

The mighty of the world do not use God for their ends; God uses them for His designs, carrying out the plans for His kingdom. In the case of Jesus, prophecy was fulfilled: Jesus was born in Bethlehem.

*O Lord, grant that we commit our ways unto Thee, trusting in Thee,
that Thou wilt bring it to pass. Amen.*

—∿∿—

December 23, 1955

DECEMBER 24

—ᨠ—

Read Matthew 1:18–25
Therefore the Lord Himself will give you a sign. Behold, the virgin shall
conceive and bear a son, and shall call His name Immanuel. *Isaiah 7:14*

THE GREAT MYSTERY

O holy night, night of mystery! The mind of man could never have conceived of such a thing. The mind of man has difficulty in receiving it. All the laws of nature are changed to bring about the wonderful event. The angels of heaven burst upon the earth to sing about it. A star of the sky is made to tell its story. But what is it, this event?

Looking at the externals, we see absolutely nothing that impresses us. A young mother who cannot find a place in the inn borrows the only shelter she can find, a stable. There, she brings forth her first Child, a baby boy, wraps Him as gently as she can, and places Him on the only thing that will serve as a bed, a pile of straw in a manger. What is so unusual? Pathetic, perhaps, but what is so unusual? Only when we look behind the externals do we see the mystery, the unusual.

The mother is a virgin. This was actually the sign whereby people could recognize the mystery—that a virgin shall have a Child. For the mystery is this: this little Child is Immanuel, God with us. Within this little Child dwelt "the whole fullness of deity . . . bodily" (Colossians 2:9). He is the only-begotten of the Father, who came in fulfillment of all the promises from the first given to Eve to the last made by Malachi. This is the Savior, the appointed Messiah, the blessed Seed, in whom all the nations of the earth would be blessed. Oh wonderful mystery! God in the flesh, born of a virgin! Great is the mystery! Great is our joy!

*Lord Eternal, grant us the grace to accept in childlike faith
this great revelation of Thy love. Amen.*

—ᨠ—

December 24, 1956

Read Luke 2:1-21
Psalm 2

*She gave birth to her firstborn son and wrapped Him in swaddling cloths
and laid Him in a manger, because there was no place for them in the inn.*
Luke 2:7

HE IS CRADLED IN A MANGER

The Christ who comes to us comes packaged in a manger. Our delightful, pastoral, and colorful nativity scenes have softened for us the offensiveness of Jesus' humble birth. But were we to imagine the odors, the crudeness, and the discomfort of that moment, we could understand something of God's purpose in the sending of this Son.

God's Son from His infancy is identified with poverty and self-denial. His life lacks the pretense, ease, and comforts that we seek and enjoy. As God had prepared His people by the vigorous disciplines of slavery in Egypt and of wilderness wanderings, so God raised His Son in the discipline of a rugged life.

However, more important: Jesus also was exposed to the hardships of the life of the plain Hebrew family that His dependence on His heavenly Father would be more evident. The human Jesus leaned trustingly upon His Father to provide His every daily need.

For our comfort, the Babe of Bethlehem became poor that we through His cross might become rich, reconciling us to His Father by bringing peace and hope into our lives. God's love laid Jesus into the Bethlehem manger.

**Heavenly Father, who didst send Thy Son to us in poverty, make us rich
in grace through Him. Amen.**

—∿—

December 25, 1964

DECEMBER 26

—〰—

Read John 17:15–21
The shepherds returned, glorifying and praising God for all they had
heard and seen. *Luke 2:20*

RETURNING FROM CHRISTMAS

When the excitement of a celebration is over, we often find it difficult to return to the routine of our daily tasks. This is especially true at Christmastime when, after weeks of preparation, decoration, and anticipation, the holiday passes with surprising abruptness. The chimes and carols suddenly stop, and we feel like asking, "What do we do now?"

The shepherds had a similar experience. They were roused from a monotonous task by a choir of angels. Then they journeyed to Bethlehem to witness the world's first Christmas. They were part of a celebration for which God Himself had made the preparations.

When it was over, the shepherds "returned." No, Christmas had not somehow abolished their need to work or even changed the nature of their task. But, as Luke tells us, there was an important difference in the way in which they now went at it. Now they worked while "glorifying and praising God."

If we let Christmas make us more aware of God's gift of His Son, the passing of the holiday will be far from a letdown. Instead, it will be a time of renewed worship and witness.

Lord Jesus, help us to make clear to the world what we saw and heard in the celebration of Thy birth. Amen.

—〰—

December 26, 1973

Read Romans 5:1–11
He Himself is our peace. *Ephesians 2:14*

DID CHRIST BRING PEACE TO EARTH?

Did Christ bring peace on earth? Does it not seem mockery on the part of the angels to sing to the shepherds of Bethlehem: "Peace on earth"? On all sides, we see nations, communities, families, and even friends at odds with one another. How then can we say that Jesus brought peace on earth?

The peace that Christ brings to us is spiritual, a reconciliation with God. "Peace I leave with you; My peace I give to you. Not as the world gives do I give to you" (John 14:27). Jesus came to free us from the guilt and curse of sin. Therefore, "the LORD has laid on Him the iniquity of us all" (Isaiah 53:6). Thus, the Father reconciled us to Himself through the Son's sacrifice on Calvary, through which we become as white as snow. Our sins are blotted out, and we no longer are afraid of God. His holiness has been satisfied through the shedding of the blood of His own Son. He is our peace.

Being at peace with God, we are at peace with ourselves. This enables us to face every problem of life with courage and confidence. The martyrs of the ages faced torture and death without fear because they had Christ's peace in their hearts.

Having this peace in his heart, Simeon of old could depart in peace. He was certain that on the other side of the grave, he would meet the welcoming Savior. This peace only Jesus can give. And He gave this peace to all. By faith in Him, we find this peace.

Lord Jesus, lead me daily to Thy cross to find peace. Amen.

—ᴀᴦᴨᴦ—

December 27, 1961

DECEMBER 28

—⁓⁓—

Read Exodus 16:14–18
I am the bread of life; whoever comes to Me shall not hunger. *John 6:35*

BETHLEHEM, THE HOUSE OF BREAD

Bethlehem, though small and unimportant, was not poverty stricken. Its people were well supplied with grain fields, vineyards, and sheep. That is why it is called "Bethlehem," which is the Hebrew for "house of bread." It was evidently with this background in mind that David said: "The LORD is my shepherd; I shall not want" (Psalm 23:1).

God is the giver of all we need. "The eyes of all look to You, and You give them their food in due season. You open Your hand; You satisfy the desire of every living thing" (Psalm 145:15–16). It is good to know that, when people are hungry or have any other need, the almighty, all-wise, and omnipresent God can do something about it.

But our greatest want is not our physical hunger. Far greater are the needs of the soul, the assurance of God's forgiveness and love. That is why Christ, who was born in the "house of bread," says of Himself, "I am the bread of life." We receive that heavenly bread whenever we read or hear His Word or are guests at His Table. There is no better thing we can do than to partake of that bread of life and then break it to others.

Lord Jesus Christ, life-giving bread,
May I in grace possess You.
Let me with holy food be fed,
In hunger I address You. Amen. (LSB 625:1)

—⁓⁓—

December 28, 1963

December 29

—∽—

Read Romans 1:14–17
Psalm 72
Let the redeemed of the LORD say so. *Psalm 107:2*

REVEALING THE GLORY OF THE LORD

The Christian faith is not something we can confine in a sealed box. The shepherds must make known abroad their holy night experience; the apostles cannot but speak the things that they have seen and heard; the redeemed of the Lord must say so. "What you hear whispered, proclaim on the housetops" (Matthew 10:27). "The glory of the LORD shall be revealed" (Isaiah 40:5).

Anything else should be unthinkable for us. Our faith has two hands, one reaching up to receive the gifts of God in Christ, the other reaching out to offer them to others—and both must be alive.

Is it not true that so often we are silent when we ought to speak? We fill the earth with the noise of our own greatness. We beat our hollow human drums and blow the tin horns of man's glory.

But where is the thunder of the Law to bring men to repentance and the music of the Gospel to bring peace to troubled hearts? Where is the chorus of the redeemed who sound it out before heaven and earth: "God's Son has made us free"?

Our eyes have seen the coming of the glory of the Lord. He is the only Redeemer. He has redeemed us. Now, let the redeemed of the Lord say so!

God, grant us grace that we may not be ashamed of the Gospel of Christ but declare it boldly and confidently. Amen.

—∽—

December 29, 1981

DECEMBER 30

—✖—

Read 2 Timothy 4:3–8
As for you, always be sober-minded, endure suffering, do the work
of an evangelist, fulfill your ministry. *2 Timothy 4:5*

LESSONS FOR AFTER CHRISTMAS

To be true Christians, we need Christmas with us all the time. We need not be celebrating it, but we need to keep it in our minds and hearts.

While our text does not say anything of Christmas, it does speak of men who kept the sound doctrine, lived by it, and were ready to die for it. The center of the doctrine by which they lived so courageously was the incarnate Christ.

When Christmas abides in the heart, it makes people strong, valiant, eager, and earnest workers for Christ and His Church. The apostle Paul and Timothy are good examples of Christian strength. All Christians can meet the challenge of life on the same grounds and on the same terms as they did.

When Christmas abides in the heart, it makes people strong, patient, and uncomplaining when bearing the cross. Paul was in prison when he wrote these words. His hands were weak and his body was worn out, but there was no complaint. The secret of his perseverance was the abiding Christ in his heart. We, too, may have a reserve of fortitude in our soul for the difficult places in life. We have it in Christ.

When Christmas abides in the heart, we may look into the future unafraid. Paul said: "There is laid up for me the crown of righteousness, which the Lord, the righteous judge, will award to me on that Day, and not only to me but also to all who have loved His appearing" (v. 8).

Jesus, lead Thou on, till our rest be won. Amen.

—✖—

December 30, 1957

DECEMBER 31

—◆—

Read Titus 3:1–8
Psalm 90
So you are no longer a slave, but a son, and if a son,
then an heir through God. *Galatians 4:7*

LEAVING THE OLD YEAR

Is it possible to maintain a casual attitude toward today and this evening? This is New Year's Eve, the final day of the year. Some people maintain that today is just like any other day. But tomorrow is a new calendar year, an unknown period of time to be explored and experienced.

In one sense, we Christians can maintain that today is like any other day—it is a day of God's grace to us. In another sense, we Christians proclaim that today is a special day. Individually and gathered as a church, we have the opportunity to thank God for His loving care this year. With joy, we recall the mercies of God each of us experienced during the year that is passing. Tonight, we, heirs of God's eternal love, sing His praise!

Today is a special day. We come to the Father through Jesus, His Son, to seek His benediction on the new year. Our prime petition is that He would help us utilize our allotted time on earth to receive His grace and proclaim His love to all people. We leave 1991 and enter into 1992 with triumphant spirits, knowing that we are heirs of God's love in Christ Jesus. We will live forever in His presence!

Lord God, we celebrate Your timeless love for us, rejoicing that You have made us heirs of eternal life in Christ. Amen.

—◆—

December 31, 1991
On this date in 1991, complete dissolution of the Soviet Union

For Special Days of the Year

We thank Thee, dear heavenly Father, for the gift of Thy Holy Spirit and the faith Thou has granted us in Christ Jesus. Amen.

The Transfiguration of Our Lord

—◊—

Read Mark 9:1–10
Psalm 99
He was transfigured before them. *Mark 9:2*

And the Glory Came Down

A magnificent event, this transfiguration of Jesus: His clothes dazzling white, His face shining like the sun! It is another example of heaven touching earth.

This had happened before. In creation, God spoke and the universe came into being. In the exodus history, God reached down and made rock-bound water flow and manna fall from above. In the announcement of Immanuel's birth, heaven's angels broke through to earth and spoke to Mary, Joseph, and the shepherds in the fields. But especially in Jesus, God broke through and clothed Himself in humanity. Heaven has indeed touched earth, and its gates are open to earthbound creatures like us.

The voice from the cloud, "This is My beloved Son; listen to Him" (Mark 9:7), speaks yet today. We listen to Jesus. We believe that indeed He has come to lead us away from slavery to sin into perfect freedom, a freedom that is ours because Jesus, the very glory of God (2 Corinthians 4:6), touched this earth with His cross. His cross set us free for glory everlasting.

Dear Lord, please continue to speak to us through Your Word and Spirit, that hearing, we might firmly hold fast to Your promise of everlasting life and glory. Amen.

—◊—

March 5, 2000

Ash Wednesday

—∞—

Read Matthew 20:17–34

How Great Is God's Love!

Today Lent begins. What does this mean? Christ died *for me*. How do I know this? "Behold, the Lamb of God, who takes away the sin of the world!" saith John the Baptist (John 1:29). I belong to the world. So I am included. Christ gave His life also for me.

How grateful ought I to be! Dead in trespasses and sins, I have been raised to newness of life and now am standing in His grace. Surely I cannot go through this day and the Lenten season without pondering upon His Passion and the great amazing love of God. I must come in spirit to the cross and worship.

But this glorious truth is too good to keep for myself. Christ dies *for all.* I must share this gladness with others.

And how wonderful! I can go to any man, woman, or child and tell each: "Christ died for you." At no time am I compelled to say: "This Gospel does not fit your case."

But why am I so cold, disinterested, and unconcerned? Why do I not get enthusiastic? Many in my acquaintance circle are still without Christ in the world. Dare I neglect them any longer?

Today Lent begins. I am standing in His grace. O Lord, at this very hour I pledge anew to serve Thee and to endeavor to share with my friends this joy, this hope, and this salvation, which Thou has purchased with Thine own blood.

—∞—

February 10, 1937
The first-ever devotion in *Portals of Prayer*

PALM SUNDAY/PASSION SUNDAY

—᙭—

Read Matthew 20:17–19
Psalm 6
But when the chief priests and the scribes saw the wonderful things
that He did, and the children crying out in the temple, "Hosanna to the
Son of David!" they were indignant. *Matthew 21:15*

THE GATHERING STORM

Like cold and warm air masses meeting in turbulent weather, the indignation of the religious leaders collide with the "Hosannas" shouted by the children. The storm was just beginning to gather. Teachers of the law would confront its fulfiller. Chief priests would be threatened by the High Priest of God. Self-righteous people would mass against the One who brings righteousness.

The gathering storm hangs heavy over the cross as Jesus willingly allows the dark deed to be done. The law's teachers were blind to the truth that by His death those under the curse of the Law would be redeemed.

Storms still gather as self-righteousness encounters the Gospel and the world's ways clash with the ways of those who are Christ's new creation. The Christian Church exists in a society that is increasingly hostile to God's message. We are kept faithful by the Holy Spirit and encouraged by the example of Jesus, who endured even the cross for us.

Righteous Lord, when we encounter the world's opposition, give us the conviction and courage to make a bold witness in Your name. Amen.

—᙭—

April 9, 1995

Holy (Maundy) Thursday

—ɯ—

Read John 13:1–20
Psalm 107:1–20
Love one another. John 13:34

A New Command

On Maundy Thursday, Christians around the world are gathered by the Word in the Upper Room in old Jerusalem. The word *Maundy* comes from the Latin word *mandatum*, meaning "command." On this day, Jesus gave a new commandment: "Love one another."

Christian love must be practiced. In everyday life we show we are Christians through deeds of kindness. "By this all people will know that you are My disciples, if you have love for one another" (John 13:35).

But such love is more than we can produce of ourselves, because its measure is Christ's love for us. The body of Jesus was broken on the cross for us; the blood of Jesus was shed on the cross for you and me. In His love, our sins are forgiven and our faith is strengthened.

To put His love in us and to strengthen that love, Jesus instituted Holy Communion. He gives us His real body and blood, together with the bread and wine, as proof positive of His forgiving love.

When we are worn down by the worries and troubles of daily life, when we find it difficult to love difficult people, He leads us to kneel at His altar, to partake of His body and blood, and then to go into the world renewed in strength, faith, and love.

Draw near and take the body of the Lord,
And drink the holy blood for you outpoured. Amen. (LSB 637:1)

—ɯ—

April 5, 2007

Good Friday

—⟋⟍—

John 19:17–30
Psalm 22
He bowed His head and gave up His spirit. *John 19:30*

Behold the Savior!

"S tricken, smitten, and afflicted, See Him dying on the tree!" (*LSB* 451:1). The drama of the trials, the mockery, the driving of the nails, and the memorable statements that Jesus made from the cross—all this is over. Jesus died.

The great irony of His terrible death is that, though it was the death of a vile criminal, Jesus was not a criminal at all. Even Pontius Pilate, acting as judge, declared that he had found no crime in Him. We who know Jesus in faith know that He was not just guiltless; He was the holy, eternal Son of God. His life on earth had not only been free of crime; it was, in fact, a perfect life of obedience to His Father's will.

Yet He died. And His death was punishment for sin, the sin that was ours along with the sin of those who lived before us, live now, and will live after us. He assumed the sin of the whole world. According to His purpose and in the will of the Father, He was guilty of every sin ever committed—all the murders, the rapes, and the more "acceptable" sins too. He was the ultimate criminal and altogether guilty by the standards of the just Judge.

Jesus, our Substitute, had to die, and He did. He died for us. He became the criminal; we are judged to be innocent saints.

By grace I'm saved, grace free and boundless. Amen. (LSB 566:1)

—⟋⟍—

April 5, 1985

HOLY SATURDAY

—ᴍ—

Read Matthew 27:57–66
Psalm 56
Joseph took the body ... and laid it in his own new tomb,
which he had cut in the rock. *Matthew 27:59–60*

THE MORNING AFTER

As Jesus' body lay in the tomb, varied thoughts must have run through the minds of men who knew Him. We can hear one man say, "You're dead now, Jesus. Dead! You're not going to bother us any more, understand? You're buried deep in the rock. That'll teach You!"

Or another: "God help us if anyone recognizes who we are. (Did I say 'God help us'? What's the use of praying? The Master prayed, and look what happened to *Him*.) Well, with a little luck we should be able to slip away from home in pairs when the crowds leave after the Passover. But *if* we get home, what do we do then?"

Jesus was in a grave, and it looked like it was all over. The Bible tells us He lay in a new grave. It was new in a sense that no one could imagine, for that grave was to make all things new. The mission of Jesus was not all over. Of that we have to keep reminding ourselves over and over.

Even as the Lord's body lay resting, the grave—His grave and that of everyone who trusts in Him—was being given new meaning. That grave had become a bed from which He would rise. So will we, to be joined with Him in the new heaven and earth, forever and ever.

Lord Jesus, through Your Spirit give new meaning to our life
and to our death. Amen.

—ᴍ—

March 28, 1970

—〰—

Read Matthew 28:1–15
Psalm 52
All that the Father gives Me will come to Me, and whoever comes
to Me I will never cast out. *John 6:37*

ARMS OPEN WIDE

He is risen! He is risen indeed! On this greatest festival of the Holy Christian Church—both on earth and in heaven—we celebrate with unbridled joy! The same arms of our Savior, which were opened wide as He hung nailed to the cross, are now opened wide to receive us forever!

Of all the comfort and meaning behind our Savior's resurrection, this is supreme: we now know for sure that God our heavenly Father is no longer separated from us by our sins. The empty tomb "sets in stone" the fact, as Jesus declared, "All that the Father gives Me will come to Me." We are drawn to know and love Jesus as our Savior by the desire of the Father through the work of His Holy Spirit in His Holy Word and Sacraments.

For the rest of our earthly lives, we now rest in the joy of knowing that "whoever comes to Me [Jesus] I will never cast out." Leaving our sins buried in the tomb, we, too, daily arise with Christ to live in and with and for Him until the day comes when our bodies will rise in glory and be gathered forever in His arms opened wide for us!

Praise to You, O resurrected Christ! Keep me forever in Your arms. Amen.

—〰—

March 31, 2002

The Ascension of Our Lord

—ᴍ—

Read Ephesians 4:7–13
When He ascended on high He led a host of captives,
and He gave gifts to men. *Ephesians 4:8*

WE ARE GLAD HE ASCENDED

Homecomings are, as a rule, happy events. Jesus' homecoming to heaven was no exception. His ascension into heaven marked His return to that glory He had left some thirty-three years before when He became our Brother. Furthermore, it represented the conquering climax in His long struggle with Satan and his evil angels. Thereby He "led captivity captive."

We rejoice with Jesus on this important day of His ascension. As we think of His holiness and the beauty of His being, we know that heaven is His rightful place of residence. We are glad He ascended, even as we rejoice over the good fortune of anyone who is dear to us. But we are glad also for ourselves. Before ascending, Jesus promised His people here on earth that He would be with them even until the end of time. He declared further: "I go to prepare a place for you. . . . I will come again and will take you to Myself" (John 14:2–3).

A third reason for rejoicing today is found in the words "gave gifts to men." A direct result of Christ's ascension was the imparting of gifts for the upbuilding of the Church. The apostle Paul lists these gifts in a later verse: "He gave the apostles, the prophets, the evangelists, the shepherds and teachers" (v. 11).

Our spiritual leaders are God's gifts to the Church. They are indeed frail human beings, but the message they proclaim is not frail. It is "the power of God for salvation to everyone who believes" (Romans 1:16).

**We thank Thee, Lord, for every faithful pastor and teacher
Thou has given Thy Church. Amen.**

—ᴍ—

May 10, 1956

THE DAY OF PENTECOST

—༝༝—

Read Acts 2:1–13
And they were all filled with the Holy Spirit. *Acts 2:4*

THE BAPTISM WITH THE HOLY SPIRIT

J ohn baptized with water; but you will be baptized with the
Holy Spirit not many days from now," Jesus had told His
disciples (Acts 1:5). This prophecy was fulfilled on Pentecost Day. St. Luke informs us: "They were all filled with the Holy
Spirit and began to speak in other tongues as the Spirit gave them
utterance."

The gift of languages was but an indication of greater gifts. The
languages served the purpose of declaring the wonders of God's
grace in Christ Jesus. The real purpose of this Baptism with the
Holy Ghost was to enlighten the disciples of Christ so that they
would be able to proclaim the truths of God to a world lost in sin.
This was the definite promise of Jesus. "The Helper, the Holy Spirit
. . . will teach you all things and bring to your remembrance all
that I have said to you" (John 14:26).

When this promise was fulfilled on Pentecost Day, the disciples
of Jesus were enabled to speak with divine authority. St. Paul sums
up this divine authority in his well-known confession: "And we
impart this in words not taught by human wisdom but taught by
the Spirit" (1 Corinthians 2:13).

The Holy Spirit has also called us, enlightened us with His gifts,
and sanctified us in the true faith.

*We thank Thee, dear heavenly Father, for the gift of Thy Holy Spirit
and the faith Thou has granted us in Christ Jesus. Amen.*

—༝༝—

May 28, 1944

The Holy Trinity

—ɷ—

Read I John 3:1–10
Psalm 8
Anyone who does not love does not know God, because God is love.
I John 4:8

God Is Love

Who is God? What is He like? On a day like Trinity Sunday we describe God as "the Holy Trinity and the Undivided Unity." We affirm that there is only one God, though there are three persons in the Godhead.

God's nature is no less a mystery when we describe Him as St. John does: "God is love." Yet that description brings God closer to us. For we have experienced love. We know how desperately we need to love and to be loved.

God is love. It is His nature to love. Out of love He created a world, that He might share His life with it. Out of love He "sent His only Son into the world, so that we might live through Him" (1 John 4:9). Out of love He has entered into intimate communion with us by giving us His Spirit.

God has shown us who He is and what He is like through acts of love. Every time we experience love, God is at work in our life. When we love others, we show that God is present in us. "Anyone who does not love does not know God, because God is love" (1 John 4:8).

God wants us to share in what He is. As God has loved us, we are to love one another. That is the Christian way of life.

**O God, whose love is our life, be present in us, that our lives
may be filled with love. For Jesus' sake. Amen.**

—ɷ—

June 9, 1968

Mother's Day

—⚬—

Read I Samuel 1:19–28
Her children rise up and call her blessed. *Proverbs 31:28*

MOTHER

Motherhood is God's noblest gift to women, at once a blessed privilege and a heavy responsibility. When Christians think of mothers, two outstanding examples immediately come to mind: Eve, the mother of all living, and Mary, the mother of our Lord. In the sight of God, and therefore also in the sight of all Christians, every mother can and ought to be great.

Mother's handiwork, which follows her, is her children and her children's children. On them she leaves inevitably and indelibly, for better or for worse, the impression of her character, her personality, her prayers, her faith, her daily living. Mother's influence is usually the first to which the child is exposed. As a rule, it is strongest during the years in which a child responds most readily. Therefore, it is also most lasting.

The words of Peter apply in special and forceful manner to all mothers, awakening them to their opportunity and obligation: "What sort of people ought you to be in lives of holiness and godliness" (2 Peter 3:11). If mothers will observe them, their children will surely rise up and call them blessed.

Lord Jesus, who didst love and cherish Thy blessed mother,
help all mothers to be more like Thine own. Amen.

—⚬—

May 13, 1951

Memorial Day

—⟋⟍—

Read 1 John 5:1–12
Psalm 115
We do not want you to be uninformed, brothers, about those who are
asleep, that you may not grieve as others do who have no hope.
1 Thessalonians 4:13

In Memoriam

The coming of Memorial Day can help to remind us of the certainty of death. Nothing is more certain than death and nothing more uncertain than the hour of our death. Death plays no favorites. Whether it be babes in arms, young men and women in the prime of life (perhaps establishing new homes), the middle-aged doing the real work of the world, the aged with natural powers dimmed but clinging desperately to life—death claims them all.

But don't "grieve as others do who have no hope," says God to the Christians. "For since we believe that Jesus died and rose again, even so, through Jesus, God will bring with Him those who have fallen asleep" (1 Thessalonians 4:14).

When the Lord's Day (the final day) comes, our Lord will make His personal appearance; "the dead in Christ will rise first" (4:16). Those who are still alive will be taken to the glories of heaven, where they "will always be with the Lord" (4:17).

"Whoever has the Son has life; whoever does not have the Son of God does not have life" (1 John 5:12).

**O God, we thank You for the promise of eternal life. Grant us
the Holy Spirit, that He may sustain our hope in Christ. Amen.**

—⟋⟍—

May 28, 1979

FATHER'S DAY

—◆—

Read Luke 15:11–31
Psalm 119:1–8
Pray then like this:"Our Father in heaven, hallowed be Your name."
Matthew 6:9

OUR FATHER IN HEAVEN

On Father's Day, we pay tribute to the role of father in family life. A good father is more than a paycheck with arms and legs. He is the head of the house, the guiding center, protector, source of love and inspiration, model and example for living. We honor fathers for good reasons.

God has paid fathers the highest tribute. He has used fathers as a picture of His relation to people. Jesus taught us to think of God as "our Father in heaven."

God is all a good father is—and more. He is the source of life; we live because of Him. Because He has put His life and Spirit in us, we are His children and rightly call Him our Father.

Like a good father, God cares for us and provides for us. He knows our deepest needs and fills them. God disciplines us the way every good father corrects his children. Would a good father not show them the difference between right and wrong?

Most important, as our Father, God is a person with whom we can share our lives. He is not an object or an impersonal force. He is someone to whom we can speak. We can pray, "Our Father in heaven," and can expect an answer.

O God, we thank Thee for being our Father in heaven through Christ Jesus and for loving us through our fathers here on earth. Amen.

—◆—

June 16, 1968

INDEPENDENCE DAY

—⚏—

Read 1 Peter 2:13–17
Psalm 117
Live as people who are free, not using your freedom as a cover-up
for evil, but living as servants of God. *1 Peter 2:16*

FREE INDEED

Today is a special day for all who live in "the good old USA." On Independence Day, we celebrate our freedom as a nation.

As American Christians, we enjoy a double freedom. As citizens, we enjoy the freedom that comes with a democratic government. As Christians, we enjoy an even greater freedom in the forgiveness that is ours through Christ's death and resurrection. The assurance that in Christ God has promised to forgive us frees us to try new ways to build a more caring community in His world.

The prophet Micah reminds us that God has shown us what He expects from His servants in both Church and state. They are to do justly, to love mercy, and to walk humbly with God (Micah 6:8).

We have a calling from our Lord as citizens of this land to bring to our community, our state, and our nation a strong voice for justice and mercy for all who are oppressed. We who enjoy a double freedom enjoy also the double opportunity to bring freedom and joy into the lives of others.

*Thank You, Lord, for freedom from civil tyranny and especially
for freedom from sin and death, which comes through Jesus' victory
for us on the cross. Amen.*

July 4, 1987

LABOR DAY (U.S. AND CANADA)

—✠—

Ecclesiastes 2:1–26
Psalm 123
Therefore, my beloved brothers, be steadfast, immovable, always
abounding in the work of the Lord, knowing that in the Lord your labor
is not in vain. *1 Corinthians 15:58*

LABOR DAY

I t seems ironic that Labor Day was designed to be a day of
rest. Why not call is Rest Day? It's a fine opportunity to sit
back and evaluate our work. Is it rewarding? Is it meaningful? Is it satisfying?

The writer of Ecclesiastes seems to be evaluating his work too.
His conclusion is full of despair. All that he has accomplished, all
of the possessions he's accumulated, he describes as meaningless.
He wonders why he should toil so hard only to leave it to those
who will follow him.

But God promises an abundant life to all who follow Him, no
matter what the work may be. When we dedicate our work and
our plans to the Lord, we can relax and leave the results to Him.
He's promised that our labor is not in vain.

Be assured that for all believers in Christ who rest in the forgiveness won for all on His cross, a great possession is already
awaiting us. It will be far greater than all the possessions we've
amassed throughout our lives. What a joy it will be to hear Jesus
say to us, "Well done, good and faithful servant."

Dear Lord, we're certainly not good, nor are we always faithful,
but thank You for the rewards You freely give! Amen.

—✠—

September 6, 1999

Thanksgiving

—ᴥ—

Read James 1:16–18
Psalm 107:1–9
Every good gift and every perfect gift is from above. James 1:17

THE BEST GIFT

Every gift is from above. If there's food on our table today and family and friends who surround us, they are all there on account of God's love toward us. We owe nothing in this life to our own worth, effort, or merit. Rather, it is all given to us from our heavenly Father.

His delivery system for these good gifts is His Word. This Word not only speaks to us of the greatest gifts—life and salvation—but it also actually transmits these gifts to us. The Word Incarnate, Christ Himself, earned for us the grace of eternal life that is now conveyed to us through Word and Sacrament.

Here on earth we gather at the Table of the Sacrament and look forward to the feasting that will commence when He comes again and takes us home.

There we will sit at a banquet table even more impressive than the one in front of us today. And all of our relatives—God's elect, our brothers and sisters in Christ—will be there too. Not one seat will be empty. We will feast with the saints who have gone before us and with the Giver of all good gifts.

Gracious God, fill us today with the blessings of this rich land and with Your unfailing love shown best in Christ, our Lord. Amen.

—ᴥ—

November 25, 2010

CHRISTMAS EVE

—⚯—

Read Luke 1:26–38
Great indeed, we confess, is the mystery of godliness: He was manifested in the flesh. *I Timothy 3:16*

SILENT NIGHT! HOLY NIGHT!

This is Holy Night. Of all the nights of the year, none so warrants that adjective as this one. For tonight we are privileged to contemplate the holiest of all mysteries.

We see a "baby wrapped in swaddling cloths and lying in a manger" (Luke 2:12). Over Him lovingly bends the Virgin Mother. The mystery is not apparent. Babies are born every day.

But what the eye beholds never tells the whole story, least of all here in Bethlehem on this holy night. God has moved in a mysterious way to perform a wonder. His Word somewhat removes the veil and gives us a glimpse of the miracle of the ages.

That Babe is God Himself, the eternal Word made flesh. God is man. The Infinite is finite. The impossible not only is possible, but actually is, because He with whom nothing is impossible so willed it. In that tiny form, cradled in the manger, Deity and humanity are one.

For reason, the mystery is too great. It staggers and balks. But faith joyously grips the mighty fact and adores the Holy Child.

For God was manifest in the flesh to save us.

O blessed Babe, open Thou my eyes, that I may behold Thy glory, a glory as of the only-begotten of the Father, full of grace and truth. Amen.

—⚯—

December 24, 1946

—⚬—

Read Galatians 4:1–7
Because you are sons, God has sent the Spirit of His Son into our hearts,
crying, "Abba! Father!" *Galatians 4:6*

REMEMBERING WHO WE ARE

L ife calls us to play various roles at the same time. We are parents, consumers, neighbors, career people, volunteer workers. It's easy to forget who we are as we move from one setting to another. What matters most is that we know who we are in relation to God. God makes so much of this issue in Holy Scripture. It's good for us that He does, because He is the one who determines who we are in relation to Him.

Jesus' coming is God's answer to our concern. God's Son became a man for all men when He was born and lived men's life. "But to all who did receive Him, who believed in His name, He gave the right to become children of God" (John 1:12). Christ became our Brother so God might claim us as His children.

God knows who we are. He remembers when we forget. He tries to assure us so we will remember. Our simplest prayer, "Abba! Father!" shows we know who we are. It's like children turning to their parents for help because they know them.

God gives a clue to help us in time of fear and doubt, especially when we feel our guilt. This is a time to consider what God has done to become our Father. In Christ, He has adopted us. Let's live according to what we are: God's children.

We thank You for the privilege of calling You our Father. In Your name we find our comfort and our calling. Amen.

—⚬—

November 26, 1973

BEFORE COMMUNION

—∿∿—

I John 3:1–11
We have an altar. *Hebrews 13:10*

THE COMMUNION IN HOLY THINGS

Some scholars say that the phrase "the communion of saints" in the Creed originally referred not to the fellowship of holy people, but to their sharing in holy things, that is, in the Sacraments. Certainly the Early Church was very careful not to cast its pearls before swine. Candidates for Holy Baptism were given an intensive course of instruction before they were even allowed to learn the Creed, and the custom of having sponsors is evidence of the Church's effort to establish the sincerity of those who asked to be baptized. As for Holy Communion, none but those eligible to receive it were permitted to remain in church for the celebration of the mystery; the deacons would, after the sermon, ask the catechumens to leave.

It is a high and holy privilege to be a member in good standing in the Christian Church. Most people in the world have not received this grace and do not enjoy its blessing. To be baptized and to receive Holy Communion is to be clothed with a tremendous dignity. St. John thought of it with awe: "See what kind of love the Father has given to us, that we should be called children of God" (v. 1). Since God has so honored us, it follows that we must not dishonor Him by unholy living. Communion in holy things requires a holy life.

By the grace given us in the Holy Sacraments, teach us to live
as those who have been called to be kings and priests
in Thy kingdom. Amen.

—∿∿—

April 21, 1964

When Seeking God's Will

Read I Kings 3:5–15
Ask, and it will be given to you; seek, and you will find; knock,
and it will be opened to you. *Matthew 7:7*

Solomon's Prayer

God appeared to King Solomon in a dream in the night and said, "Ask what I shall give you" (v. 5). Solomon therefore had the choice of anything he desired in heaven above or on earth beneath. He took advantage of this offer and asked for the largest and most important thing, a wise and understanding heart to rule the people whom God had entrusted to his care. His prayer was answered. He received even much more, namely, riches and honor in large measure, things for which he had not asked.

Our God appears to us in His Word with the same offer: "Whatever you ask in prayer, you will receive, if you have faith" (Matthew 21:22). And lest God be misunderstood, He offers again: "Whatever you ask in prayer, believe that you have received it, and it will be yours" (Mark 11:24). Let us therefore take Him at His Word. Let us ask for the greatest treasure, a wise and understanding heart. With such a heart we shall be able to discern between good and evil. With such a heart we shall have the correct philosophy of life, putting first things first. With such a heart we shall set our affections on things above, on the eternal treasures of forgiveness and salvation, where moth and rust do not corrupt and where thieves do not break through and steal. Then, if it is the Lord's will, and if it be good for us, other things also, even riches and honor and length of days, will be added.

Create in me a clean heart, O God, and renew a right spirit within me.
Amen.

October 2, 1943

THE PASSION OF OUR LORD JESUS CHRIST IN FORTY READINGS

—⧕—

1. Matthew 20:17–34
2. Luke 18:31–43
3. Luke 19:1–10
4. Matthew 26:1–16
5. Luke 19:28–40
6. John 12:23–36
7. Luke 22:1–14
8. John 13:1–20
9. John 13:21–30
10. John 13:31–38
11. Matthew 26:26–35
12. Luke 22:31–38
13. John 14:1–14
14. John 14:15–31
15. John 15:1–16
16. John 15:17–27
17. John 16:1–16
18. John 16:17–33
19. John 17:1–12
20. John 17:13–26
21. Matthew 26:36–46
22. Matthew 26:47–56
23. Mark 14:51–54
24. John 18:19–24
25. Matthew 26:69–75
26. Luke 22:63–71
27. John 18:28–38
28. Luke 23:5–18
29. Matthew 27:3–10
30. Matthew 27:11–26
31. John 19:1–16
32. Luke 23:26–37
33. John 19:17–27
34. Luke 23:39–44
35. Matthew 27:45–49
36. Matthew 27:50–56
37. John 19:25–37
38. Mark 15:42–47
39. Matthew 27:57–66
40. Mark 16:1–8

—⧕—

This list first appeared in 1938, issue 8.

Scripture Index

Index of Devotion Titles

—m—

A

—m—

B

—⚹—

C

—〰—

D

—〰—

E

—〰—

F

—ιν—

G

—⚹—

H

—ᴍ—
L

—ᴍ—
M

—⟋⟍—

N

—⟋⟍—

O

—⟋⟍—

P

—ɷ—

Q

—ɷ—

R

—ɷ—

S

—ɯ—

T

—✠—

Y

—✠—

Z